INTERNATIONAL ASSOCIATION OF AUTO THEFT INVESTIGATORS

1952 • 2002

TURNER PUBLISHING COMPANY

TURNER PUBLISHING COMPANY

Copyright © 2002
Publishing Rights: Turner Publishing Company
This book or any part thereof may not be
reproduced without the written consent of the
publisher.
Turner Publishing Company Staff:
Editor: Randy Baumgardner
Designer: Peter A. Zuniga
Library of Congress Catalog Card No.
2002100991
ISBN: 978-1-68162-562-1
Additional copies may be purchased directly from the
publisher. Limited Edition.

TABLE OF CONTENTS

THE WHITE HOUSE

WASHINGTON

July 19, 2002

I send greetings to those gathered for the annual seminar of the International Association of Auto Theft Investigators (IAATI). Congratulations on your 50th anniversary.

As local and national authorities continue to work together to protect the American people, police agencies and concerned industries must cooperate to fight auto theft. By uniting investigative professionals, IAATI is working toward the important goal of reducing global auto theft.

I commend the members of IAATI for your commitment to addressing the costly incidents of auto theft. Through education, training, and shared resources, your efforts help secure our property and promote the rule of law worldwide.

Laura joins me in sending our best wishes for a successful seminar.

INTERNATIONAL ASSOCIATION AUTO THEFT INVESTIGATORS

Dear IAATI Members:

As the IAATI Director of Marketing, I volunteered for the task of developing a book reviewing the first 50 years of this dynamic organization in August of 2000. Now, exactly two years later, I am putting the finishing touches on the book and I am finally seeing the fruits our labor.

I would like to sincerely thank all of you that provided input and guidance throughout the past two years. Also, I would like to thank Dave Turner and Randy Baumgardner of Turner Publishing. Although, I have a BA in Marketing and have developed many 3M marketing publications and videos, I had no idea on how to design a book. Dave and Randy were truly professionals and are the reason the book looks as great as it does.

This has been an overwhelming process and at times frustrating. However, the excitement of the challenge, the discovery, and getting to know many of you and our predecessors much better has far out weighed the difficult issues. I can honestly say that this has been a great joy for me and I hope you are as pleased with the results as I am.

My goal is that this book, reinforces for you what a great, strong organization that you are a member of. I am extremely proud to be a member of IAATI for the past 12 years, look forward to future, and most of all I am grateful for all my wonderful IAATI friends.

Enjoy the book!

Tracie Mortenson
Director of Marketing.

Executive Offices • P.O. Box • Clinton, NY 13323-0223 • Phone (315) 853-1913 • Fax (315) 793-0048 •
www.iaati.org

Established 1952

INTERNATIONAL ASSOCIATION AUTO THEFT INVESTIGATORS

Presidents Message

As the 50th President of the International Association of Auto Theft Investigators, I am proud to be able to look back with you at the accomplishments of IAATI since that historic first meeting in 1952, in Dallas, Texas. I am sure that the subsequent formation of IAATI in Oklahoma City, Oklahoma and the ideals of those founding members never dreamed that IAATI would ultimately become the most recognized Auto Theft Organization around the world.

The passing years have been a testament of our commitment as an organization. Our membership has grown and is now approaching 4000. Eight Chapters and Branches later, IAATI has continued to further our goals, objectives and the spirit of cooperation on a global scale.

As proud as we are, we cannot rest on the laurels of the past 50 years. I and future Presidents must look forward to the future. We must strive to keep IAATI's objectives in the forefront while leading the organization and its membership.

I am confident that as an organization, IAATI will do just that. The commitment of our Executive Boards worldwide continue to improve as well as grow. It is with that commitment that I am confident that IAATI will be as proud an organization 50 years from now as it has been in the last 50 years.

Congratulations to all of you for achieving this most exciting benchmark in IAATI's history.

David M. Ecklund

David M. Ecklund
IAATI President
2001-2002

Executive Offices • P.O. Box 223 • Clinton, NY 13323-0223 • Phone (315) 853-1913 • Fax (315) 793-0048 • www.iaati.org
Established 1952

INTERNATIONAL ASSOCIATION

AUTO THEFT INVESTIGATORS

Incoming President's Message to the Membership:

Our Golden Anniversary! What a grand milestone to achieve as a volunteer organization. Although we must never forget the past, it is our vision of the future that will drive us to continued success in our efforts to achieve our goals of unity, information sharing, cooperation and integrity. IAATI's success will depend on our capacity as members to promote our interests throughout our spheres of influence and manage the many geopolitical forces that present themselves throughout the world. We must seek opportunities to collectively provide our vast knowledge and resources through training and networking –the two areas that really determine how well we achieve our goals.

There are numerous issues that will confront our Association in the future, but here are a few of almost immediate consideration. First, technology has and will provide us with an avenue never before available to provide training. We must seize the opportunity to adopt innovative ideas to provide education through the ever-expanding media of the Internet and related conduits. The ability to provide real time viewing of our annual seminar and other training venues to someone thousands of miles away is very powerful. Second, historical events have created the need to share information as never before envisioned. Our existing network of professionals across the globe can provide a powerful tool in targeting not only vehicle theft, but also other organized crime such as terrorism. We must expand our pool of members and use this tool for the benefit of everyone. And third, our growing Web presence has begun to place our organization in a position to communicate more efficiently than ever before with the membership. In addition to the obvious use of our web site, I believe the future includes its expansion to include features such as intelligence sharing services and portals to other data sources that would allow for a common interface for all members across the globe.

It is imperative that we recruit committed and active members to continue the goals and objectives of IAATI in the next fifty years. As you well know the success of our organization is dependent on you, the volunteer, to make it happen. We must mentor our prospective members to provide them the ability and encourage innovation to pick-up the reins as IAATI gallops into the future. Ultimately it is the leaders of this Association that will provide the future direction for IAATI, not just this year, but for many years to come. Not only must we do things right— we must do the right things, for the right reasons and at the right time. Right now is the time to plot IAATI's course for the future. Become a part of its future with your vision, participation and desire to grow both personally and professionally.

There is little doubt that IAATI provides valuable service to its members, the private sector and to the various levels of government across the world. We, the consortium of individual members, branches and chapters, will determine the future path that links the many disparate countries together to form a common bond to achieve the objectives established in 1952 by a few extremely visionary men. It is our task to take their legacy and build it to an entirely different level, but never forgetting our seminal beginning.

Kent W. Mawyer

Established 1952

Gene Rutledge and Ed Sparkman

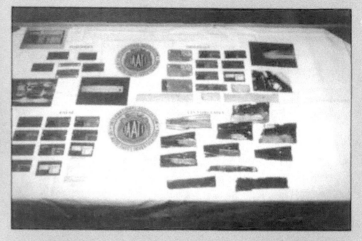

Jim Spanel and Glenn Wheeler

John Hanchett Kent, England

Proud Bobbie Hat winner

Roger Van Drew (left) and Jack deRemer (right) at the Oklahoma seminar in 1998.

2001 Virginia Beach Seminar Banquet

2000 Vancouver BC Police drum and pipe band

1998 Tulsa Seminar

2001 Virginia Beach Opening Ceremony

1998 Tulsa Seminar: Roger Van Drew and Steve Gobby

IN MEMORIAM

THE INTERNATIONAL ASSOCIATION OF AUTO THEFT INVESTIGATORS HAS SEEN TRAGIC DEATHS AND CAREER ENDING INJURIES TO MANY PEOPLE WHILE CONDUCTING VEHICLE THEFT INVESTIGATIONS THROUGH OUT THE WORLD.

IAATI EXTENDS OUR DEEPEST AND MOST HEARTFELT SYMPATHY TO "OUR FALLEN HEROES" WHO HAVE SUFFERED WHILE CASTING THEIR STONE IN AN EFFORT TO REDUCE VEHICLE THEFT.

THIS ORGANIZATION SHALL BE EVER GRATEFUL FOR YOUR EFFORTS AND DEDICATION. IAATI PLEDGES OUR LOYAL SUPPORT AND DEDICATION IN CONTINUING OUR EFFORTS TO COMPLETE THE ASSIGNMENTS TAKEN FROM YOUR HANDS SO ABRUPTLY. MAY YOUR SOULS, AND ALL THE SOULS OF THE FAITHFULLY DEPARTED, REST IN PEACE

National Insurance Crime Bureau

July 18, 2002

Dear Colleagues in the International Association of Auto Theft
Investigators:

The National Insurance Crime Bureau (NICB) and its 317 employees wish to extend its
heartiest congratulations to the International Association of Auto Theft Investigators
(IAATI) on their 50th Anniversary.

The partnership between IAATI and the NICB that was established 50 years ago in
Oklahoma continues to grow stronger each year. Working together, we have seen
outstanding accomplishments, including improved training, increased public awareness
of vehicle theft issues, and a mutual support for the common goals and objectives of
IAATI and NICB.

As we all know, vehicle theft and fraud does not stop at state or national borders. In
response to this, IAATI has grown into a truly international association with over 3,600
professional members in over 40 countries representing law enforcement agencies at all
levels, the insurance industry, rental car companies, the vehicle manufacturing industry,
and other interested groups.

I have attended several IAATI annual conferences and find them to be informative and
an outstanding network for addressing vehicle theft and fraud issues.

On behalf of all NICB employees, past and present, we wish you much continued
success in the future.

Warmest Regards,

Robert M. Bryant
President and Chief Executive Officer

National Office
901 N. Stuart Street, Suite 1150
Arlington , VA 22203

Phone: (703)469-2200
(703)469-2206
www.nicb.org

11

Sandy Thompson, Tommy Hanson, ??

1995 Orlando Seminar-Karen Metz, Denny Roske, Russ Suess, Kevin Curry, Dave Ecklund, Tracie Lucking, Bob Grimm, Mike Arbit

1992 Toronto Seminar, Charles Kelly, ??, Steve Gobby

2000 Vancouver Seminar-Jim Gavigan, Ron Powell

Joanie Pitts, Don Robertson, Karen Metz, Marianne Finnay, Roger VanDrew, and Denny Meyer

Tommy Hanson, Pat Ethridge, J.C.

1993 Boise Seminar-Ziggy gets a laugh at Kevin Curry's expense.

??,??, Jim Cadigan, Don Kessler, Ziggy Zablocki, Paul Dehesandro

Joanie Pitts and Vancouver City P.D. friends.

Greg White and Tommy Hansen

Sandra Thompson, Bill Larocque, Tracie Mortenson, Russ Suess,
Karen Metz, Ari Huhtinen, Jack de Remer

Denny Roske swearing in his Executive Board Members

CODE OF ETHICS

- I WILL, AS AN AUTO THEFT INVESTIGATOR, REGARD MYSELF AS A MEMBER OF AN IMPORTANT AND HONORABLE PROFESSION.

- I WILL CONDUCT BOTH MY PERSONAL AND OFFICIAL LIFE SO AS TO INSPIRE THE CONFIDENCE OF THE PUBLIC.

- I WILL NOT USE MY PROFESSION AND MY POSITION OF TRUST FOR PERSONAL ADVANTAGE OR PROFIT.

- I WILL REGARD MY FELLOW INVESTIGATORS WITH THE SAME STANDARDS AS I HOLD FOR MYSELF. I WILL NEVER BETRAY A CONFIDENCE NOR OTHERWISE JEOPARDIZE THEIR INVESTIGATIONS.

- I WILL REGARD IT MY DUTY TO KNOW MY WORK THOROUGHLY. IT IS MY FURTHER DUTY TO AVAIL MYSELF OF EVERY OPPORTUNITY TO LEARN MORE ABOUT MY PROFESSION.

- I WILL AVOID ALL ALLIANCES WITH THOSE WHOSE GOALS ARE INCONSISTENT WITH AN HONEST AND UNBIASED INVESTIGATION.

- I WILL MAKE NO CLAIMS TO PROFESSIONAL QUALIFICATIONS WHICH I DO NOT POSSESS.

- I WILL SHARE ALL PUBLICITY EQUALLY WITH MY FELLOW INVESTIGATORS, WHETHER SUCH PUBLICITY IS FAVORABLE OR UNFAVORABLE.

- I WILL BE LOYAL TO MY SUPERIORS, TO MY SUBORDINATES, AND TO THE ORGANIZATIONS I REPRESENT.

- I WILL BEAR IN MIND ALWAYS THAT I AM A TRUTH SEEKER, NOT A CASEMAKER; THAT IT IS MORE IMPORTANT TO PROTECT THE INNOCENT THAN TO CONVICT THE GUILTY.

Cpl Tom Quinn, OPP, Demo fingerprinting of suspect vehicle

Australia

Austria

Bahamas

Belgium

Bosnia–Herzegovina

Bulgaria

Canada

Costa Rica

Denmark

England

Estonia

Finland

France

Germany

Gibraltar

Greece

Guatemala

Holland

Honduras

Hungary

Ireland

Israel

Italy

Jamaica

Kenya

Kosovo

Malaysia

Mexico

Northern Ireland

New Zealand

Norway

Philippines

Poland

Portugal

Russia

Scotland

South Africa

Spain

Sweden

Switzerland

The Netherlands

Ukraine

United Arab Emirates

United Kingdom

United States of America

MOTOR TREND

The Car Owners Magazine

DECEMBER 1952
25c

FBI EXPOSES INTERNATIONAL CAR THIEVES!

By J. Edgar Hoover

NEW WONDER MATERIAL
Sports Car Builders Turn to Fiberglas

Book found by Tommy Hansen in junk shop.

16

What Does It Cost to Customize Your Car?

The Red-Hot Steamers!

1981 Houston: Lyman Ross, NATB; Gene Rutledge, CHP.

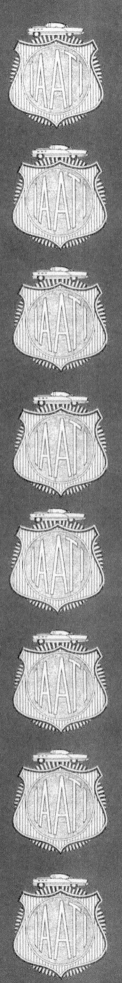

BEGINNINGS OF THE INTERNATIONAL ASSOCIATION OF AUTO THEFT INVESTIGATORS

by Detective Thomas J. Horrigan, D.C. Metropolitan Police

FOUNDERS

Glen McLaughlin, Texas Department of Public Safety
Vincent Moncrief, Oklahoma City Police Department
C.C. Benson, NATB
James Sullivan, NATB
John Daniel, Dallas Police Department

In 1952, a group of law enforcement officers, concerned with the rising volume of automobile thefts, decided to hold a three-day conference to discuss the problem and exchange experiences. Response to the meeting in Dallas, Texas was gratifying, and the enthusiasm of the participants was stimulating. All believed the conference was worth continuing and enlarging.

A planning session was held for organizing a new association which would be dedicated to uniting those interested in the investigation of automobile thefts. A constitution and by-laws were drafted and plans made for the first annual conference to be held in Oklahoma City, in 1953. The group was comprised of Chief Glen McLaughlin, Texas Department of Public Safety; Vincent Moncrief, Oklahoma City Police Department; C.C. Benson, Manager; James Sullivan of the National Auto Theft Bureau; and, John Daniel, Dallas P.D.

The organizational meeting was held in May 1953 at the Biltmore Hotel in Oklahoma City. The constitution and bylaws of the International Association of Auto Theft Investigators (IAATI) were adopted and the organization was chartered under the laws of Oklahoma. Captain John F. Daniel, Dallas Police Department, was elected the first president.

STATE OBJECTIVES OF THE ASSOCIATION WERE, AND ARE:

1. To unite for mutual benefit, persons who are regular salaried law enforcement officers of munici pal, county, state and federal agencies; those honorably retired therefrom; agents of the National Auto Theft Bureau; and administrative officers of State Motor Vehicle Departments.

2. To exchange technical information and developments.

3. To cooperate with all law enforcement agencies and associations engaged in the prevention and suppression of auto thefts and kindred crimes.

4. To encourage a high professional standard of conduct among theft investigators and to strive con tinually to eliminate all factors interfering with the administration of auto theft suppression.

IAATI, in the intervening years, has demonstrated that the most effective weapon to combat the crime of auto theft, as well as other crimes, is cooperation—the combined efforts of all law enforcement agencies with the support and understanding of the public. No police agency is so big, or so small, that it does not need the assistance of another. Through an exchange of information and ideas, the initiative, the intelligence and the industry of all persons of like interest and ambition can attain remarkable achievements.

Since the very nature of he crime of automobile theft is one of transportation, the involvement of more than one agency is the rule, not the exception. Even the simple crime of "joy riding" calls for the cooperation of more than one agency. For example, registration records are kept and handled by one agency, another takes the theft report, the recovery may be made by another agency, and the apprehension can be made by still another. Good intentions never caught a thief, or recovered a stolen automobile, and ideas are useless unless they are expressed. IAATI has served as such a medium of expression, holding annual seminars since 1953.

WANTED
DEAD OR ALIVE

PREFERABLY ALIVE, KICKING AND FULL OF ENERGY THAT YOU WOULD LIKE TO DEDICATE TO MAKING IAATI A STRONGER ASSOCIATION. IF YOU HAVE A DESIRE TO BECOME MORE ACTIVE IN IAATI, PLEASE CONTACT OUR PRESIDENT, KEN MACKENZIE. HE WISHES TO APPOINT INTERESTED MEMBERS TO THE FOLLOWING COMMITTEES: CONSTITUTION AND BY-LAWS; CORPORATE INVOLVEMENT; EXHIBIT; FINANCE & AUDIT; LEGISLATIVE; MARINE MARKETING; MEMBERSHIP; PROTOCOL; PUBLIC RELATIONS(MEDIA); RESOLUTIONS; SITE SELECTION; AND 3M AWARD COMMITTEE.

IAATI FOUNDERS

IAATI THANKS C.C. BENSON AND MRS. JOHN DANIEL FOR THE HISTORICAL INPUT.

CARROLL C. (C.C.) BENSON

C.C. was born Jan. 29, 1915 in Coke Co., Texas, the son of Clyde and Beulah Benson. His father was a railway station telegraph agent. The family eventually settled in Clay Co. (Petrolia), Texas. He graduated from Petrolia High School.

During the Great Depression, he worked at any odd jobs available, and made application to the Wichita Falls State Mental Hospital. He was accepted as an "attendant" and began work on August 2, 1932. He worked his way up within the rank of the company, from dining room supervision, dairy and vegetable farming, transportation, and ultimately to the accounting department. During this time he met another hospital employee, Ada Grace Rutherford, whom he married on Oct. 6, 1934.

In 1937 C.C. became a patrolman with the Texas Dept. of Public Safety and was assigned to Dallas, Corpus Christi, Victoria and Amarillo over the next three years. He returned to the Dallas District in 1940 as a Sergeant. He joined the U.S. Navy in 1942 as a Warrant Officer, on active duty with the 12th District Naval Intelligence. He served as a Naval Intelligence Investigator, and after several training schools was assigned to Naval Transport Service serving as assistant to the Commander of Troops on the SS *President Tyler*. Additional assignments included Honolulu, Hawaii and San Pablo Bay in the south Philippines. He returned to the States in December 1945 and was released from active duty.

He returned to the Texas Highway Patrol as a sergeant in Fort Worth. In June 1946, he was offered a position as a special agent for the National Automobile Theft Bureau (NATB) in Dallas by the late Ed Gormley, with the assurance that his relations with the DPS would remain steadfast. In conjunction with this assignment, he was commissioned a Special Texas Ranger by the Texas Legislature. He remained an active Ranger after retirement from the NATB, now called the National Insurance Crime Bureau.

In his years with the NATB, he was fortunate to work with all branches of law enforcement and to participate in a number of law enforcement training programs at the local, state and Federal level. The NATB felt a great responsibility to share all information and intelligence they could gather. This conviction was manifest, in part, by the great interest and support the NATB gave in the creation of the IAATI.

1981 Houston: Tom Horrigan, John Hoover, Magician, Bob Olson, and Gene Rutledge

1989 Seminar BBQ (Foreground) Lily Bell, Rose Heaword, Gerry Wood, Brian Wood, Gene Rutledge

1976 San Jose: Clarence Brickey, Mayland State Police, and George Hees, LAPD

The Evolution of the IAATI Logo

International Association of
Auto Theft Investigators

Seeking solutions to the growing problem of vehicle theft, 181 attendees from the southwestern region of the United States met at Dallas in November 1951. The three day conference was sponsored by the Texas Police Association, Texas Sheriff's Association, Dallas Police Department, Federal Bureau of Investigation, and NATB. The seminar was composed of a cross section of law enforcement. A major topic of discussion was control of vehicle crime.

According to C.C. Benson, retired NATB Southwestern Division Manager, the conference was well received. Attendees expressed interest in having a similar meeting the following year. A committee was formed consisting of Captain John Daniel, Dallas PD; Chief Glen McLaughlin, Texas Department of Public Safety; Chief Robert Lester, Oklahoma Department of Public Safety; Vince Moncrief, Oklahoma City PD; Bill Sterzing, Austin PD; and Jim Sullivan and C.C. Benson, NATB. While meeting in Ardmore, Oklahoma, the committee prepared a constitution and bylaws for the

NATB ceased efforts in traffic safety in 1952. This 1949 Ford ended its useful life at an Arizona scrap yard.

Pacific Coast Division Special Agents Meeting at San Francisco in 1951. Seated (L to R): E.F. Zimmmerman, Comptroller and Dennis N. Key, Manager. Standing Special Agents, Lyman C. Ross, Ernest Hout, A.O. Peterson, W.L. Payne, Ruth Assalena, A.S. Ekern, E.J. Halm, G.F. Potts, Jim Allen, B.H. Germain and R.M. Newsome.

new organization. Benson observed that, "From the beginning, the association members exhibited keen interest and desire for strong educational programs. With much work from many people, the 1952 conference was most successful and the delegates formalized the International Association of Auto Theft Investigators (IAATI), which was chartered in Oklahoma." John Daniel was elected president and Vince Moncrief was elected secretary.

Today, IAATI continues to be a forum for those who are working to control vehicle crime. The purpose of the organization is to formulate new methods to attack and control vehicle theft and fraud. The organization has grown to include more than 1,200 professional members representing law enforcement agencies, insurance companies, car rental companies, the automobile manufacturing industry and other interested organizations. NATB personnel regularly assist IAATI by serving as speakers and instructors at international and regional seminars. Since its inception, IAATI's membership has continued to meet annually to look for solutions to the international problem of vehicle theft.

Western Division Manager William J. Davis and Special Agent Alfonso Rincon Pina, discuss the return of recovered stolen vehicles from Mexico.

NATB personnel attending the 1951 Auto Theft Conference which led to the founding of IAATI. Front row (L to R): Ken Johnson, Martin Koonsman, Royce Calvert, Guy Shirley, and Jim Sullivan. Back row (L to R): Burwell Avara, Gary Potts, William J. Davis, C.C. Benson, and Don Armstrong.

PROGRAM

☆

*Conference on
Automobile Theft*

☆

November 19-20-21, 1951
BAKER HOTEL
Dallas, Texas

☆

Sponsored by the
Texas Police Association

In Cooperation with
FEDERAL BUREAU OF INVESTIGATION
TEXAS DEPARTMENT OF PUBLIC SAFETY
SHERIFFS' ASSOCIATION OF TEXAS

Automobile Theft Conference

FIRST DAY
November 19, 1951

8:00-10:00 A.M.—Registration
Mr. J. F. Daniel, Captain, Auto Theft Bureau, Dallas Police Department.

10:00-10:45 A.M.—Opening
Mr. J. W. Dellinger, Chief of Police, Taylor, Texas.
—Introductions
Mr. C. F. Hansson, Chief of Police, Dallas, Texas.
—Address
Mr. Charles C. Ford, City Manager, Dallas, Texas.

11:00-11:45 A.M.—Auto Theft Trends
Mr. F. H. McIntire, SAC-FBI, San Antonio, Texas.

NOON

1:15-2:00 P.M.—Recent Case Histories
Mr. W. C. Doss, Detective, Houston Police Department.
Mr. S. P. Jones, Detective, Fort Worth Police Department
Mr. G. A. Bates, Detective, Dallas Police Department.
Mr. Royce Calvert, Field Representative NATB, Dallas, Texas.
Mr. J. K. Mumford, SAC-FBI, Dallas, Texas.

2:15-3:00 P.M.—Centralization of Information
Mr. Glen H. McLaughlin, Chief, Bureau of Identification and Records, Department of Public Safety, Austin, Texas.
Mr. Bob Brewer, Texas Highway Department, Austin, Texas.
Mr. Bennie Williams, Texas Department of Public Safety, Austin, Texas.
Mr. D. Armstrong, NATB, Chicago, Illinois.
Mr. L. O. Heard, Captain Louisiana State Police, Baton Rouge.

3:15-4:00 P.M.—Title Information
Mr. Bob Brewer, Texas Highway Department, Austin, Texas.
Mr. J. H. Clark, NATB, Atlanta, Georgia.
Mr. Gordon Carlson, Texas Highway Department, Austin.
Mr. Bob Townsley, Texas Highway Department, Austin.

4:15-5:00 P.M.—Modus Operandi
Mr. Royal G. Phillips, Chief, Bureau of Intelligence, Department of Public Safety, Austin, Texas.
Mr. N. K. Woerner, Chief of Statistical Division, Department of Public Safety, Austin, Texas.
Mr. A. N. Boggs, Lieutenant of Detectives, Dallas Police Dept.

SECOND DAY
November 20, 1951

9:00-9:45 A.M.—Identification and Tracings as Related to Motor Vehicles
Mr. C. C. Benson, Manager, NATB, Dallas, Texas.

10:00-10:45 A.M.—Coordination of Work Programs
Mr. D. A. Loe, Inspector CID, Dallas Police Department.
Mr. Joe S. Fletcher, Assistant Director, Department of Public Safety, Austin, Texas.
Mr. D. K. Brown, SAC-FBI, El Paso, Texas.
Mr. R. D. Thorp, Chief of Police, Austin, Texas.
Mr. C. C. Maxey, Sheriff, Waco, Texas.

11:00-11:45 A.M.—Administrative Policies and Procedures
Mr. J. F. Daniel, Captain of Detectives, Dallas Police Dept.
Mr. C. G. Connor, Inspector, Texas Highway Department, Austin, Texas.
Mr. E. G. Huckabay, Chief of Police, Shreveport, Louisiana.
Mr. H. A. Spradley, Lieutenant of Detectives, Houston Police Department.
Mr. C. E. Hightower, Chief of Detectives, Fort Worth Police Department.
Mr. J. E. (Bill) Decker, Sheriff, Dallas County, Texas.

NOON

1:15-2:00 P.M.—Surveillances and Blockades
Mr. R. D. Allen, Captain in Charge of Operations, San Antonio Police Department.
Mr. E. P. Bogasch, Inspector, San Antonio Police Department.
Mr. Jack Larned, Sergeant of Detectives, San Antonio Police Department.

2:15-3:00 P.M.—U. S. Customs Service
Mr. Tully Garner, Customs Agent, Laredo, Texas.

3:15-4:00 P.M.—Investigative Techniques
Mr. A. L. Lorton, SAC-FBI, Houston, Texas.
Mr. R. A. Crowder, Captain, Texas Rangers, Dallas, Texas.
Mr. V. A. Moncrief, Detective, Oklahoma City Police Dept.
Mr. Bill Sterzing, Sergeant of Detectives, Austin Police Dept.
Mr. H. J. Cobb, Detective, Fort Worth Police Department.
Mr. M. N. Koonsman, Field Representative NATB, Abilene, Texas

---

4:15-5:00 P.M.—Motor Vehicle Inspection and Driver Responsibility Laws
Mr. G. W. Busby, Chief, Motor Vehicle Inspection Division, Department of Public Safety, Austin, Texas.
Mr. J. B. Alderdice, Chief Accountant, Department of Public Safety, Austin, Texas.

5:00-'til—Barbecue and "Trimmins'"
Catering Service by:
Lieutenant V. S. Smart of the Dallas Police Dept.
Lieutenant O. R. Brown of the Fort Worth Police Dept.
Entertainment: Uncle Lee (Pop) Myers, Official Master of Ceremonies—Texas Police Association.

THIRD DAY
November 21, 1951

9:00-9:45 A.M.—Functions of the Highway Patrol
Mr. W. J. Elliott, Chief, Texas Highway Patrol, Austin, Texas.

10:00-10:45 A.M.—Training Programs
Mr. William S. Brogdon, Assistant Chief of Police, Dallas.
Mr. F. H. McIntire, SAC-FBI, San Antonio, Texas.
Mr. T. C. Laws, Chief, Training Division, Department of Public Safety, Austin, Texas.
Mr. E. P. Bogasch, Inspector, San Antonio Police Department.
Mr. Carl Shruptine, Captain, Training Division, Houston Police Department.
Mr. J. D. Galloway, Lieutenant, Fort Worth Police Dept.
Mr. R. B. Laws, Lieutenant, Police Department, Austin, Texas.
Mr. C. H. Meyer, Sheriff, Beaumont, Texas.

11:00-11:45 A.M.—Police Ethics
Mr. C. F. Hansson, Chief of Police, Dallas, Texas.

NOON

1:15-5:00 P.M.—Panel Discussions

No. 1. Recovery of Vehicles from Mexico
Mr. Wm. J. Davis, Manager, NATB, Chicago, Illinois.
Mr. D. K. Brown, SAC-FBI, El Paso, Texas.

No. 2. Training Programs
Mr. Charles Batchelor, Inspector, Dallas Police Dept.
Mr. F. H. McIntire, SAC-FBI, San Antonio, Texas

No. 3. Administration
Mr. Joe S. Fletcher, Assistant Director, Department of Public Safety, Austin, Texas.
Mr. Harry Riddell, Deputy Chief of Police, Commanding Criminal Investigation Division, Dallas Police Department.

POLICE STUDY AUTO THIEVERY

By FRANK X. TOLBERT

There was the $20,000-a-year businessman who had a kind of hobby, stealing a half dozen or so automobiles every month.

This and dozens of other cases were scientifically considered Monday in Dallas by officers specializing in automobile theft cases.

The officers came from sixty-six police departments of the Southwest to the first annual conference on vehicle theft sponsored by the Texas Police Association, in cooperation with the FBI, the Texas Department of Public Safety and the Sheriffs' Association of Texas.

Among them Monday, the 135 officers had almost a thousand years' experience combatting car thieves.

Still, despite careful police work, automobile theft is alarmingly on the increase.

Fred H. McIntire, agent-in-charge for the FBI in San Antonio, told the conference that Texas, Arkansas, Louisiana and Oklahoma accounted for one third of the nation's increase in stolen vehicles last year.

"We're getting more car thieves down this way. We don't know where they're coming from," declared McIntire.

McIntire said the age bracket of the majority of the car thieves is known, though. He said that 69 per cent of the nation's arrested car thieves are under twenty-one years old. And there are more 18-year-old car thieves than in any other age bracket.

Giving a brief history of car thieving in this country, McIntire said the picture was a lot brighter today than back in 1918-1919, before passage of the Dyer Act. This law makes it a federal offense to transport a stolen vehicle from one state to another.

In the year just before the Dyer Act was passed, McIntire said $25,-000,000 worth of cars were stolen in the United States. In contrast, he said $15,400,000 were stolen last year, although the number of vehicles in the country has increased many times since 1918. In 1918, 18 per cent of the cars stolen were

See POLICE, Page 14, Col. 6

POLICE

Continued from Page 1

never recovered, while now about 8 per cent completely disappear.

McIntire told of the $20,000-a-year businessman, who made about as much from his car thefts. And when he was finally caught he admitted to police: "If I couldn't open a locked car in thirty seconds, I figured I deserved to be caught."

Royce Calvert, field representative of the National Automobile Theft Bureau in Dallas, told of the high-powered car thief who once stole a car in Detroit, sold it to a San Antonio dealer, stole it from the San Antonio dealer immediately, and then sold it to an Oklahoma City man.

Speaking of the conflicting testimony of witnesses, Detective G. A. Bates of the Dallas police department told of the 6-foot 4-inch car thief who was persistently described by his victims as being about 5 feet 8 inches in height.

The conference, conducted in as scientific an atmosphere as a college professors' convention, will continue through Wednesday. Much of the information before the conference would be of value to criminals and can not be reported.

In an interview, Detective Escajeda of the El Paso police department told of the international difficulties in recovering stolen cars taken into Mexico.

El Paso had 295 cars stolen last year. In comparison, Austin an inland city of about the same size had only 111 stolen. Escajeda, who has pursued car thieves all over Mexico, says he gets splendid cooperation from Mexican authorities.

Working through the treaty between Mexico and the United States it often takes from one to two years, though, to recover a stolen auto.

"It would be impractical to check each car going through customs to see if it is stolen," said McIntire. To illustrate, he said that in border cities close to San Antonio last year, about 15,000,000 crossed the border into the United States and about 14,000,000 crossed into Mexico.

"Car thieves often take cars off the street of San Antonio and the car is in Monterrey, Mexico, before the theft is even reported," said McIntire.

City Manager Charles C. Ford welcomed the officers to Dallas. Police Chief Carl Hansson also spoke. Inspector D. A. Loe of Dallas Police was master-of-ceremonies for the conference in the Peacock Terrace of Baker Hotel. Hansson said the conference was the first of its kind in the Southwest

—Dallas News Staff Photo.

Fred H. McIntire, FBI agent from San Antonio, is pictured speaking Monday at a conference in Dallas of Southwest police officers on automobile thefts.

Police Arrive From 9 States For Meeting

Police officers from nine states were arriving in Dallas Sunday for a 3-day conference on auto thieves.

Sessions will begin at 10 a.m. Monday in the Baker Hotel, said Asst. Police Chief William S. Brogdon of Dallas. Brogdon is secretary-treasurer of the Texas Police Association, principal sponsor of the conference. The Federal Bureau of Investigation, the Texas Department of Public Safety and the Sheriff's Association of Texas are assisting.

Morning speakers will include J. W. Dellinger, chief of police at Taylor, Williamson County; Capt. J. F. Daniel of the Dallas Police Department auto theft bureau; Dallas Police Chief Carl Hansson and Dallas City Manager Charles C. Ford.

The afternoon session will begin at 1:15 with a recital of recent auto theft case histories.

Glen H. McLaughlin, chief of the bureau of identification and records of the Department of Public Safety at Austin, will speak at 2:15 p.m. on how information on stolen vehicles is centralized.

An attendance of 2,000 has been predicted. States to be represented are Texas, Louisiana, Arkansas, New Mexico, Oklahoma, Tennessee, Missouri, Alabama and Mississippi.

AT A 9-STATE police confab here on auto thefts, the officers got to talking about old case histories. One of them told of a $20,000-a-year businessman whose hobby was stealing half a dozen autos a month. "If I couldn't open a locked car in thirty seconds, I figured I deserved to be caught," he said. Another well-known car thief was a 6-foot 4-inch fellow who somehow had the knack of making witnesses remember that he was 5 feet 8 inches.

A SAN ANTONIO detective sitting in on the auto theft conference at the Baker passed on some tips about how he tails a stolen car. He travels in an inconspicuous car. He carries extra license plates and changes occasionally so the absconder won't catch on. Also carries a can of extra gasoline and some money. His car has a special switch so he can make either headlight dimmer than the other, to hide its appearance in the dark. So if the car behind you starts changing its dim headlight back and forth, you know what.

—Dallas News Staff Photo.

Between these three veteran Texas policemen there is more than 100 years' experience in chasing car thieves and other criminals. There are, left to right, H. J. Cobb of Fort Worth, who started combatting car thieves in 1924; Lt. H. A. Spradley of Houston police, and Police Chief J. W. Dellinger of Taylor, Williamson County. They were in Dallas for a conference of Southwest officers on automobile thefts, sponsored by the Texas Police Association.

SEIZURE OF AUTO THIEF LIKENED TO RAT CHASE

By JIM STEPHENSON

You catch an auto thief much the same way a farmer heads off a rat that's stealing his corn, Senior Investigator Walter Naylor of the Texas Department of Public Safety, explained in Dallas Thursday.

Naylor spoke before officers from nine southern and southwestern states, assembled just to discuss the type of rat that steals automobiles. The sessions, started Monday, will run through Wednesday. They are being held on the Peacock Terrace of the Baker Hotel.

"When a farmer discovers a hole in a sack of corn, he hurries to shut off all avenues of escape—a hole in a window, a crack in the floor—clears things away so he can operate, then closes in on the thieving rat," Naylor said.

"When we're notified of a car theft, we do about the same thing. Allowing for the time element, we back off, blockade roads leading away from the vicinity, then close in on the car thief."

Policy of the Safety Department, Naylor reminded the officers, is to assist local officers whenever possible.

"And the department has the technique, equipment and manpower to do it," Naylor said.

See THIEF, Page 16, Col. 5

THIEF

Continued from Page 1

"We're ready at any time to move up a secondary line of defense."

Jack Larned, San Antonio sergeant of detectives, gave some ABC's of surveillance.

"A car being used to trail another car should be inconspicuous," Larned said. "And the two investigators operating it—there should be two—ought to have some special equipment. This includes some extra license plates (to fool the followed person), a can of extra gasoline (to keep from getting stranded), and some money (handy stuff)."

His own car, Larned said, has a few special touches, like a switch to dim one light at a time, giving the vehicle a different appearance at night.

The conference, sponsored by the Texas Police Association in co-operation with the Federal Bureau of Investigation, the Texas Department of Public Safety and the Sheriffs' Association of Texas, emphasized again and again the importance of reporting a theft the minute it is discovered.

"Even a 1940 Chevy can go a long way in just a few hours," Dallas County Sheriff Bill Decker pointed out, telling about one in particular that did so, with a young thief at the wheel.

D. K. Brown of the FBI office at El Paso, urged that the FBI be notified promptly of thefts.

"Even though the case may not come up in federal court," he said, "we can often give you the benefit of a background check."

Brown said the FBI was not satisfied with light sentences sometimes handed car theives for lack of time to prepare the fullest possible cases against them.

Joe S. Fletcher, assistant director of the safety department, reminded the officer that car thievery is pretty big busines in Texas—around thirty cars a day stolen, or ten to twelve thousand a year, worth about $15,000,000.

Fletcher emphasized the need for good public relations.

"Our problems will be easier," he said, "if we tell the public about them.

"A car thief looks first for easy pickings—the car parked at a drug store with the engine still running. If people are asked to co-operate and to report thefts promptly they'll usually do it."

B. E. Williams, chief deputy sheriff of Harris County, said he hoped Harris County and the City of Houston could work out a deal like Dallas', whereby expenses of going out of the state for a fugitive are shared.

"It takes money," Williams said.

Bill Decker jokingly told Williams if he'd stay away from Galveston he'd have more money.

"It's different with you, Bill," Williams razzed back. "You don't need money to go after thieves, because all your thieves are right here in Dallas."

Organization of a Modern Auto Theft Bureau

by CARL F. HANSSON, *Chief of Police, and* CAPT. JOHN DANIEL, *Auto Theft Bureau, Dallas, Tex., Police Department.*

Automobile thefts represent a greater property loss than the combined totals of all other offenses. It is one of the major offenses holding a top position of responsibility for the alarming nationwide crime rate.

Generally, there are three categories of auto theft, depending upon the purpose for which the auto is stolen: joyriding; commercial or transportation theft; and theft of vehicles to be used in committing other crimes. While joyriding is a local problem, commercial theft and thefts for the commission of other crimes are largely of national significance, since the cars involved generally are transported interstate; therefore, it is imperative that cooperation and a close liaison be maintained among all law enforcement agencies in order to attack the auto-theft problem successfully.

The problem, both locally and nationally, is not one for the auto-theft investigators only, but for all police officers. It is not enough to train the auto-theft investigator to a specialist degree—all members of a department must be instructed in the basic problems related to auto-theft investigation.

Officers of the Dallas Police Department are instructed in the techniques of interviewing subjects suspected of auto theft. They are acquainted with the danger signs of auto thefts—the manner in which license plates are attached, if the license was issued before the car was manufactured, dirty licenses on clean cars and vice versa. They are familiarized with the automobile factory numbering system, especially important to the officers in the field who have increased opportunity to observe changes in motor and serial numbers on vehicles. Much of the officers' instruction is received through informal classroom discussions conducted by trained, experienced auto-theft investigators who relate some of their experiences and advise on tested techniques of uncovering auto thefts and their successful investigation.

This instruction has definitely been fruitful.

Many cases of auto theft have been solved even before the crimes were discovered and reported by the owners.

Specialists of the Auto Theft Bureau are given training in inventorying wrecking yards, used-car lots, and automobile dealers to determine if salvaged vehicles are being used in commercial theft rings. Through this process investigators uncover many misrepresented titles which were issued to wrecking yard operators but had been sold to other persons. It has been necessary, at times, to inventory an entire business to determine and remedy discrepancies in vehicle numbers corresponding with title papers in the dealer's possession. Through this technique alone several stolen vehicles have been recovered and valuable information gained, leading to the recovery of many more cars which otherwise would have been almost impossible to detect.

Chief Carl F. Hansson.

Howard Apple and Dan Ryan, FBI undercover agents, buy nine stolen new Buicks, 1981, Baltimore, MD.

Detection
of the
Stolen Automobile

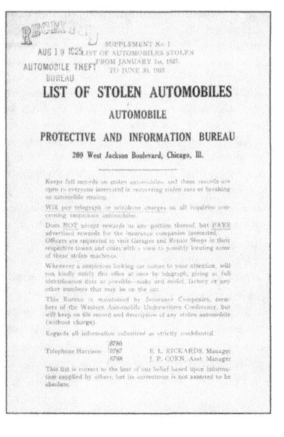

SUPPLEMENT No. 1

AUG 19 1925 LIST OF AUTOMOBILES STOLEN
FROM JANUARY 1st, 1925,
TO JUNE 30, 1925

LIST OF STOLEN AUTOMOBILES

AUTOMOBILE

PROTECTIVE AND INFORMATION BUREAU

209 West Jackson Boulevard, Chicago, Ill.

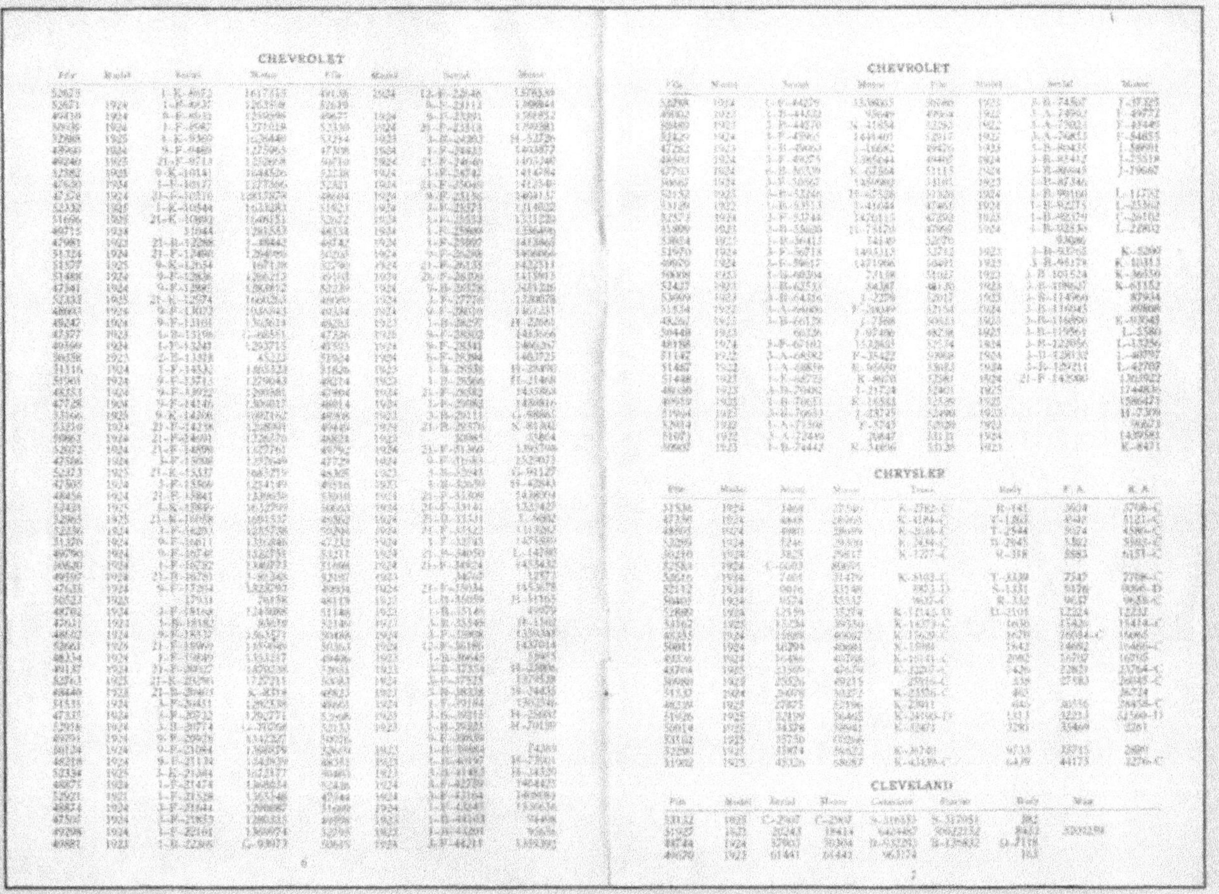

CHEVROLET

CHEVROLET

CHRYSLER

CLEVELAND

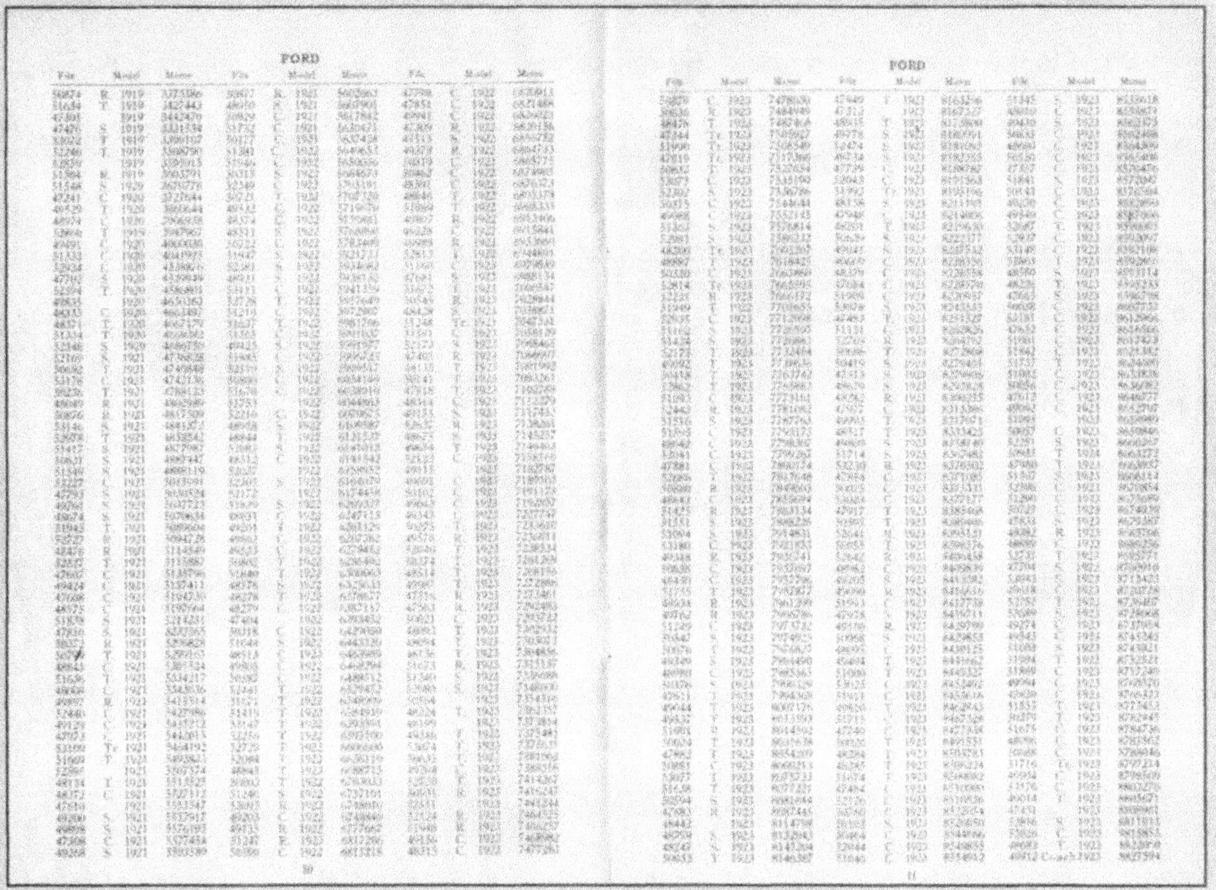

FORD

FORD

List of stolen automobiles, printed in August 1925 by the Automotive Protective and Information Bureau

AUTO THEFT QUESTIONS AND COMMENTS

BY R.B. KING, CAPTAIN, VIRGINIA STATE POLICE

Originally printed in Texas Police Journal, November 1955

1. **Do Automobile Theft Crimes Pay?**
   No one is arrested in 72.5 out of every 100 auto thefts, and of the 27.5 arrested, only about two-thirds are convicted.

2. **When is it a Theft?**
   Although it varies from state to state, in general these elements are necessary to prove larceny:
   a. There must be an "unlawful taking."
   b. There must be a "carrying away" of the stolen property.
   c. There must be intent to permanently deprive another of his property.

3. **What are the Motives for Auto Theft?**
   Although motives may vary, some of the more prevalent ones are:
   a. Joy riding.
   b. Essential transportation in which an individual has no other means of transportation.
   c. To commit other offenses of a criminal nature.
   d. To flee after committing another criminal offense.
   e. Commercial thefts.

4. **What is the Modus Operandi of the Auto Thieves?**
   Some of the well known methods involve counterfeit titles, fraudulently obtained titles through junk operations or obtaining a title before the vehicle is stolen. Some means of starting the cars are with foil, paper clips, hair pins, jumpers, and crossing the wires.

5. **Who Commits the Auto Thefts?**
   The predominant car thief is the juvenile white male.

6. **Some Things to Look for:**
   a. The driver is frequently not dressed in keeping with the vehicle being operated.
   b. The vehicles are out of place, such as new vehicles in slum areas.
   c. Cracked glasses.
   d. License tags are not properly secured.
   e. Freshly painted vehicles.
   f. Operators who are unusually observant of the police, particularly juveniles.
   g. An operator doing a natural thing in an unnatural manner.
   h. Two vehicles obviously traveling close together so that one may be used for a blocker in the event of a chase.

AUTO THEFT IS BIG BUSINESS

SINCE THE CLOSE of World War II, more than one million automobile thefts have been reported to law enforcement agencies throughout the United States. The prey of amateur and professional criminals alike, automobiles now are among the largest items on the nation's ledger of annual losses due to theft.

The magnitude of the automobile theft problem is shown in reports which have been received by the Federal Bureau of Investigation from law enforcement agencies in 381 U.S. cities. These reports reveal that the value of automobiles stolen in the 381 cities totaled more than $95,000,000 during 1951, while all other property taken by robbers and thieves was valued at little more than $61,000,000.

Over the entire nation an estimated 196,960 automobiles, valued at more than $190,000,000, were stolen last year. Even when it is considered that an estimated 180,810 stolen automobiles were recovered during 1951, the citizens of the United States still suffered a net loss of $15,600,000 through theft of automobiles alone in that 12-month period.

Statistics such as these certainly do not adequately portray the true picture of the losses suffered by law-abiding citizens through the theft of automobiles. Each of the 196,960 cars which were stolen resulted in police investigation, financed by public funds. In addition, many of the owners of these cars were dependent upon them in their vocations. Others suffered severe inconvenience which cannot be estimated in dollars due to the loss of their automobiles.

Statistics showing the total estimated value of automobiles stolen in the United States demonstrate that car theft is a major law enforcement problem. Aggressive action has been taken in the past to combat the auto thief, and such action has been

By J. Edgar Hoover
DIRECTOR, FEDERAL BUREAU
OF INVESTIGATION

stepped up to further combat this menace. Like all criminal acts, automobile theft is not solely the concern of the police or of the person who suffers the loss. It is also the concern of the public and must be met with vigorous and constructive action.

Armed with Federal legislation which makes illegal the inter-state transportation of stolen motor vehicles, the FBI has been active since 1919 in smashing auto theft rings which have operated on a national or international basis. The investigative jurisdiction of the FBI is limited to those cases in which the stolen automobile has been transported from one state to another; however, through cost-free services provided by the FBI Laboratory and Identification Division, the FBI has been able to assist state and municipal law enforcement agencies in identifying and convicting numerous auto thieves whose operations have not extended across state lines.

Each year it has become increasingly more obvious that the challenge presented by automobile thieves can be adequately met only through united action. As a first step in effecting a more concentrated offensive against automobile thieves, the FBI called upon state and local law enforcement agencies to meet with its agents in regional conferences which are now being held throughout the nation. Also participating in these conferences are state motor vehicle bureaus, the National Automobile Theft Bureau, and other interested agencies. Devoted solely to open forum discussion of car thefts, the conferences are meeting everywhere with interest and enthusiasm. An encouraging number of fine solutions to this problem have already been proposed at these conferences, and there has been universal agreement that an alert, educated public is the greatest asset available to the law enforcement officer in coping with this type of crime. *(Continued on next page)*

Article taken from Motor Trend, December 1952

Editor's Note: This chapter details the past 50 years of IAATI, presented by annual term. Due to varying amounts of information available, the number of pages will vary from year to year. We apologize for any inconvenience this may cause.

1952–1953

PRESIDENT J. F. DANIEL, DALLAS POLICE DEPARTMENT

Daniel began his career as a bicycle patrolman in 1929 in Dallas, Texas, working the 11 p.m. to 7 a.m. shift and earning $135 a month. Five months later he was promoted to the motorcycle squadron. Soon afterward, he was assigned as an auto theft detective. Then, in 1932 he joined the new robbery and homicide division as a lieutenant.

J.F. Daniel, Dallas (TX) Police Department

One of Daniel's most interesting tales was a run-in with the Clyde Barrow gang, in which Barrow's V-8 outmatched Daniel's old 490 Chevy. That same night Barrow was credited with the second murder. Daniel went on to be promoted to captain, and worked with the Dallas Police Dept. until his retirement in 1959. He became the first president of the International Association of Auto Theft Investigators in 1952.

EXECUTIVE BOARD

1st Vice President:	E.L. Hutchinson, Memphis Police
2nd Vice President:	R.B. King, Virginia State Police
3rd Vice President:	A.T. Nelson, Los Angeles Police
Secretary/Treasurer:	V.E. Moncrief, Oklahoma City Police
Directors:	Richard Jerabek, St. Louis Police
	Edward Leestma, Grand Rapids Police
	Melvin Larson, Wisconsin Dept. of Motor Vehicles
	E.G. Huckabay, Shreveport Police
	Gerald Akeman, Indianapolis Police
	N.C. Sturgeon, Tulsa Police

SEMINAR

Oklahoma City, Oklahoma
May 26–28, 1953

ROSTER OF ATTENDEES AT THE FIRST ANNUAL IAATI CONVENTION

Robert C. Abla, Oklahoma Highway Patrol
Jerry Akeman, Indianapolis Police
Roy M. Ambers, McAlester, Oklahoma Police
Jack M. Annis, Woodward, Oklahoma Police
Don Armstrong, Chicago NATB
Avara Burwell, Tyler, Texas NATB
John A. Baker, Norman, Oklahoma USN
C.C. Benson, Dallas NATB
Roy J. Bergman, Oklahoma City Police
O.K. Bivins, Oklahoma City Police
Eldon Boyer, Anadarko, Oklahoma Sheriff
Charles S. Black, New York City NATB
William T. Bowling, North Little Rock NATB
Robert L. Brandenburg, Alva, Oklahoma Police
Bob Brewer, Texas Highway Dept.
Herbert D. Brigham, Missouri Highway Patrol
William S. Brogdon, Dallas Police
Richard B. Brooks, Aradia County California Sheriff
W.W. Brown, Houston Police
George B. Buell, Fort Sill, Oklahoma
Royce L. Calvert, Dallas NATB
E.A. Capshaw, Oklahoma City Sheriff's
Russell L. Carleton, Oklahoma City Ofc. of Special Investigations
H.C. Carmichael, McAlester, Oklahoma Highway Patrol
William H. Chennault, Shreveport, Louisiana
Julian H. Clark, Atlanta NATB
C.D. Cochran, Oklahoma City Special Agent
E.F. Creech, Abilene, Texas Police
Paul V. Danigan, Casper, Wyoming Police
John F. Daniel, Dallas Police
William J. Davis, Chicago NATB
H.G. Dankenling, East St. Louis, Illinois Police
Leonard Ferris, Oklahoma Bureau of Investigation
Dennis K. Fitch, Kansas Bureau of Investigation
B.J. Gibson, Oklahoma Highway Patrol
Bert Giddens, Oklahoma City Police
A.M. Gilbert, North Carolina Dept. of Motor Vehicles
S.T. Grayson, Texas Highway Patrol
Wilfred A. Grusich, Sr., New Orleans Police
S.E. Gunn, Oklahoma City Police
Jack D. Hansford, Fort Sill, Oklahoma
Wayne Harbolt, Oklahoma City Police
Walker W. Harrison, Oklahoma City Police
Asa Dee Hickman, Beaumont, Texas Sheriff's
C.E. Hodges, Amarillo, Texas Police
E.G. Huckabay, Shreveport, Louisiana Police
Ted M. Hunt, Edenburg, Texas Police
E.P. Hutchinson, Memphis Police
Gordon R. Ivey, Grand Rapids Police
Richard Jerabek, St. Louis Police
S.P. Jones, Ft. Worth Police
G.L. Kennedy, Oklahoma Bureau of Investigation
Kennie Johnson, Houston NATB
Dennis N. Key, San Francisco NATB
Joe Klepper, Wichita, Kansas Police

R.B. King, Virginia State Police
Martin Koonswan, Abiline, Texas NATB
M.A. Larson, Norman, Oklahoma US Navy
Melvin Larson, Wisconsin Motor Vehicle Dept.
Edward Leestma, Grand Rapids Police
D.A. Loe, Dallas Police
S.E. Long, Guthrie, Oklahoma Police
R.J. Luther, Dallas District Attorney's Ofc.
Frank J. Masur, Jr., Austin Police
Wilford Matlock, Ft. Worth Police
Paul R. McDonald, Arkansas State Police
H.W. McFarling, TX DPS
Glen H. McLaughlin, TX DPS
J..A. May, Oklahoma City Police
C.C. Miller, Oklahoma City Police
V.E. Moncrief, Oklahoma City Police
George McNally, Kansas City NATB
A.T. Nelson, Los Angeles Police
Carl E. Nutt, Joplin, Missouri Traffic Dept.
Ralph F. Oberlichnu, Joplin, Missouri Police
Edward L. Oldham, Baton Rouge, Louisiana Police
Clyde W. Oliver, Jr., Illinois State Police
Kyle Oasman, Dallas Detective Bureau
Ray H. Page, Oklahoma Bureau of Investigation
Arthur G. Phillips, Jr., Oklahoma Ofc of Special Investigations
Alfonso Rincon Pina, NATB
G.F. Potts, San Diego NATB
J.B. Powers, Oklahoma State Police
R.B. Price, Wichita, Kansas Police
M. Rear, Oklahoma City NATB
Wilfred E. Reardon, New Orleans Police
Jack E. Rickards, Detroit NATB
Ed Riley, California Auto Manufacturers Association
Jack Roberts, Oklahoma Highway Patrol
Henry J. Schmidt, Oklahoma Police
J. Earl Scroggin, Arkansas State Police
Worth Seaman, Texas Dept. of Public Safety
Tom S. Secrest, Raleigh, North Carolina Theft Bureau
Earl Sellers, Oklahoma Bureau of Investigation
Claud Seymour, Oklahoma Bureau of Investigation
Lynn R. Shelby, Monterey Park, California Police
W.H. Shepperd, Houston Police
Ellis Slater, Oklahoma Air Provost Marshal
A.E. Slosson, Los Angeles Police
Bill Sterzing, Austin, Texas Detective Bureau
Chester Stringer, Oklahoma Bureau of Investigation
Thomas L. Stuart, Anadarko, Oklahoma Sheriff's Ofc
N.C. Sturgeon, Tulsa, Oklahoma Police
James R. Sullivan, Oklahoma City NATB
William T. Thorne, Oklahoma Bureau of Investigation
Don Thurber, Ponca City, Oklahoma Police
Joel Tisdale, Texas Department of Public Safety
Sam E. Tranum, Montgomery, Alabama NATB
Bob Turner, Oklahoma County Sheriff's Dept.
Carl H. Tyler, Oklahoma Dept. of Public Safety
Duke C. Vincent, Memphis Police
Arvel M. Walker, Edmond, Oklahoma Police
Amos G. Ward, Rogers County Sheriff's Dept.

Raymond Webb, Borger, Texas Police
Gene Wells, Oklahoma County Sheriff's Dept.
Steele F. Westbrook, Oklahoma Governor's Office
Johnnie D. Whittle, Oklahoma Bureau of Investigation
R. T. Williams, Oklahoma Highway Patrol
Milburn Shaver, Oklahoma Air Provost Marshal
Roy Patterson, Oklahoma Police
Sid Wilson, Oklahoma Bureau of Investigation
Gene Good, Oklahoma Police
E.L. Bumpass, Oklahoma Highway Patrol
N.C. Holt, Oklahoma Highway Patrol
W.D. Hamilton, Oklahoma Highway Patrol

Official Letterhead

1953—1954

PRESIDENT J. F. DANIEL, DALLAS POLICE DEPARTMENT

(see biography, 1952-53)

EXECUTIVE BOARD

1st Vice President:	Herbert D. Brigham, Missouri State Highway Patrol
2nd Vice President:	R. B. King, Virginia State Police
3rd Vice President:	A. T. Nelson, Los Angeles Police
Secretary/Treasurer:	V. E. Moncrief, Oklahoma City Police
Directors:	Richard Jerabek, St. Louis Police
	Edward Leestma, Grand Rapids Police
	John J. Barton, Indiana State Police
	Melvin Larson, Wisconsin Motor Vehicle
	Ben F. Ragusa, Louisiana State Police
	N. C. Sturgeon, Tulsa, Oklahoma Police

SEMINAR

Kansas City, MO
July 19–21, 1954

This article appeared on page 12 of the July 1952 issue of the Oklahoma State FOP Journal.

439 AUTOS STOLEN IN TULSA IN 1952; 97% RECOVERED

Careless Tulsa car owners lost 439 automobiles to car thieves during 1952 – almost 100 more than in 1951 – but hard-working police returned all except a dozen of them to their owners.

The slightly over 97 per cent recovery rate ranks Tulsa with the best in the nation, FBI reports show.

Detectives Frank Yeager and N.C. Sturgeon, the only full-time officers on the auto theft detail, fear that the dozen autos still missing fell prey to the easy -going operations of a small theft ring. Sturgeon said that the thieves were slow and careful, usually taking only about one car a month. "But rings of commercial thieves do the job thoroughly, and never leave clues."

Adding to the excellent rate of recovery during 1952 was the breakup by Yeager and Sturgeon of the Travis-Taylor ring. The pair recovered 15 automobiles after discovering the ring's operations, which included the clever forgery of valid car titles.

"They would buy old, almost worthless junk heaps just for the title that went with them," Sturgeon said.

"Then they would carefully erase the automobile named on the title and substitute a newer make auto that they had stolen and re-finished. "When they sold the car, they of course got a new title, making it almost impossible to trace."

Yeager and Sturgeon said a majority of the cars stolen during the year were taken by juveniles, often using them only for a joy ride.

Of the 439 autos taken during 1952, 139 of them were taken by joy riders who found parked cars with keys in them and sometimes with the motor still running, and just drove them off. They usually were found abandoned a few hours later, with an empty tank.

Sturgeon said the days when cars were stolen to be stripped of parts and accessories, then junked in ditches and ponds or lakes, are almost gone.

The officers noted that thieves during 1952 seemed to pick on newer model cars.

"A few years ago, we seldom found anyone stealing new or almost new cars, " Sturgeon said. "This year the majority of the thefts are of 1949-1950 and '51 models – usually the Fords and Chevrolets."

He noted that a new ignition switch found in the newer model cars made it very easy for the thieves.

"Many of the new cars have switch panels with three key positions – only one of them locking the ignition. Most drivers do not bother to turn the key to "lock" and in the other two positions the car can be started without the key," Sturgeon said.

"We have also found the juveniles are much more adept at wiring around a switch than most adults," Sturgeon added.

Total value of autos stolen during the past year was $362,300, with the recovery value amounting to $349,100 – leaving a gross loss of 12 cars valued at $13,200 during 1952.

Seminar Companion's Luncheon

1954—1955

PRESIDENT H. D. BRIGHAM,
MISSOURI HIGHWAY PATROL

EXECUTIVE BOARD
not found

SEMINAR

Grand Rapids, Michigan

No archives for this year could be found.
Please accept our apologies

1955–1956

PRESIDENT R. B. KING, VIRGINIA STATE POLICE

EXECUTIVE BOARD

1st Vice President:	A. T. Nelson, Los Angeles Police
2nd Vice President:	Edward Leestma, Grand Rapids Police
3rd Vice President:	N. C. Sturgeon, Tulsa Police
Secretary/Treasurer:	V. E. Moncrief, Oklahoma City Police
Directors:	Richard C. Jerabek, St. Louis Police
	Clyde W. Oliver Jr., Illinois Highway Police
	Wilford Matlock, Fort Worth Police
	S. D. McCleary, Memphis Police
	H. J. Gibbons, Sioux City Police
	M. Gilbert, North Carolina
	Department of Motor Vehicles

SEMINAR

Los Angeles, California
August 6–9, 1956

Executive Board of Directors 1955-1956

1956—1957

PRESIDENT

A.T. NELSON, LOS ANGELES POLICE DEPARTMENT

Born in a log cabin on a Minnesota farm, Captain Nelson joined the Los Angeles Police Department in 1925, and the detective bureau of that department in 1930. He has worked every detective assignment from homicide to checks and has in his career been

A.T. Nelson

in command of detective divisions covering every field of criminal investigation. In and out of the Auto Theft Division throughout his career, he assumed what appears to be permanent command of that division in 1947. During his career, Captain Nelson took part in such precedent establishing events as the stolen car blockades along the Mexican-American border in 1931 and again with the Border Patrol in 1935. Captain Nelson is largely responsible for the methods, techniques and approaches to vehicle investigation which have caused the Los Angeles Police Department to be acclaimed as the leader in this field. He pioneered such ordinances as Los Angeles' famous false-report ordinance and repossessions reporting ordinance. Captain Nelson was one of the first administrators in the vehicle theft field to realize the importance of the problem of theft from motor vehicle and the growing problem connected with salvage operations having to do with vehicles. In order to combat problems in these fields, he initiated such things as specialized "contingent surveillance" teams, a program of stolen property market control on used auto parts and accessories and auto accessory identification programs. On the auto theft side, in addition to sustaining a constantly improving program in regard to auto records, communications and statistics, he initiated the first well organized and widespread programs of auto wrecking and salvage control directed both toward the legitimate business of auto wrecking and toward the elimination of illegal "wild-cat" wreckers.

Captain Nelson is the first President of IAATI to rise to that position through the chairs.

UNITED STATES DEPARTMENT OF JUSTICE
FEDERAL BUREAU OF INVESTIGATION

WASHINGTON 25, D. C.

In Reply, Please Refer to
File No.

August 12, 1957

It is indeed a pleasure to extend greetings to the International Association of Auto Theft Investigators on the occasion of your fifth annual seminar.

Automobile theft is one of the most complex, costly and widespread problems ever to confront law enforcement. During 1956, a year in which the estimated major crime total for the Nation topped the two and one-half million mark for the first time, the auto theft total reached a new all-time high of more than 250,000.

The automobile plays a very important part in the everyday life of America. It has assumed an even greater role in the life of the criminal. With rare exception, the most vicious hoodlums in America today are accomplished car thieves. Many began their underworld careers by stealing automobiles. Others--such as bank robbers or fleeing felons who need getaway cars--develop this criminal specialty as an essential sideline. In many instances, the automobile is more important to the criminal than a gun.

The local officer should be alert to the fact that automobiles found in the possession of law violators and suspected criminals may very well be stolen property. Often, the alert and properly trained officer may find that in recovering a stolen car and apprehending the thief, he has taken into custody not merely a car thief but a criminal responsible for more vicious crimes.

John Edgar Hoover
Director

IAATI Conference Los Angeles, 1955, Biltmore Hotel. Standing: Capt. Nelson, Los Angeles Police, S/A Jimmie Sullivan NATB Oklahoma, C.C. Benson NATB. Seated: Sgt. Brigham, Missouri State Police, Charlie Black NATB New York, Capt R.B. King, Virginia State Police, Bill Sturgeon, Tulsa P.D.

EXECUTIVE BOARD

1st Vice President: Edward Leestma; Grand Rapids Police
2nd Vice President: N. C. Sturgeon; Tulsa Police
3rd Vice President: A. M. Gilbert; North Carolina Dept. of Motor Vehicles
Secretary/Treasurer: V. E. Moncrief; Oklahoma City Police
Directors: Clyde W. Oliver, Jr.; Illinois Highway Police
Wilford Matlock; Fort Worth Police
W. T. Fulghum; Tacoma Police
H. J. Gibbons; Sioux City Police
W. Alexander; Kansas City Police
H. Knight; Miami Police

SEMINAR

Fort Worth, Texas
Texas Hotel, 8th and Main Sts., ED 2-3151

Stolen Hubcaps Traced—Thief Convicted

William L. Johnson "BJ" Western Chapter IAATI member pictured at the 2002 IAATI Conference with his membership card issued in 1956. BJ has been an active member since that time.

1957–1958

PRESIDENT EDWARD LEESTMA, GRAND RAPIDS POLICE DEPARTMENT, MICHIGAN

Notes from Past President, from IAATI News Bulletin, May–June 1958

I wish at this time to express my appreciation to all the officers who served with me in the past year, also all the members who assisted to make it an enjoyable year.

My heartiest best wishes go out to our President Sturgeon and all the new officers elected at Memphis, for a successful and enjoyable year.

I wish to state that I will certainly assist any or all the officers at any time that I may be called upon.

If I may make one suggestion that would make the work of your officers easier and help to advance our association, it is that you answer you correspondence promptly. Since we are all so far removed from each other it is very difficult to make major decisions where several persons thoughts on the matter are needed.

I would certainly like to publicly thank our fine Secretary Tom Secrest for the outstanding job that he did during the past year. Only after having held office can you realize the time and effort that Tom has put into his work and (I) am certainly happy that we are fortunate enough to have him as our Secretary for the coming year.

I regret that it was necessary for me to leave the Seminar without being able complete the program and to have had an opportunity to express my thanks in person, but that was one of the things that we have no control over.

Our thanks go to those people who so ably participated in the Memphis program, and know that all of us brought back some new ideas, which is one of the basic reasons for having our organization.

EXECUTIVE BOARD

1st Vice President:	N.C Sturgeon, Tulsa Police
2nd Vice President:	A.M. Gilbert, License & Theft Enforcement, Raleigh, NC
3rd Vice President:	Glen McLaughlin, Texas Dept. of Public Safety
4th Vice President:	Clyde W. Oliver, Jr., Illinois Highway Patrol
5th Vice President:	C.H. Knight, Miami Police
6th Vice President:	S.D. McCleary, Memphis Police
Secretary:	T.S. Secrest, Dept. of Motor Vehicles, Raleigh, NC
Treasurer:	V.E. Moncrief, Oklahoma City Police

SEMINAR

Memphis, Tennessee

Interesting Facts:
IAATI Annual Dues were $3
Communication with members was done via the "News Bulletin"

From the IAATI News Bulletin, Vol. V, No. 5, May-June 1958

This News Bulletin is the official organ of the International Association of Auto Theft Investigators, a nonprofit organization, chartered in the State of Oklahoma and devoted to the following objectives and purposes:

1. To unite for mutual benefit those individuals who are eligible for membership.

2. To provide for exchange of technical information and developments.

3. To cooperate with all law enforcement agencies and associations who are engaged in the prevention and suppression of automobile thefts and kindred crimes.

4. To encourage high professional standards of conduct among auto theft investigators and to continually strive to eliminate all factors which interfere with the administration of crime suppression.

The Association shall not be operated for profit and its funds may not be used in an attempt to influence legislation.

```
                          -33-

      INTERNATIONAL ASSOCIATION OF AUTO THEFT INVESTIGATORS

                    POLICE HEADQUARTERS
                  OKLAHOMA CITY, OKLAHOMA

                  FINANCIAL STATEMENT, 1957

FUNDS RECEIVED:

     FUNDS ON HAND JANUARY 1, 1957----------$ 971.39
     DUES RECEIVED DURING THE YEAR---------- 723.00
     1957 CONFERENCE SURPLUS----------------  89.00
              TOTAL FUNDS------------------------------$ 1,783.39

FUNDS EXPENDED:

     OFFICE SUPPLIES-----------------------$ 273.03
     POSTAGE------------------------------   97.57
     MISC:  HOWARD SMITH CONF.EXP.$50.00
            V. E. MONCRIEF CONF.EX.50.00
            SECRETARIAL WORK      30.00
            BANK SERVICE CHARGE    .50  130.50
              TOTAL EXPENDITURES--------------------$  501.18

FUNDS ON HAND DECEMBER 31, 1957,---------------------$ 1,282.21

FUNDS OBLIGATED-------------------------------------       -0-

FUNDS ON HAND & UNOBLIGATED-------------------------$ 1,282.21


            STATEMENT OF ASSETS & LIABILITIES

ASSETS:

     FUNDS IN BANK-----------------------$ 1,282.21
     OFFICE EQUIPMENT--------------------     364.48
              TOTAL ASSETS----------------------------$ 1,646.69

LIABILITIES:---------------------------------------        -0-

NET ASSETS:-----------------------------------------$ 1,646.69


                    Signed:
                           V. E. Moncrief,
                           Treasurer.
```

1958—1959

PRESIDENT
N. C. STURGEON, TULSA POLICE
DEPARTMENT

Obituary, from the Tulsa Tribune, July 17, 1986.
Sturgeon–N. Curtis, 82, formerly of Tulsa, retired Tulsa Police Detective, (died) Thursday in Bentonville, Arkansas. Services today, Bentonville Cemetery (Burns, Bentonville).

EXECUTIVE BOARD

1st Vice President: A.M. Gilbert, Tulsa Police
2nd Vice President: Glen McLaughlin, Texas Dept. of Public Safety
3rd Vice President: C.H. Knight, Miami Police
4th Vice President: S.D. McCleary, Memphis Police
5th Vice President: A.E. Slosson, Los Angeles Police
6th Vice President: John G. Williams, D.C. Metropolitan Police
Secretary: T.S. Secrest, License & Theft Division, Raleigh, NC
Treasurer: V.E. Moncrief, Oklahoma City Police

SEMINAR

Miami, Florida, McAllister Hotel
July 19 – 24, 1959

Interesting...
Membership at 242

N.C. Sturgeon, Tulsa Police Dept.,1924-1959. Courtesy of Ron Trekell, TPD Historian.

This article appeared on page 12 of the July 1952 issue of the Oklahoma State FOP Journal.

439 Autos Stolen in Tulsa in 1952; 97% Recovered

Careless Tulsa car owners lost 439 automobiles to car thieves during 1952 – almost 100 more than in 1951 – but hard-working police returned all except a dozen of them to their owners.

The slightly over 97 per cent recovery rate ranks Tulsa with the best in the nation, FBI reports show.

Detectives Frank Yeager and N.C. Sturgeon, the only full-time officers on the auto theft detail, fear that the dozen autos still missing fell prey to the easy -going operations of a small theft ring. Sturgeon said that the thieves were slow and careful, usually taking only about one car a month. "But rings of commercial thieves do the job thoroughly, and never leave clues."

Adding to the excellent rate of recovery during 1952 was the breakup by Yeager and Sturgeon of the Travis-Taylor ring.

The pair recovered 15 automobiles after discovering the ring's operations, which included the clever forgery of valid car titles.

"They would buy old, almost worthless junk heaps just for the title that went with them," Sturgeon said. "Then they would carefully erase the automobile named on the title and substitute a newer make auto that they had stolen and re-finished.

"When they sold the car, they of course got a new title, making it almost impossible to trace."

Yeager and Sturgeon said a majority of the cars stolen during the year were taken by juveniles, often using them only for a joy ride.

Of the 439 autos taken during 1952, 139 of them were taken by joy riders who found parked cars with keys in them and sometimes with the motor still running, and just drove them off. They usually were found abandoned a few hours later, with an empty tank.

Sturgeon said the days when cars were stolen to be stripped of parts and accessories, then junked in ditches and ponds or lakes, are almost gone.

The officers noted that thieves during 1952 seemed to pick on newer model cars.

"A few years ago, we seldom found anyone stealing new or almost new cars, " Sturgeon said. "This year the majority of the thefts are of 1949-1950 and '51 models – usually the Fords and Chevrolets."

He noted that a new ignition switch found in the newer model cars madeit very easy for the thieves.

"Many of the new cars have switch panels with three key positions – only one of them locking the ignition. Most drivers do not bother to turn the key to "lock" and in the other two positions the car can be started without the key," Sturgeon said.

"We have also found the juveniles are much more adept at wiring around a switch than most adults," Sturgeon added.

Total value of autos stolen during the past year was $362,300, with the recovery value amounting to $349,100 – leaving a gross loss of 12 cars valued at $13,200 during 1952.

1959—1960

PRESIDENT A. M. GILBERT,
NORTH CAROLINA DEPARTMENT OF
MOTOR VEHICLES

EXECUTIVE BOARD
not found

SEMINAR

Norman, Oklahoma
October 24-28, 1960

University of Oklahoma

I. A. A. T. I. Seminar   October 24-28, 1960

1960—1961

PRESIDENT GLEN H. MCLAUGHLIN, TEXAS DEPARTMENT OF PUBLIC SAFETY

Glen McLauglin is a founding member of the Association and former Past President. Glen, along with other officers from about 15 different states, conducted an auto theft training conference in Dallas, Texas in 1951. A product of that conference was the desire of many attendees to continue on a formal basis. In 1952, Glen and four other founding members met in Lake Murray, Oklahoma one weekend to formalize what is now known as the International Association of Auto Theft Investigators.

Glen began his law enforcement career in 1939, with the Texas Department of Public Safety as a chemist/toxicologist. In 1945, Glen was promoted to the Chief of the Identification and Criminal Records Division. It was during this period that Glen became involved with auto theft investigation from an identification perspective. In 1957, during reorganization he became the Chief of the Personnel & Staff Services of which Training Section was a component. In 1973, he became the Chief of Administration which encompassed all of his previous duties and then some. Glen retired in 1977, in Austin, Texas, where he still resides.

EXECUTIVE BOARD
not found

SEMINAR

Dallas, Texas

Glen McLaughlin

Benson and McLaughlin 1961, IAATI Seminar at S.M.U. Dallas.

50 YEARS OF HISTORY

1961–1962

PRESIDENT W. P. SCANLAND, CALIFORNIA DEPARTMENT OF JUSTICE

EXECUTIVE BOARD
not found

SEMINAR

Norman, Oklahoma – University of Oklahoma
October 1-5, 1962

First Row: Walter D. Arnold, Okla. City, OK; Ronald L. Walker, Carlsbad, NM; N.E. Swackhamer, Jefferson City, MO; George H. Harkness, Kansas City, MO; R.C. Morgan, Tulsa, OK; B.J. Jones, Tulsa, OK; R.C. Jerabek, St. Louis, MO; Nat A. Pinkston, Dallas, TX; John J. Amend, Amarillo, TX; Art Fitzpatrick, Los Angeles, CA; Eugene Sache, Evansville, IN; T.A. Bates, Ft. Worth, TX; Worth Seaman, Austin, TX; Howard A. Watson, Columbus, OH; Tom Secrest, Raliegh, NC. Second Row: M.K. Alexander, Santa Fe, NM; Bill G. Melton, Tulsa, OK; James Clayton, Carrizozo, NM; Julian Clark, Atlanta, GA; G.F. "Gary" Potts, San Francisco,CA; Jesse W. Divers, Ft. Hood,TX; Harold W. Olsen, Tacoma,WA; Carey C. Hagler, Charlotte, NC; Walter B. Broome, Charlotte, NC; Harry A. Hansen,Columbia,MO; H.G. Wright, South Bend, IN; George F. Kinesey, Fort Hood, TX; Lloyd F. Palmer, Okla City, OK. Third Row: Olen Rawls, Baton Rouge, LA; Malcolm A. Hallard, Baton Rouge, LA; K.A. Stoner, Warren, MI; Donald F. Handy, Brighton, CO; George H. Prince, Commerce City, CO; Royce Cahuent, Dallas, TX; H.W. Jordan, Ft. Worth, TX; Terry Thomas, Amarillo TX; S.R. Mayhugh, Sacrament, CA; Richard D. Fullington, Ft. Bragg, NC; John E. Davidson, Ft. Bragg, NC; Nolan J. DeVine, Washington, D.C., A.M. Gilbert, Raleigh, NC. Fourth Row: Glenn S. Smith, Edmond, OK; Carl White, Okla City, OK; James Robinson, Norman, OK; William J. Davis, Chicago, IL; Glenn H. Smith, Baton Rouge, LA; Charles P. Cave, Ft. Sill, OK; Paul Lopez, El Paso, TX; Norman Taylor, Tacoma, WA; John G. Williams, Washington, D.C.; Bill Sterzing, Austin, TX; Gary Roberson, Norman, OK; H.W. McFarling, Austin, TX; John S. Paszek, Reno, NV; Stanley Hornberg, Madison, WI; W.G. Hunter, Okla City, OK; W.P. Scanland, Sacramento, CA; Bud Tatum, Okla City, OK.

1962–1963

PRESIDENT JOHN G. WILLIAMS,
WASHINGTON D.C. TRANSIT AUTHORITY

EXECUTIVE BOARD
not found

SEMINAR

Norman, Oklahoma

No archives for this year could be found.
Please accept our apologies.

1963–1964

PRESIDENT GEORGE R. HARKNESS

EXECUTIVE BOARD
not found

SEMINAR

Chapel Hill, North Carolina

International Association of Auto Theft Investigators, Chapel Hill, N.C.

1964—1965

PRESIDENT S. RAY MAYHUGH, CALIFORNIA HIGHWAY PATROL

EXECUTIVE BOARD
not found

SEMINAR

Baton Rouge – Louisiana State University
August 9-12, 1965

INTERNATIONAL AUTO THEFT INVESTIGATION SEMINAR
INTERNATIONAL ASSOCIATION OF AUTO THEFT INVESTIGATORS
LOUISIANA STATE UNIVERSITY

First Row: Capt. Malcom Ballard, Baton Rouge, LA; Gene Sachs, Evansville, IN; Leonard Thames, Jackson, MS; R.E. Swackhamer, Jefferson, MO; George R. Harkness, Kansas City, MO, S.R. Mayhugh, Sacramento, CA. Second Row: Henry Lipe, Corpus Christ., TX; Carl White, Okla City, OK; Harry A Hansen, Columbia, MO; Donald E. Pemberton, Chattanooga, TN; Charles B. Merriman, Chatanooga, TN; Leo Harris, Little Rock, AR; Thomas J. Horrigan, Wheaton, MD; James E. Sullivan, Jr., Chattanooga, TN; Lionel D. Kelleher, Baton Rouge, LA. Third Row: Nat A. Pinkston, Dallas, TX; D.R. Archer, Dallas, TX; J.C. Nichols, Dallas, TX; George J. O'Connor, Baton Rouge, LA; M.T. Baker, Baton Rouge, LA; H.L. Donaldson, Chattanooga, TN; Eugene E. Pedigo, Abbeville, LA; Francis S. Hebert, Morgan City, LA; L.B. Baymard, Baton Rouge, LA; Paul E. Lopez, El Paso, TX. Fourth Row: Det. Raymond J. Hubbard, Rochester, NY; Roy McDowell, Gadsden, AL; Troy F. Pounder, Mobile, AL; Edward M. Valentine, Columbus, OH; W.W. Peterson, Saskatoon, Sask; Joe Williamson, Des Moines, IA; B.M. Pike, Atlanta, GA; James B. Ragsdale, Atlanta, GA; Major S. H. Berthelot, Baton Rouge, LA; William J. Salathe, New Orleans, LA; Edelbert Kirkpatrick, Baton Rouge, LA; Ralph E. Sprinkle, Raliegh, N.C. Fifth Row: Jim Harris, Toronto, Canada; Clarence Barton, Tuscaloosa, AL; Ronald Bruce DeLaughter, Baton Rouge, LA; Bert Miller, West Trenton, NJ; Ray A Hoevelmann, Rolla, MO; John J. Scarisbrick, Jr., New York, NY; Charley Evans, Baton ROuge, LA; Lee S. Cole, San Francisco, CA; Bill Murray, Baton Rouge, LA; Larry Waldt, Oakland, CA; Nick Gudmunds, Sacramento, CA; Henry A. Guinn, Knoxville, TN; Henry J. Rentschler, Springfield, IL; Charles Springer, Morton, IL. Sixth Row: Det. Robert P. Lambiase, Rochester, NY; Thomas E. Posey, Montgomery, AL; Harley Foster, MObile, AL; James A. Wollenberg, Jefferson City, MO; John A. Paden; Raymond W. Dreher, Jefferson City, MO; C.C. Benson, Dallas, TX; Theodore H. Johnstone, Detroit, MI; Joe E. Richter, Topeka,, KS; P. Stuart Meyer, Warren, MI; Julian Clark, Atlanta, GA; George L. Mortimer, Tallahassee, FL.

1965—1966

PRESIDENT MALCOLM A. BALLARD, BATON ROUGE POLICE DEPARTMENT

EXECUTIVE BOARD
not found

SEMINAR

Knoxville, Tennessee

Fourteenth Annual Seminar
INTERNATIONAL ASSOCIATION OF AUTO THEFT INVESTIGATORS
The University of Tennessee•Knoxville•August 8-11, 1966

1966–1967

PRESIDENT RICHARD JERABECK, ST. LOUIS POLICE DEPARTMENT

EXECUTIVE BOARD

1st Vice President:	Gene Sachs, Evansville, IN Police Department
2nd Vice President:	Thomas J. Horrigan, D.C. Metropolitan Police
3rd Vice President:	Clyde Oliver, Illinois State Highway Police
Secretary/Treasurer:	Robert E. Swackhamer, Missouri Highway Patrol
Directors:	James Harris, Ontario Provincial Police
	Henry Guinn, Knoxville Police
	B. Sturgeon, Mobile, Alabama Police

SEMINAR

College Park, Maryland

No archives for this year could be found.
Please accept our apologies.

1967—1968

PRESIDENT THOMAS J. HORRIGAN, WASHINGTON DC METROPOLITAN POLICE DEPARTMENT

Joined the Metropolitan Police Department in August 1949, and spent five years with the Patrol Division until transferred to the Juvenile Bureau. He spent several years at Juvenile and while so assigned was detailed to the United States Attorneys Special Squad for two years. Went back to Juvenile for a while before being transferred to the Criminal Investigations Division, Auto Theft Unit.

He attended his first IAATI seminar in Chapel Hill, North Carolina, found it very interesting, and asked a lot of questions, but most of all, met a lot of people with similar interests—auto theft investigations. The following year, while attending the seminar he was nominated and elected to the position of 4th Vice President. Progressed up through the chairs, until becoming President at San Jose, California in 1968.

About the same time, IAATI Chapters were coming into formation. The North-Central and North-East Chapters had already been formed. Several people approached him to write up a chapter for the formation of a South-East Chapter. At the 74-75 seminar the charter was approved, and W.S. Plowden of the South Carolina Law Enforcement Division (SLED) was elected as President and Horrigan was elected as First Vice President along with a slate of other officers. The following year, he became President of the South-East Chapter.

A few years later he was asked to take over the duties of Executive Secretary for the International, a position he occupied for eight years. The duties included maintaining the membership rolls, collecting dues, preparing the quarterly newsletter, getting it printed and mailed out, attending the seminars and recording the minutes, publishing the seminar presentations and mailing them out to the members,

Retired from the Metropolitan Police in June 1974 and went to work for Government Employees Insurance Co. as a field investigator. Two years later he was inside as a Theft Examiner and as such, was responsible for all vehicle thefts reported to the company in Maryland, Northern Virginia and the District of Columbia. Later, he was transferred to the Home Office as a Vehicle Theft Auditor and traveled to all seven company offices auditing theft files.

Presently, and for the past seven years, he has been employed as a golf starter at the Congressional Country Club just outside of Washington, D.C.

He states that he could have done nothing without the support of his wife, Agnes, with whom he celebrated his 50th wedding anniversary in 2002.

EXECUTIVE BOARD
not found

SEMINAR

Sacramento, California

T.J. Horrigan

1968–1969

PRESIDENT CLYDE W. OLIVER JR., ILLINOIS STATE POLICE

Captain Oliver joined the Illinois State Police in January 1950. In 1955 after prior promotions and assignments, he was promoted to Lieutenant in charge of the stolen car section, later called the Vehicle Investigation Bureau of the Illinois State Police.

In 1964 he was promoted to Captain and he was elected President of the International Association of Auto Theft Investigators, having served prior on its Executive Board. Prior to this election, he had been a leading force in promoting the Midwest Auto Theft Seminar that initially was held at the University of Illinois Police Training Institute in 1963, then later at the Illinois Building at the Illinois State Fairgrounds until 1974. He also instructed auto theft investigation to the Illinois State Police and outside agencies, promoting professionalism.

In 1972 he, along with Special Agent Robert Sadler of the National Auto Theft Bureau, initiated the formation of the North Central Regional Chapter of IAATI. In 1975, under his initiative, the annual IATTI Conference was held in Springfield, cohosted by the Illinois State Police.

Captain Oliver retired in 1983 and died due to health problems in 1986. He was a U.S. Navy veteran. In 1989 the North Central Regional Chapter initiated the Clyde Oliver Award to recognize individuals for distinguished service to the North Central Regional Chapter.

Examining transmission numbers

EXECUTIVE BOARD

1st Vice President: Henry A. Guinn, Knoxville Police Department
2nd Vice President: James W. Harris, Ontario Provincial Police
3rd Vice President: R.W. Dreher, Missouri State Highway Patrol
4th Vice President: B.M. Pike, Georgia Bureau of Investigation
Secretary/Treasurer: J.A. Wollenberg, Missouri State Highway Patrol
Directors: William C. Brennan, New Jersey Division of Motor Vehicles
                       Jesus Medina Fuentes, Tijuana Police
                       Edward L. Geyer, California Highway Patrol

SEMINAR

Toronto, Ontario, Park Plaza Hotel
July 28 – 31, 1969

Henry Guinn, Allen Grassman, Clyde Oliver, Mrs. Oliver

Henry A. Guinn, Knoxville Tenn-IAATI President 1969-1970; James Mackie, Chief of Police-Metro Toronto P.D.; Allen Grassman-Solicitor General Province of Ontario; James H. Harris-Asst. Chief Superintendent Ont. Provincial Police. President of IAATI 1970-71.

AUTO THEFT PREVENTION CAMPAIGN

KAR KEY SEZ:

How stolen cars are traced instantly

Officer spots suspicious car -- radios license to control desk

Control desk queries NCIC in Washington

PROMPT REPORT OF THEFT --

Will insure theft report getting into National Crime Information Center (NCIC)

Will aid in faster recovery of car

At NCIC headquarters computer automatically searches memory bank

```
LIC/ 8P5108 TENN
OWNER/ JOHN F DOE 15 E 4TH
        MEMPHIS TENN
STOLEN/ 11-28-68 * MEMPHIS TENN
YEAR/ 65
MAKE/ DODGE
STYLE/ 4D
VIN/ 4242100762
CASE NBR/ 12543
NCIC NBR/ V0000145365
```

Answer received in seconds

KAR KEY SEZ: "Take Me Along!"

AN UNLOCKED CAR INVITES A THIEF.

Remember your keys campaign

LOCK YOUR CAR!

PREVENT THEFT

Friends:

Most car thieves are opportunists looking for an easy dollar. Your car is their favorite target, because quickly removed parts can be sold for these easy dollars. These thieves are constantly on the prowl, along the sidewalks and unattended parking lots looking for cars where keys have been carelessly left in the ignition. This is also the major cause of so many juveniles stealing cars, youngsters who may never be in trouble but can't resist the temptation.

CATO S. HIGHTOWER
Chief of Police

Cato S. Hightower

HELP THE POLICE PROTECT YOUR PROPERTY

by

Locking your ignition and your car doors

DON'T GIVE THESE THIEVES A CHANCE

LOCK YOUR CAR!

Lock your car campaign

1969—1970

PRESIDENT

HENRY A. GUINN, KNOXVILLE POLICE
DEPARTMENT

EXECUTIVE BOARD
not found

SEMINAR

Knoxville, Tennessee

Mobile, Alabama, 1978 Seminar, Stan Moats-1st VP and Henry Guinn-Past Pres.

Eighteenth Annual Seminar
INTERNATIONAL ASSOCIATION OF AUTO THEFT INVESTIGATORS
The University of Tennessee*Knoxville*August 3-6, 1970

1970—1971

PRESIDENT

JAMES. W. HARRIS, ONTARIO PROVINCIAL POLICE

Jim formed the first Auto Theft Squad in the early 1960s for the Ontario Provincial Police. Soon after, he began attending IAATI seminars to increase his knowledge until his police force sponsored the first IAATI conference outside the U.S., in Toronto, 1969.

While president of IAATI, Jim suffered a heart attack at the Detroit seminar, which forced his retirement from active police work. He retired as Assistant Chief Superintendent of the Special Services Division of the Ontario Provincial Police.

After retirement, his health improved and he enjoyed his 50th Wedding Anniversary with wife Edith in 1988. Jim passed away in the early 1990s of natural causes. He was in his late 80s.

Courtesy of Louis Spry

EXECUTIVE BOARD
not found

SEMINAR

Detroit, Michigan

I. A. A. T. I. CONVENTION
August 2, 1971 DETROIT, MICHIGAN

1971—1972

PRESIDENT

RAYMOND W. DREHER, MISSOURI HIGHWAY PATROL

Lt. Ray Dreher entered service with the Missouri Highway Patrol in 1948. After 32 years with the patrol, Ray retired as a Lieutenant in August 1980. He spent many of those years working as an auto theft investigator. Shortly after his retirement, Ray died of cancer on Sept. 2, 1980. He was on IAATI's Board of Directors for many years and worked his way through the chairs before serving as president in 1971-72.

After Ray became a past-president, his devotion to IAATI remained steadfast, helping in any way possible and increasing recognition of IAATI in the law enforcement community.

In 1983, IAATI established the Ray Dreher Memorial Award. The award, not necessarily annual, is IAATI's most prestigious award, and is presented to an individual who most personifies the principles, ideals and dedication that Ray showed as an IAATI leader. The recipients are listed elsewhere in this volume.

EXECUTIVE BOARD
not found

SEMINAR

Tallahassee, Florida

Ray Dreher

Left to Right: David Brickell, Gene Rutledge, Tom Horrigan, C.O. Brickey, Seated Ray Dreher, 1972 San Jose

1972–1973

PRESIDENT

BONNIE M. PIKE,
GEORGIA BUREAU OF INVESTIGATION

Past President Pike first joined IAATI at the Chapel Hill, NC seminar in 1964. He was elected president at the Tallahassee, FL seminar in 1972, and presided over the 21st Annual Seminar in Arlington, TX. He was the first president to organize standing committees in the IAATI organization.

Pike began his auto theft investigations career with the development of the auto theft squad in 1964. He spent 10 of his 30–year career working auto theft with the Georgia Bureau of Investigation. He retired in 1989 with the rank of Inspector.

EXECUTIVE BOARD

1st Vice President:	Gonzalie Rivers
2nd Vice President:	Harry J. Brady, Sr.
3rd Vice President:	Don R. Campbell
4th Vice President:	Clarence O. Brickey
Secretary:	Clyde W. Oliver, Jr.
Treasurer:	Louis Spry

SEMINAR

Arlington, Texas
170 attendees

Bonnie M. Pike

Ron Van Raalte and Red

Arlington Heights, IL Seminar, 1980.

50 YEARS OF HISTORY

1973–1974

PRESIDENT

HARRY J. BRADY, SR., PORT AUTHORITY OF NEW YORK & NEW JERSEY (RETIRED)

Brady first started in the Port of New York Authority Police Department in October 1952 as a detective working out of Kennedy Airport. In March 1974 he joined the Maryland Port Administration, attaining the rank of Lieutenant. He later worked as Chief of Police in Stewartstown, York County, Pennsylvania.

Brady joined IAATI in 1961 and found a home, as well as numerous friends. In 1972 he and several others founded the Northeast Chapter, the first Chapter of IAATI, comprised of the several of the Northeast States and several Provinces from Canada. Its membership grew and at times exceeded 1,500 members. He was also instrumental in starting the hospitality room for the organization, a great place to meet new friends and "discuss" business. He has received the Ray DREHER award from IAATI and the John SCARISBRICK(sic) Award from the Northeast Chapter.

He is the proud father of six lovely children and 19 grandchildren, and has a wonderful, lovely wife, Alice.

EXECUTIVE BOARD

1st Vice President:	D.R. Campbell, Indianapolis Police Dept.
2nd Vice President:	C.O. Brickey, Maryland State Police
3rd Vice President:	G.F. Hees, Los Angeles Police Dept.
4th Vice President:	L.W. Spry, Ontario Provincial Police
Secretary:	C.W. Oliver, Jr., Illinois State Police
Treasurer:	L.W. Spry
Directors:	T.W. Baehni, Topeka Police Dept.
	R.D. Burke, Las Vegas Police Dept.
	R. Cadieux, Montreal Urban Community Police
	P.J. Collins, Canadian Automobile Theft Bureau
	M.J. Murphy, National Automobile Theft Bureau
	W. Seaman, Texas Dept. of Public Safety

SEMINAR

Newark, Delaware

John F. Daniel, Harry Brady Sr., and C.C. Benson (1989 Galveston, TX)

1974—1975

PRESIDENT

DONALD R. CAMPBELL, INDIANAPOLIS POLICE DEPARTMENT

Donald worked as an auto theft investigator since 1965 and became commanding officer of his auto theft unit in 1968. During his career in auto theft, he participated in the preparation of a training film on the detection and recovery of stolen cars and also assisted in the writing of two auto theft suspects manuals.

Lt. Campbell is married and the father of three children. He has been a member of IAATI since 1969.

EXECUTIVE BOARD

1st Vice President:	C.O. Brickey, Maryland State Police
2nd Vice President:	G.F. Hees, Los Angeles Police
3rd Vice President:	L.W. Spry, Ontario Provincial Police
4th Vice President:	S.D. Moats, University of Tennessee Police
Secretary:	R.C. Van Raalte, Arlington Heights, Illinois Police
Treasurer:	J.J. Scarisbrick, Avis Rent A Car
Directors:	P.J. Collins, Canadian Automobile Theft Bureau
	M.J. Murphy, National Automobile Theft Bureau
	R. Cadieux, Montreal Urban Community Police
	D.E. Finney, Indiana State Police
	S.V.B. English, Maryland State Police
	D.R. Mueller, Lakewood, Colorado DPS

SEMINAR

Springfield, Illinois
August 25–29, 1974
Registration Fee was $40

Donald R. Campbell

Dan Ryan with a Baltimore City Auto Detective

George Hees, Stanley Moats, C.O. Brickey, Harry Brady, Scott V.B. English, Ray Dreher, Tom Horrigan, Don Finney.

1975–1976

PRESIDENT

CLARENCE O. BRICKEY,
MARYLAND STATE POLICE (RETIRED)

Brickey joined the Maryland State Police in January 1963, working both traffic and criminal assignments. After a short stint in the U.S. Army, rejoined the Maryland State Police where his work included garage inspections for stolen vehicles. He was assigned as a full-time auto theft investigator in Feb. 1976. Retired from MSP in July 1994

He attended his first IAATI seminar in August 1967 at the University of Maryland and was elected to IAATI Board of Directors in August 1971. He also served as chairman of IAATIs legislative committee and training coordinator, among other positions. He was instrumental, working for IAATI in legislation passage of the Law Enforcement Act of 1984 and Anti-Car Theft Act of 1992. In August 1975 helped form the Southeast Chapter, serving as president (1981-82) and secretary (1985-2000).

He and his wife, the former Willie Sue Woods, have been married since July 1963, and have three children. They currently live in Virginia.

EXECUTIVE BOARD

1st Vice President:	G.F. Hees, Los Angeles Police
2nd Vice President:	L.W. Spry, Ontario Provincial Police
3rd Vice President:	S.D. Moats, University of Tennessee Police
4th Vice President:	R.C. Van Raalte, Arlington Heights Police
Secretary:	D. R. Finney, Indiana State Police
Treasurer:	J.J. Scarisbrick, Avis Rent A Car
Directors:	P.J. Collins, Canadian Automobile Theft Bureau
	S.V.B. English, Maryland State Police
	R.H. Klemm, Illinois State Police
	F.L. Letterman, Raleigh, North Carolina DMV
	M.J. Murphy, National Automobile Theft Bureau
	K.S. Platt, Hamilton-Wentworth, Canada Regional Police

SEMINAR

San Jose, California
August 8–13, 1976

Interesting...

Southeast Chapter holds their first seminar June 14-15, 1976 in Raleigh, North Carolina.

Clarence O. Brickey

L to R: Sam Gonzales-Sgt. Dallas PD, Unidentified, John Hoover-Lt. Louisiana SP.

1976–1977

PRESIDENT

GEORGE F. HEES, LOS ANGELES (CA) POLICE DEPARTMENT

George Hees joined the Los Angeles Police Department in November 1946 and rose to the rank of Detective Lieutenant in 1967. He assisted in the formation of the department's first specialized auto theft unit, which was assigned to the Burglary Auto Theft Division, and this unit became known as "Bad Cats". George commanded this unit until his retirement in November 1976.

George's interest and dedication in combating auto theft led to his being elected president of the Southern Chapter of WSATI in 1970, and the president of IAATI in 1976–77.

EXECUTIVE BOARD

1st Vice President:	L.W. Spry, Ontario Provincial Police
2nd Vice President:	S.D. Moats, University of Tennessee Police
3rd Vice President:	R.C. Van Raalte, Arlington Heights Police
4th Vice President:	S.V.B. English, Maryland State Police
Treasurer:	J.J. Scarisbrick, Avis Rent A Car
Secretary:	T.J. Horrigan
Directors:	P.J. Collins, Canadian Automobile Theft Bureau
	G. DeLarochelliere, Montreal Urban Community Police
	G.C. Ruddell, Oregon Law Enforcement Data Systems
	W.E. Rutledge, California Highway Patrol
	W. Seaman, Texas Dept. of Public Safety
	S.S. Zablocki, Jr., Broward County Sheriff's Office

SEMINAR

Montreal, Quebec, Loews La Cite Hotel
August 8 – 12, 1977

G.F.Hees

George Hees - President, Ron Van Raalte - 3rd VP and Program Chairman.

Head Table - L to R: John Scarisbrick - Treasurer, Tom Horrigan - Ex Sec., Agnes Horrigan, Scott English - 4th VP, Stan Moats - 2nd VP.

Bill Lovold, Gene Rutledge, Unidentified, George Hees.

Capt Ralph Beasley - Baton Rouge Police, on-site Chairman for 1978 Seminar, Mobile, Alabama.

C.C. Benson and wife, Ada.

Ray Dreher - Past President, Vivian Rutledge, Emille Maasen - So. Calif Auto Club Security.

John Hoover - LA State Police, Ziggy Zablocki - Director, Bob Olson - Houston PD, Guy DeRochelliero - Montreal On Site Chairman.

Gil Mardilla - Calif DMV, Barbara Mardilla

Mrs. Robin Rerie, Robin Rerie - LAPD BADCATS.

Mary Ann Brickell, Sgt. Dave Brickell - San Jose, Cal PD 1976 on -site Chairman - San Jose

Seminar on-site Committee

Board 76-77: Brickey, Hees, Spry, Moats, Van Raalte, Scarisbrick, Horrigan, English, Dreher.

50 Years of History

1977–1978

President

Louis W. Spry, Ontario Provincial Police

Spry's police career began way back in 1949 when he transferred to the Ontario Provincial Police (OPP) from another Gov't Ministry in Ontario. He served at Perth, Brockville, Cayuga, and Crystal Beach in General Law Enforcement duties before transfer to the Special Services Division at GHQ Toronto in January 1965, when he was assigned to the Auto Theft Branch as a Det. Sgt. He stayed there thru several promotions until 1971, when he was made a Chief Inspector and given command of the branch upon the retirement of Asst. Chief Superintendent James Harris, another Past President of IAATI, now deceased.

He remained with the Auto Theft Branch until 1974, when promoted to Staff Superintendent and given command of the Special Investigations Branch which specialized in Drugs, Illegal Gambling, Liquor, Horse Racing and Pornography, Province wide.

Spry served in that capacity until February 1978 when he was assigned as Second-in-Command of our Staff Development Division, where he remained until retirement in September 1982 after over 35 years in the employ of the Province of Ontario.

His first exposure to IAATI was in 1968-69 when the OPP Auto Theft Branch sponsored a seminar in Toronto. He was soon elected Treasurer and from there progressed through nearly all the elected offices until elected President in 1976-77. He also served as President of the North East Regional Chapter of IAATI, which he and Ray Dreher had been involved in getting a Regional Charter, the first in IAATI history, back in the early 70's.

He and his wife, Margo, have two children and two grandchildren.

Executive Board

1st Vice President:	S.D. Moats, University of Tennessee Police
2nd Vice President:	R.C. Van Raalte, Arlington Heights Police
3rd Vice President:	S.V.B. English, Maryland State Police
4th Vice President:	W.E. Rutledge, California Highway Patrol
Treasurer:	J.J. Scarisbrick, Jr, Avis Rent A Car
Secretary:	T.J. Horrigan
Directors:	R.G. Beasley, Alabama Dept. of Public Safety
	H.L. Burr, Boston Dept. of Motor Vehicles
	G. DeLarochelliere, Montreal Urban Community Police
	R. Irvine, Royal Canadian Mounted Police
	W. Seaman, Texas Dept. of Public Safety
	S.S. Zablocki, Jr., Broward Co. Sheriff's Office

Seminar

Mobile, Alabama

Lou Spry and wife.

Virgil Luke-cooking shrimp

L to R: Larry Potts - Spec. Agent FBI, Vivian Rutledge, FBI NCIC Representative.

L to R: Mrs. Robin Rerie, Robin Rerie - LAPD, Mrs. John Hoover, John Hoover - LA State Police.

Past Presidents table. L to R: Bonnie Pike - 1973, Harry Brady - 1974, Ray Dreher - 1972, Unidentified, Vivian Rutledge, Willie Brickey, C.C. Benson in back.

```
              INTERNATIONAL ASSOCIATION
           OF AUTO THEFT INVESTIGATORS

                FINANCIAL STATEMENT

           August 1, 1977 to July 31, 1978


Funds on Hand as of August 1, 1976

Checking Account  -  Suburban Trust Company       $     639.01
                     Hyattsville, Maryland

Savings Account   -  The Central Trust Bank       $ 7,557.50    $ 8,196.51
                     Jefferson City, Missouri

Funds Received

Memberships (includes foreign currency exchange)  $ 9,632.36
N.E. Chapter Assessment                               166.00
S.E. Chapter Assessment                               101.00
IAATI Emblem/Book Contribution                        121.25
Interest (savings account)                            285.84    $10,306.45

                                                                $18,502.96


Expenditures

Printing                                          $ 5,081.36
Postage                                             1,380.95
Secretarial Expense                                 2,246.00
Bank Charges & Currency Exchange                      104.29
Treasurer's Bond                                      190.00
Miscellaneous Supplies & Expenses                     117.58    $ 9,120.18

Funds on Hand as of July 31, 1978

Checking Account  -  Suburban Trust Company       $ 4,039.44
                     Hyattsville, Maryland

Savings Account   -  University National Bank     $ 5,343.34    $ 9,382.78
                     Rockville, Maryland

                                                                $18,502.96


                              John J. Scarisbrick, Jr.
                              Treasurer
```

1978—1979

PRESIDENT

STANLEY G. MOATS,
UNIVERSITY OF TENNESSEE POLICE

Stanley Moats was a man who wanted to make a name for himself. After joining the United States Marine Corp, Stanley served in the Pacific Theatre of WW II, and helped put up the flag on Iwo Jima.

While in the service, he met a beautiful woman, Clestia L. Holt, at a USO party and asked her to marry him after the party. Three days later they were married. In October 1953 their son, Donald, was born.

Moats continued his military career as a military police officer, and after discharge continued his career in law enforcement. He is remembered as a good and honest officer who stood behind the law all the way.

Submitted by Donald L. Moats.

EXECUTIVE BOARD

1st Vice President:	R.C. Van Raalte, Arlington Heights Police
2nd Vice President:	S.V.B. English, Maryland State Police
3rd Vice President:	W.E. Rutledge, California Highway Patrol
4th Vice President:	S.S. Zablocki, Broward Co. Sheriff's Dept.
Treasurer:	J.J. Scarisbrick, Jr., Avis Rent A Car
Secretary:	T.J. Horrigan, Government Employees Insurance Co.
Directors:	R.G. Beasley, Alabama Dept. of Public Safety
	D.T. Brickel, San Jose Police
	H.L. Burr, Boston Dept. of Motor Vehicles
	P.J. Collins, Canadian Auto Theft Bureau
	P.W. Gilliland, National Auto Theft Bureau
	R.M. Irvine, Royal Canadian Mounted Police
	R.D. McQuown, Kentucky State Police
	D.E. Norman, Indiana State Police

SEMINAR

Denver, Colorado, Denver Hilton Hotel
July 30 – August 3, 1979

Charlie Banks

L to R: Terry La Casse-Pompano PD, C.B.-Ft. Lauderdale PD, Tad Rice-Miami PD, Ike Ivkovich-IL St. Pol., Gordon Rice-Broward SO, Ziggy Zablocki-Broward SO, Man facing camera unknown.

L to R: MO State Trooper and wife, Ray Dreher-Past President.

```
INTERNATIONAL ASSOCIATION
OF AUTO THEFT INVESTIGATORS

FINANCIAL STATEMENT

August 1, 1978 to July 31, 1979

Funds on Hand as of August 1, 1978

Checking Account  -  Suburban Trust Company       $ 4,039.44
                     Hyattsville, Maryland

Savings Account   -  University National Bank      $ 5,343.34   $ 9,382.78
                     Rockville, Maryland

Funds Received

Memberships (Includes foreign currency exchange)  $ 9,707.00
N.E. Chapter Assessment                                150.00
N.C. Chapter Assessment                                165.00
Seminar Surplus                                      1,821.54
IAATI Emblem/Book Contributions                          4.55
Interest (Savings Account)                             207.25   $12,055.34

                                                                $21,438.12

Expenditures

Printing                                          $ 5,636.69
Postage                                             1,466.89
Bank Charges & currency exchange                      111.35
Secretarial Expense                                 1,926.00
Membership Emblems                                    875.00
IACP Dues                                              35.00
President's Award                                      77.23
Seminar Expense                                        32.10
Miscellaneous Supplies & Expenses                     284.74   $10,445.00

Funds on Hand as of July 31, 1979

Checking Account  -  Suburban Trust Company       $ 5,442.53
                     Hyattsville, Maryland

Savings Account   -  University National Bank      $ 5,550.59   $10,993.12
                     Rockville, Maryland

                                                                $21,438.12
```

- John J. Scarisbrick, Jr.
Treasurer

INTERNATIONAL ASSOCIATION AUTO THEFT INVESTIGATORS

NEWS LETTER

EXECUTIVE OFFICES
12415 Feldon Street, Wheaton, MD 20906
(301) 946-4114

PRESIDENT
L. W. Spry
Ontario Provincial Police
Toronto, Ontario, Canada

FIRST VICE-PRESIDENT
S. D. Meath
University of Tennessee Police
Knoxville, Tennessee

SECOND VICE-PRESIDENT
R. C. Van Raalte
Arlington Heights Police Dept.
Arlington Heights, Illinois

THIRD VICE-PRESIDENT
S. V. B. English
Maryland State Police
Pikesville, Maryland

FOURTH VICE-PRESIDENT
W. E. Rutledge
California Highway Patrol
Visalia, California

TREASURER
J. J. Scarisbrick, Jr.
Avis Rent A Car
Garden City, New York

EXECUTIVE SECRETARY
T. J. Horrigan

DIRECTORS
R. G. Beasley
Alabama Dept Public Safety
Montgomery, Alabama

H. L. Burr
Department Of Motor Vehicles
Boston, Mass

G. DeLarochelliere
Montreal Urban Community Police
Montreal, Quebec, Canada

R. Irvine
Royal Canadian Mounted Police
Vancouver, British Columbia, Canada

W. Seaman
Dept. of Public Safety
Austin, Texas

S. S. Zablocki, Jr.
Broward County SHeriffs Office
Fort Lauderdale, Florida

IMMEDIATE PAST PRESIDENT
G. F. Hess
Los Angeles Police Dept.
Los Angeles, California

BOARD OF ADVISERS
P. J. Collins
Canadian Automobile Theft Bureau
Toronto, Ontario, Canada

P. McManus
Inpol Automobile Theft Bureau
.... ho, New York

APRIL - MAY 1978

GILLILAND NAMED PRESIDENT : Paul W Gilliland has been
named President of the National Automobile Theft Bureau
Mr Gilliland joined the NATB in 1963 as a special
agent assigned to Ohio and Indiana area. Before being
named Vice-President of the bureau in 1976, he was the
manager of NATB's Eastern Division Office. Prior to
that he was manager of the bureaus national systems division. Congratulations Paul & the best of luck in
your new task.

DOT LOOKS AT A NEW VIN:
There is in the making a proposal for a new motor vehicle identification number, says the US Department of
Transportation. A proposal by DOTs National Highway
Traffic Safety Administration to amend the federal vehicle standard # 115, to specify the structure and the
meaning of numbers and letters used in the vehicle's
VIN
Standard 115 presently only requires that the number
be on passenger vehicles, that it be unique to a particular manufacturer for a 10 year period and be so loc-
ated that it is readable from the outside of the vehicle. The new proposal would require manufacturers to provide a VIN that would be unique to each motor vehicle,
without duplication, for 30 years.
The new VIN would contain 16 characters plus a check
digit. On passenger vehicles, it would identify the
manufacturer, make, class of vehicle, model, line, ser-
ies, body type, engine, weight, transmission, year of
manufacture and restraint type.
In addition to its value in the recovery of stolen vehicles, it is important to state motor vehicle administrators, the International Association of Auto Theft
Investigators, US Treasury agents and other state, local
and international law enforcement agencies, said NHTSA
The effective date of the proposal is 1-1-80 for passenger vehicles and 9-1-81 for other types of vehicles.
(It appears that IAATI is starting to be recognized as
a leader in this field........editor)

MAKE PLANS: The next seminar for the International
Association of Auto Theft Investigators will be August
6th through 12th 1978 in Mobile, Alabama. Plan now to
attend, it will be a big one and from the reports its
will be interesting to all.

SEMINAR WARNING

Denver Post
Aug 6, 1979

1979 Could Be Record for Car Thefts

By GEORGE LANE
Denver Post Staff Writer

Automobile thefts in the United States during the past two years had dipped to below a million vehicles annually. But an official of the National Automobile Theft Bureau said in Denver this week that if this year's trend continues, 1979 could be a record year for stolen cars with the number of thefts at more than a million.

Auto-theft investigators from 43 states and four foreign countries—Great Britain, Australia, Japan and Canada—met in Denver last week to discuss the increasing problem of stolen vehicles and exchange ideas on how to catch the thieves.

The auto-theft seminar was sponsored by the International Association of Auto Theft Investigators, the University of Colorado Denver Center, the Denver Police Department and a number of other metropolitan-area police and sheriff's departments.

Organizers of the seminar said the meetings have been conducted nationwide for 27 years to help keep auto-theft investigators informed of new techniques.

REPRESENTATIVES OF auto investigation units from the foreign countries attended the sessions, a spokesman said, because auto theft also is becoming a major problem in their countries.

Paul Gilliland, a National Automobile Theft Bureau representative from Jericho, N.Y., said auto thefts nationally for the first quarter of this year are 15 percent higher than at the same time last year.

He said auto thefts are actually down about 16 percent in Denver because of efforts by the Denver Police Department.

"When you work those types of cases and let the criminal know you're going to be around, obviously it's got to be a deterrent," he added.

Gilliland, who was a keynote speaker during the seminar, said that about three years ago 1.5 million cars were stolen each year throughout the United States, but the figure dropped to fewer than a million for each of the past two years.

"FOR THE FIRST quarter of 1979," he said, "auto theft is up 15 percent and all crime is up 11 percent. Now if this holds, this may be the peak of all years."

He said the economy-inflation and the rising cost of gasoline—are contributing to the increasing number of car thefts. For example, he said, there are many cases recorded where a car is rented from an auto renting agency, driven until the full tank of gasoline is gone and then abandoned.

"You still have the thefts of cars from the agency storage lot," he said, "but we now have a growing number of cars

Denver Post Photo
PAUL GILLALAND
Cites changes in auto theft.

stolen from the agencies just because they have a full tank of gas."

Gilliland and W. E. Ruthlege, a California highway patrolman and a conference organizer, said there also is a difference today in the type of vehicle being stolen and from whom they are being stolen.

Prime targets are late-model cars and sporty models, Ruthlege said. But since the energy crisis, more economy cars and compacts are being stolen.

THE CALIFORNIA patrolman said there also is a serious problem nationwide of thefts of tractors, bulldozers and other farm and heavy off-road equipment.

The two seminar participants also said there has been in the past few months an increasing number of auto-theft insurance frauds. Already there have been several convictions for this kind of crime.

Gilliland explained that the insurance fraud occurs when someone owns a large, old, gas-eating automobile that he can't get rid of, so he abandons it or hires someone to steal it in order to obtain insurance money that can be used to purchase an economy car.

He said New York state recently has passed a law making it a felony to file false police reports or false insurance claims.

Gilliland said that in addition to a change in the kinds of auto thefts being reported to police departments, there also is a change in the location of most thefts.

HE SAID MANY people now are moving from the cities to the suburbs because they feel more secure, but auto thieves also are moving to the suburbs because that is where they can find the kind of cars they are looking for.

Another thing being changed by the car thief is what is being done with the stolen vehicle.

Gilliland said triple steering-wheel locks that manufacturers began putting on vehicles about 10 years ago have thwarted the juvenile or occasional thief, as they were intended to do, "but, given enough time, the pro is going to get your car."

Ruthlege said once a professional auto thief gets a car it is very likely it never will be seen again in one piece because it is more profitable to sell it part by part. A $5,000 car sold this way could bring as much as $25,000.

According to statistics presented to seminar participants, an estimated 38 percent of the stolen cars are stripped for parts, 35 percent are used for transportation, 3 percent are used in other crimes, with the use of the remaining 24 percent unknown.

GILLILAND SAID a great percentage of the cars stolen are chosen by the auto thief because they have the keys in them.

He said among the simple steps a car owner can take to make the job of the car thief more difficult are:

—Park in a well-lighted area.

—Park with front wheels turned sharply to the right or left, making it difficult for the professional thief to tow your car away.

—Close all windows and lock all doors.

—Put all packages or valuables out of sight. CB radios, tape decks and other expensive items in full view invite theft.

—If you park in a commercial lot or garage, leave only the ignition key with the attendant.

—Keep driver's license and registration in your wallet or purse. If left in the car, thieves can use these documents to sell the car.

—If you have a garage, use it and lock both the vehicle and the garage.

1979–1980

PRESIDENT

RONALD C. VAN RAALTE, ARLINGTON HEIGHTS POLICE DEPARTMENT

Ron's first IAATI was 1968 in Sacramento, CA. He was a patrolman at the Arlington Heights (IL) Police Department (joined in 1966). He also had attended an auto theft conference in Cleveland at Case Western University and met Paul Gilliland. After joining in 1969, he also met Ray Dreher, Tom Horrigan, Clyde Oliver, Lou Spry, and some others who took him "under their wings".

In 1969, Ron was promoted to Detective and began investigating auto theft cases. Being from a small department, they were expected to work all cases, but Ron thrived working auto theft related cases.

In 1974 he was elected to the office of IAATI secretary, succeeding Clyde Oliver. The position became a presidential appointed position in 1975, so that IAATI would have a permanent address rather than changing every year. As secretary, Ron focused on improving the quality, frequency of the newsletters and the annual membership directory, and recruiting members.

In 1977 Ron was elected to 3rd Vice President and moved through the chairs to President. During his year as president, he initiated presidential attendance at chapter seminars (at his expense), got IAATI involved with the IACP, started monthly written communication with the board, and continued recruitment efforts.

Over the years, Ron has stayed involved with IAATI and also contributed to other law enforcement organizations by writing articles for *The Police Chief* and *Law* and founding the Law Enforcement Memorial Research Project, which became the Law Enforcement Memorial Association, Inc. in 1989.

In 1983 he was employed by Avis Rent A Car System, Inc. In 1984, he became the first recipient of the Raymond Dreher Memorial Award and in 1995, received the IL Association of Chiefs of Police Private Security Award. Ron has also chaired the Dreher Memorial Award Committee for a number of years.

Ron has a BA and Masters degree in Public Administration. He has been married 30 years to Carol, "Big Red" as she is known in airline circles and to friends at IAATI. Carol has attended many seminars and played a crucial role in the spouse program for the 1980 international seminar.

EXECUTIVE BOARD

1st Vice President:	S.V.B. English, Maryland State Police
2nd Vice President:	W.E. Rutledge, California Highway Patrol
3rd Vice President:	S.S. Zablocki, Broward County Sheriff's Dept.
4th Vice President:	R.D. McQuown, Kentucky State Police
Treasurer:	J.J. Scarisbrick, Jr., Avis Rent A Car
Secretary:	T.J. Horrigan, Government Employees Insurance Co.
Directors:	R.G. Beasley, Alabama Dept. of Public Safety
	D.T. Brickell, San Jose Police
	H.L. Burr, Boston Dept. of Motor Vehicles
	G.L. Cole, Lakewood, Colorado Dept. of Public Safety
	P.J. Collins, Canadian Auto Theft Bureau
	P.W. Gilliland, National Auto Theft Bureau
	D.E. Norman, Indiana State Police
	D.A. Sandberg, Insurance Corp. of British Columbia

SEMINAR

Arlington Heights, Illinois
August 3-8, 1980

Ray Dreher Committee, L to R: Ziggy Zablocki-P/P, V. Ivkovich, Gene Rutledge, Ron Van Raalte.

28th annual seminar

1980—1981

PRESIDENT

SCOTT V. B. ENGLISH,
MARYLAND STATE POLICE

EXECUTIVE BOARD

1st Vice President:	W.E. Rutledge, California Highway Patrol
2nd Vice President:	Z. Zablocki, Broward County Sheriff's Dept.
3rd Vice President:	R.D. McQuown, Kentucky State Police
4th Vice President:	G.E. Cole, Lakewood Dept. of Public Safety
Treasurer:	J.J. Scarisbrick, Jr., Avis Rent A Car
Secretary:	T.J. Horrigan, Government Employees Insurance Co.
Director:	P.J. Collins, Canadian Auto Theft Bureau
	J.A. Cumby, Texas Dept. of Public Safety
	P.W. Gilliland, National Auto Theft Bureau
	J.L. Hoover, Louisiana State Police
	F.L. Letterman, North Caroliina Dept. of Motor Vehicles
	D.E. Norman, Indiana State Police
	R.A. Pope, Cincinnati Police
	B. VanDoleweerd, Durham, Canada Regional Police Force

SEMINAR

Houston, Texas
August 3-7, 1981

Scott English-President

Bob Olson, John Hoover, Tom Horrigan and Gene Rutledge

Gene Rutledge and Jerry Williams, Houston

Vivian Rutledge, Gene Rutledge, Ziggy, Zablocki, Rick and Betty McQuown, and Jery Cole

Bob Olson-On Site Chairman

Larry Barksdale John Hoover, Ike Ivkovich, Jerry Cole, Rick McQuown, Ziggy Zablocki, Gene Rutledge

1st VP Gene Rutledge presents award to Jim Zurek, International Harvester.

Guest magician, Tom Horrigan, Bob Olson, and Vivian Rutledge

Guest magician and Gene Rutledge

Bob Olson and Sgt. Brian Wood, Valley Constabulary, Thames, England

Gene Rutledge and Jim Zureck (International Harvester)

Peter Birse, Australia Capital Territory Police, with Gene Rutledge

Bob Olson and ??

Gene Rutledge and Jerry Jones

Lyman Ross and Gene Rutledge

Scott English and Gene Rutledge

1981–1982

PRESIDENT

W. E. "GENE" RUTLEDGE,
CALIFORNIA HIGHWAY PATROL (RETIRED)

Rutledge began his law enforcement career on June 6, 1957 when he joined the Tulare Country Sheriff's Office, Visalia, CA, as a Deputy Sheriff. He worked as a Deputy Sheriff until March 1, 1962 when he was promoted to Sergeant and became a shift supervisor.

On March 1, 1963 he entered the California Highway Patrol Academy, graduating as a Traffic Officer on June 28, 1963. Rutledge was assigned to the San Bernardino office and served there until June 1965, when he transferred back to the Visalia area. He was promoted to Vehicle Theft Investigator on August 13, 1967 and remained at that rank until retirement on December 7, 1992.

From December 1992, until permanent retirement, he worked in the insurance industry as a Senior Special Investigator, for AAA, CalFarm and Nationwide Insurance Companies respectively, specializing in fraudulent agricultural crimes.

His IAATI career began in 1967 with the invitation to join by Ed Geyer, also a CHP investigator, and a Director on the IAATI Board. In 1968, the annual seminar was held in Sacramento, Ca. and hosted by Ed. He became a Regional Director in August 1975, a Director in 1976 and was elected Fourth Vice-President in August 1977, eventually becoming the IAATI President for the 1981-82 year.

In August 1978, he was appointed by President Stanley Moats to head a new IAATI committee on heavy equipment, which he chaired until August 2000. In 1984, he became IAATI's first exhibit coordinator, appointed by President Rick McQuown. In 1985, he was appointed by President Ike Ivkovich to be the first Newsletter Editor, a job held for seven years.

In 1978, at the annual seminar held in Denver, Colorado he met Brian Wood, a Sergeant in the Thames Valley Police, Oxford, England and they developed a lasting friendship. In 1979, Brian invited him to England where we met with several individuals interested in auto theft and this lead to the formation of the European Branch in 1979-80. In 1989, he and Brian journeyed to South Africa and met with several law enforcement and insurance personnel, leading to the formation of the South African Chapter.

In 1982 while President of IAATI, he initiated the Raymond Dreher Award in recognition and memory of close friend and IAATI Officer, Sergeant Raymond Dreher of the Missouri Highway Patrol. He has personally funded this award since its inception. In 1984, he approached the Associated General Contractors of America with the suggestion that an award be established to honor an individual or group who had distin-

Gene Rutledge

1982 Baltimore, Pres. Rutledge passes gavel to Ziggy Zablocki

guished themselves in the field of heavy equipment investigation. As a result, the AGC/IAATI Award became a reality. In 1989 he met with Kevin Curry of the 3M Corporation who wanted to establish an award in recognition of an IAATI member involved in auto theft investigation that utilized 3M product(s) to aide in their investigation. As a result the 3M Award became a reality.

He is most proud of his wife of 44 years, Vivian. They have three wonderful daughters, a grandson and granddaughter.

EXECUTIVE BOARD

1st Vice President: Z. Zablocki, Broward County Sheriff's Department
2nd Vice President: R.D. McQuown, Kentucky State Police
3rd Vice President: G.E. Cole, Lakewood Department of Public Safety
4th Vice President: V. Ivkovich, Illinois Secretary of State Office
Treasurer: J.J. Scarisbrick, Jr., Avis Rent A Car
Secretary: T.J. Horrigan, Government Employees Insurance Co.
Directors: L. Barksdale, Lincoln, Nebraska Police
P.J. Collins, Canadian Auto Theft Bureau
J.A. Cumby, Texas Dept. of Public Safety
P.W. Gilliland, National Auto Theft Bureau
J.L. Hoover, Louisiana State Police
F. L. Letterman, N. Carolina Dept. of Motor Vehicles
R.A. Pope, Cincinnati Police
W. VanDoleweerd, Durham, Canada Regional Police Force

Virgil Luke-Miss. State Police, Gene Rutledge, Roy Barnett-Harley Davidson Co.

SEMINAR

Baltimore, Maryland, Hyatt Regency
August 1–6, 1982

Ziggy Zablocki, Inner Harbor, Baltimore,MD

Dan Ryan trying to record VIN's on stolen Buicks

1982–1983

PRESIDENT

ZIGGY ZABLOCKI,
BROWARD COUNTY SHERIFF'S DEPT.

Ziggy started his career in law enforcement in 1966 after three years as a reserve special officer. In 1969 he was promoted to Detective 1st/Class, the youngest Detective in Woodbridge (NJ) history. He was also named the department expert on vehicles. While in this assignment he became friends with several NATB agents who took him under their wing.

In 1970, he relocated to Ft. Lauderdale and took assignment as a road patrol officer with the Broward County Sheriffs Office. After about six weeks on the job, a vicious murder occurred. The Detective Bureau supervisors scanned all personnel for detective experience and he was selected. During that time he was able to continue his insight into vehicles and upon completion of the murder investigation was given the green light to begin an auto theft unit.

All went well, and in 1972 he attended his first IAATI conference in Tallahassee, FL. Ziggy soon became active with the organization, becoming a member of the board soon after. He was elected as a Director at the annual conference held in Irving (Dallas) TX. During the Tallahassee conference, a group of us Florida people recognized the need for a state unit and initiated what is now known as the Florida Auto Theft Intelligence Unit (FATIU).

Ziggy rose up the ranks to Lieutenant as commander of the Broward County Sheriffs Office Auto Theft Unit, maintaining that grade through eight years and three different sheriffs. Around 1990, he was told that his position did not require a Lieutenant and that he was going to be transferred to a district as a commander with the possibility of greater rank. He asked that consideration be given to his remaining with the unit, even if it required a drop in grade to Sergeant. After several

hours, administrators agreed that he could remain with the unit if he dropped to the Sergeant grade with no reduction in pay. This was done within twenty minutes and he was able to stay status quo.

He was President of FATIU for six, two year terms and has met literally thousands of the most determined investigators one can imagine. Since 1972, he has only missed the Ontario (work), Australia (cost), and the Vancouver (illness) seminars, and can usually be found near or around my almost-lifelong best friend, Charlie Banks in the Hospitality Suite.

EXECUTIVE BOARD

1st Vice President:	R.D. McQuown, Kentucky State Police
2nd Vice President:	G.E. Cole, Lakewood Department of Public Safety
3rd Vice President:	V. Ivkovich, Illinois Secretary of State's Office
4th Vice President:	R.A. Pope, Cincinnati Police
Treasurer:	J.J. Scarisbrick, Jr., Avis Rent A Car
Secretary:	T.J. Horrigan, D.C. Metropolitan Police
Directors:	L. Barksdale, Lincoln, Nebraska Police
	D. Bradley, Tulsa, Oklahoma Police
	J.C. Cloutier, Canadian Auto Theft Bureau
	J.A. Cumby, Texas Dept. of Public Safety
	P.W. Gilliland, National Auto Theft Bureau
	J.L. Hoover, Louisiana State Police
	F.L. Letterman, North Carolina Dept. of Motor Vehicles
	R.C. Roloson, Ontario, Canada Provincial Police

SEMINAR

Little Rock, Arkansas, Little Rock Excelsior Hotel
July 31 – August 5, 1983

1983 Seminar. 1st Row: Charlie Banks, Gene Rutledge,Tom Horrigan; Second Row: Lloyd Letterman, Ziggy Zablocki, Ron Van Raalte, John Scarisbrick; Third Row: Clarence Brickey, Rick McQuown, Bob Pope, ---, ---, Jean Claude, Larry Barksdale, Jerry Cole.

Auto theft investigators gather at Hyatt

By Rafael Alvarez

Ziggy Zablocki's wife doesn't like going to shopping centers with her husband. It's not because he's tight with a dollar, she just can't get the Fort Lauderdale auto theft detective off the parking lot and into the store.

"I keep on walking down the aisles, checking this and that. It gets in your system," Detective Lieutenant Zablocki said of looking for stolen cars.

He is in Baltimore this week with about 200 other detectives to attend the 30th annual convention of the International Association of Auto Theft Investigators at the Baltimore Hyatt Regency. The Florida detective is to be installed as the new president of IAATI.

Dedicated auto detectives, he said, are like dedicated watchers of the opposite sex: They inspect every model that passes by.

When out on the road, he tries to match a car with the person behind the wheel.

If he sees a 15-year-old zipping down the freeway in a Cadillac Coupe de Ville, rock music blaring out the windows, there's a good chance it's not the kid's car.

"I try to make eye contact, confront them. A kid that's out with his father's car has no problems looking at you," he said. If the car or driver looks suspicious, he'll cruise around to the right of the car to check for keys in the ignition, he said.

The rugged-looking detective—his baby-blue sports clothes accented

by heavy gold jewelry, his eyes fixed seriously beneath wispy bangs of salt-and-pepper hair—used to drive a coveted Chevrolet Corvette.

Now he travels in a battered pick-up truck.

"I got tired of worrying about somebody stealing it," he said of his sports car.

Vladimir Ivkovich's reward for sticking his nose into organized auto theft in Illinois for the past 19 years was a bomb left on his doorstep and gunfire aimed at his moving car.

"On July 8, 1978, my dog came jumping up on my bed very excited," said Detective Ivkovich, who works for the Illinois State Police.

"I thought he had to go out. When I opened the door there was a smok-

See AUTO, D5, Col. 1

1983–1984

PRESIDENT

RICK McQUOWN,
KENTUCKY STATE POLICE

This being the first newsletter since our annual seminar in Little Rock, it is my first opportunity to address the membership. I am very honored to be the 1983-84 president of IAATI and look forward to the new year. IAATI has come a long way in recent years in being recognized as the voice in the vehicle theft field. The experience of all our membership when combined and brought forth at the annual seminars shows what can be done through communication. Without out annual seminar and our chapter seminars, we would never be able to ex-

Rick McQuown

change information and ideas as we do. The Little Rock seminar was probably the best attended as far as interest of the membership and expertise in instruction. Almost every instructor spoke to a full house; each year it seems to get better.

I would like to ask all our members to attempt to increase the membership. Those on the Executive Board have recognized the need to provide more to the membership, and we are dedicated to improving IAATI. We still need your help. The members are IAATI; members are what make any organization work. We cannot do it once a year at the annual seminar.

I urge each member to submit useful and informative articles for the newsletter. I would also like for the membership to advise me of any new personnel or commanding officers assigned to an auto theft section. I want to personally contact them about IAATI.

Let's all try to make this a better year for IAATI. I hope to see many of you at different seminars around the country.

—President McQuown's comments from APB.

EXECUTIVE BOARD

1st Vice President:	G.E. Cole, Lake Department of Public Safety
2nd Vice President:	V. Ivkovich, Illinois Secretary of State Office
3rd Vice President:	R.A. Pope Cincinnati Police
4th Vice President:	P.W.Gilliland National Auto Theft Bureau
Treasurer:	J.J. Scarisbrick, Jr, Avis Rent A Car
Secretary:	T.J. Horrigan D.C. Metropolitan Police
Directors:	L. Barksdale, Lincoln, Nebraska Police
	D. Bradley, Tulsa, Oklahoma Police
	L. Capp, Arizona Dept. of Public Safety
	J.C. Cloutier, Canadian Auto Theft Bureau
	P. Ethridge, Tennessee Dept. of Safety
	D. Robertson, Virginia Dept. of Motor Vehicles
	D. Ryan, Federal Bureau of Investigation
	J. Streitch, Oklahoma Tax Commission

SEMINAR

Reno, Nevada, Eldorado Hotel
August 26 – 31, 1984

Registration Table 1984, London meeting to form European IAATI; Ian Ramsey and Gerry Wood.

London 1984, Registration Desk; Vivian Ruttledge, Gerry Wood, Frankie Jones

1984 London, Brian Wood speaks to delegates

1984–1985

President

Gerald Cole,
Lakewood Police Department

Cole was born in Denver and arrived at Lakewood, Colorado as a police recruit in 1970, following a college career that included the Arapahoe Jr. College, Northern Arizona University, an internship with the Flint, Michigan PD, and a BS degree from Cal State LA.

Bill Borman-Treasurer and John Scarisbrick-Past Treasurer.

Jerry Cole, (right) welcomes incoming president Ike Ivkovich.

His IAATI career began at an auto theft seminar at Case Western University in Cleveland, in 1973. His recruiters were Clyde Oliver & Paul Gilliland. He was immediately hooked on how interesting and challenging vehicle theft investigations were and how great the IAATI organization was. That same year he threw in with a group of investigators who established the Colorado Auto Theft Investigators, based on the IAATI model, and helped along considerably by IAATI's Ray Dreher and Bob Saddler.

During his time with Lakewood he's passed through patrol, investigation, intelligence and administrative assignments both as an Agent and as a Sergeant. His details have included patrol, auto theft detective, two undercover multi-agency sting operations, supervisor for K-9 and Special Enforcement Teams, internal affairs, patrol sergeant and supervisor for the auto theft unit on two occasions, including the present.

His IAATI duties have included being host to the Annual Seminar in Denver in 1979 and program chair at Baltimore in 1981. He describes the role as IAATI President as being a runner in a middle leg of an unending relay race: in 1984 at Reno he received the baton from Rick McQuown and carried it to Des Moines were it was passed to Ike Ivkovich.

Cole has a beautiful wife, Sue, who is a High School computer teacher and a website designer, and they have three lovely daughters.

Gene Rutledge recieving Ray Dreher Award.

Joanie Pitts

EXECUTIVE BOARD

1st Vice President:	V. Ivkovich, Illinois Secretary of State Police
2nd Vice President:	R.A. Pope, Cincinnati Police
3rd Vice President:	P.W. Gilliland, National Auto Theft Bureau
4th Vice President:	L. Barksdale, Lincoln Nebraska Police
Treasurer:	J.J. Scarisbrick, Jr., Avis Rent A Car
Secretary:	T.J. Horrigan, D.C. Metropolitan Police
Executive Director:	H. Lee Ballard
Directors:	D. Bradley, Tulsa, Oklahoma Police
	L. Capp, Arizona Department of Public Safety
	J.C. Cloutier, Canadian Auto Theft Bureau
	J. Duff, Georgia Bureau of Investigation
	P. Ethridge, Tennessee Dept. of Public Safety
	J.H. Jones, Utah Highway Patrol
	K. MacKenzie, Richardson, Texas Police
	D. Robertson, Virginia Dept. of Motor Vehicles
	D. Ryan, Federal Bureau of Investigation

SEMINAR

Des Moines, Iowa, Hotel Fort Des Moines
August 10 - 16, 1985

Ziggy Zablocki

The Brickey's

Paul Gilliland

1985–1986

PRESIDENT

VLADIMIR "IKE" IVKOVICH, ILLINOIS SECRETARY OF STATE POLICE

Ike was born in the state of West Virginia, but moved to Virginia at age four months. He later moved to Chicago in 1941, and attended schools in the Chicago area before joining the U.S. Air Force in 1948.

Vladimir "Ike" Ivkovich

He began his law enforcement career with the Secretary of State Police as a field investigator in April 1964. In January 1966 he was promoted to Lieutenant and assigned to the truck enforcement section. In 1971 he was transferred to the stolen car section as its commander, and led this group for eight years. In January 1981 was transferred to be the zone supervisor for the Northern District of Illinois. After retiring from the SOS Police he served as Chief of Police in Bridgeview, IL.

Ike's career with IAATI began when he joined the North Central Chapter in 1975, and later served as chapter president. After service as director, he was elected as fourth vice president in 1981, before moving up the chairs to president.

He has been married to Joan since July 1950, and they three daughters and three grandchildren.

EXECUTIVE BOARD

1st Vice President:	R.A. Pope, Cincinnati Police
2nd Vice President:	P.W. Gilliland, National Auto Theft Bureau
3rd Vice President:	L. Barksdale, Lincoln Nebraska Police
4th Vice President:	L. Capp, Arizona Department of Public Safety
Treasurer:	J.J. Scarisbrick, Jr., Avis Rent A Car
Secretary:	T.J. Horrigan, D.C. Metropolitan Police
Executive Director:	H. Lee Ballard
Directors:	D. Bradley, Tulsa, Oklahoma Police
	J.C. Cloutier, Canadian Auto Theft Bureau
	J. Duff, Georgia Bureau of Investigation
	P. Ethridge, Tennessee Dept. of Public Safety
	J.H. Jones, Utah Highway Patrol
	K. MacKenzie, Richardson, Texas Police
	D. Robertson, Virginia Dept. of Motor Vehicles
	D. Ryan, Federal Bureau of Investigation

SEMINAR

Hartford, Connecticut, Sheraton Hotel
August 3 – 8, 1986

John Scarsbrick retires as IAATI Treasurer 1986 Hartford, Conn.

Jim Cadigan, FBI, and wife Kathy

Clarence Brickey, Willy and daughter

Aggie and Tom Horrigan, Lou Spry and John Scarisbrick and Margo Spry.

European Chapter President, Brian Wood entertains wife Gerry and Gene Rutledge.

Past President Lou Spry presents Ray Dreher award to Past President Gene Rutledge.

Horrigan and Scarisbrick in deep conversation.

The McQuown's

Lou Spry

EXECUTIVE DIRECTOR

H. LEE BALLARD

After graduating from Loyola College and a tour of duty in the Army, Lee Ballard started his insurance career in Baltimore, MD. He started with Motors Insurance Company (GM) in 1955. He joined the Americam Road Insurance Company - Taric (Ford) in 1963. He was the first claims adjuster hired by Taric. He rose to claim supervisor (1966) and then to district manager in the Detroit district office. (1969). Ballard moved from there to staff claims in Tarics' home office in Dearborn, MI in 1973.

In the mid '70's, Ford Credit recognised the increasing problem of theft from their new car dealerships. After studies, a loss prevention activity was established in Taric to reduce this problem. Ballard was assigned the task of identifing the causes and effect some solutions.

Ballard was introduced to IAATI in Baltimore. He met with Clarence Brickey, MDSP and Harry Harper, Baltimore Police and subsequently joined IAATI in 1975.

Ballard attended his first seminar (NCRC) in the Chicago area. His first international seminar was in Montreal, Canada in 1977, where he was invited to make a presentation on auto dealership security. He has attended 22 subsequent international seminars in addition to numerous chapter and state theft association meetings.

In 1985, then NCRC president Paul Seiler appointed Ballard as an advisory director, the first civilian member to serve on an IAATI board. The honor of being first was repeated in 1986 when he was appointed executive director (then executive secretary) of the international board.

During his tenure he served on manyIAATI committees and saw IAATI grow from aproximently 950 members to over 4000. Records were computerised during this time also.

In addition to Ford and IAATI Ballard was engaged in other law enforcement related activities. He attended the Dearborn, MI reserve police officers training and was appointed a reserve officer in 1982. He also taught a basic auto theft course for reserve police officers at Schoolcraft College in Michigan. He has lectured on auto theft and tractor and equipment (farm) theft on several occasions.

Ballard became involved in scuba diving in the early 1970's and became an instructor. He taught basic scuba for the Ford Seahores. He was a visiting professor (scuba) at Eastern Michigan University for several years. He was on the scuba instructor training staff at Northern Michigan University (NMU) for 10 years. This latter position resulted in

H. Lee Ballard

his being one of the first certified law enforcment diving instructors. He was involved in the training of several police dive team officers from all over the US and Canada at the law enforcement diving training institute at NMU. He is an honorary Ontario (OPP) force diver.

He has written several theft related magazine articles and produced a booklet "Loss Prevention for Ford Motor Company Dealers" which was endorsed by the Federal Bureau of Investigation and used as a reference by NICB (formerly NATB) for all auto dealers. This variety of endevors contributed to Ballard's success at Ford as well as his contribution to IAATI. He retired from Ford as manager of loss prevention in 1990. Theft losses for Ford Credit were reduced by approximately $200 million from 1975 to 1990.

Ballard moved to an emeritus position with IAATI in 2001. He has been recognised by the NCRC with a service award and the Clyde W. Oliver award. The international honored him with a life membership, a presidential award (2001), and the presitigous Drehr Award (1993).

1986–1987

PRESIDENT

R. POPE, CINCINNATI POLICE DEPARTMENT

Bob Pope

EXECUTIVE BOARD

1st Vice President: P.W. Gilliland, National Automobile Theft Bureau
2nd Vice President: L. Barksdale, Lincoln Nebraska Police
3rd Vice President: L. Capp, Arizona Department of Public Safety
4th Vice President: P. Ethridge, Tennessee Department of Public Safety
Treasurer: W.G. Borman, Avis Rent A Car
Executive Director: H. Lee Ballard, The American Road Insurance Co.
Directors: R.L. Bloss, Michigan State Police
J.C. Cloutier, Canadian Auto Theft Bureau
P.J. Crepeau, New York City Police
H.H. Fronk, Travelers Insurance Co.
T. Hansen, Galveston County, Texas Organized Crime Unit
J.H. Jones, Utah Highway Patrol
K.B. MacKenzie, Richarson, Texas Police
D.F. Ryan, Federal Bureau of Investigation

SEMINAR

Salt Lake City, Utah, Radisson Hotel
July 19 – 24, 1987

Marianne Finney and Joan Pitts.

Ziggy Zablocki, and Carol and Ron Van Raalte

Ziggy Zablocki, Howie Fronk, Ann Banks, Pat Mitchell

John Scarisbrick, Harry Brady and wives.

L-R Rear: Rutledge, MacKenzie, Barksdale, Bloss, Brickey, Ryan, Cloutier, Van Raalte, Cadigan, Hansen, Meyer, Pike, McQuown, Zablocki, Ivkovich. L-R Front: Frank, Pope, Borman, Brady, Mitchell, Crepeau, Ballard

Ray Dreher Award presented to Charlie Banks. From left: Ike Ivkovich, Ziggy Zablocki, Charlie Banks, Gene Rutledge, Ron Van Raalte

1987–1988

President

Paul W. Gilliland, National Automobile Theft Bureau

Paul joined the NATB in 1963 as a special agent assigned to the Ohio and Indiana area. Before being named vice-president of the bureau in 1976, he was the manager of NATB's Eastern Division Office. Prior to that, he was commissioned an Ohio Highway Patrol Officer in December 1954, and was later manager of the NATB's national systems division.

A veteran of the Korean War, he served in the U.S. Marines. A graduate of the State University of New York, he also served as a member of the Auto Theft Committee of the International Assoc. of Chiefs of Police, the American Assoc. of Motor Vehicle Administrators, the society of Automotive Engineers, and the International Standards Organization.

Paul and his wife, Jan, have three children—Paul Jr., Nancy and Peggy.

Paul W. Gilliland

Executive Board

1st Vice President:	L. Barksdale, Lincoln Nebraska Police
2nd Vice President:	L. Capp, Arizona Department of Public Safety
3rd Vice President:	P. Ethridge, Tennessee Department of Public Safety
4th Vice President:	D.F. Ryan, Federal Bureau of Investigation
Treasurer:	W.G. Borman, Avis Rent A Car
Executive Director:	H. Lee Ballard, The American Road Insurance Co.
Directors:	R.L. Bloss, Michigan State Police
	J.J. Cadigan, FBI
	J.C. Cloutier, Canadian Auto Theft Bureau
	P.J. Crepeau, CARCO Group, Inc.
	H.H. Fronk, Travelers Ins. Co.
	T. Hansen, Galveston Co., Texas Organized Crime Unit
	K.B. MacKenzie, Richardson, Texas Police
	D.L. Meyer, Illinois State Police

L to R: John Daniel, Harry Brady Sr., and C.C. Benson

Seminar

Galveston Island, Texas, The San Luis Hotel
August 7 – 12, 1988

C.C. Benson, P. Gilliland, J. Daniel

A.T. Phillips recieves Dreher Award (L-R) Zablocki, Rutledge, Van Raalte, and Phillips

Western Chapter receives Charter from President Paul Gilliland with Western Chapter President J.J. Jones and Gene Rutledge, ??, Jerry Bayer, Ken MacKenzie, ??, ??

IAATI Board; Galveston, TX; August 11, 1988. Back Row(L to R): G. Cole, L. Ballard, D. Meyer, B. Borman, T. Hansen, J.C. Cloutier, C.C. Benson, L. Barksdale, V. Ivkovich, P. Crepeau, G. Rutledge, P. Gilliland, D. Robertson. Seated (L to R): K. MacKenzie, H. Fronk, J. Cadigan, D. Ryan, P. Ethridge, H. Brady, Sr., R. McQuown, G. McLaughlin, J. Daniel

Judy and Tommy Hansen

P. Gilliland, J. Daniel and C.C. Benson

Nominating Committee 1988, Brickey, McQuown, Zablocki, Brady, Van Raalte, Cole

L-R: Tommy Hansen, Kate Dawdowitz, Mike Creech "Creecher". Conference was held in honor of Kate's late husband Sam, TX City Fire Dept.

P. Gilliand, J.C. Clouter, Ike Ivkovich, Gene Rutledge

Seminar Equipment display

Odd street Galveston

Jerry Boyer, Kevin Curry, Gene Rutledge

A.T. Phillips and John Amazzo

1988—1989

PRESIDENT

L. E. BARKSDALE,
LINCOLN NEBRASKA POLICE DEPARTMENT

Larry was born in Dodge City, Kansas, on September 27, 1946, and raised on a chicken ranch on the outskirts of town. He attended public schools up through the local Community College.

After graduating from Community College, he was drafted in 1966 into the United States Army. The Army trained him to be an Explosive Ordinance Disposal Specialist, and sent him to Chicago. In the Chicagoland area he frequently worked with law enforcement agencies on situations involving explosion events, participated in security details for dignitaries, and experienced the civil disturbances taking place in the United States at that time.

After leaving the Army in 1968, he went back to college in Kansas. While in college he had the good fortune to meet Connie Lincoln, who he married in 1972. During this time, in 1971, became an official member of the Lincoln Police Department.

Although he had intended to stay on with the police for only about three years (until he finished college and could get another job), he remained on the job for the past 30 years. Along the way he picked up a Bachelor's Degree in Criminal Justice, and a Master's Degree in Political Science.

Barksdale worked as a Sergeant in the Criminal Investigations Team as a Case Manager, and as Supervisor of the Crime Scene Tech Unit. He spends his spare time as an Adjunct Instructor, Nebraska Wesleyan University, in the Forensic Science Program.

Although he has been unable to attend IAATI seminars over the past several years, he looks back on the active years as the best of his police career, and the people met through IAATI as largely influential in instilling in him the love of the job.

Larry Barksdale

EXECUTIVE BOARD

1st Vice President:	L.L. Capp, Arizona Department of Public Safety
2nd Vice President:	P.A. Ethridge, Tennessee Department of Public Safety
3rd Vice President:	D.F. Ryan, FBI
4th Vice President:	J.C. Cloutier, Canadian Auto Theft Bureau
Treasurer:	W.G. Borman, Avis Rent A Car
Executive Director:	H. Lee Ballard, The American Road Insurance Co.
Directors:	J.J. Cadigan, Federal Bureau of Investigation
	P.J. Crepeau, CARCO Group, Inc.
	H.H. Fronk, GE–CAA
	T.J. Hansen, Galveston Co., Texas Organized Crime Unit
	K.B. MacKenzie, Richardson, Texas Police
	D.L. Meyer, Illinois State Police
	D.W. Robertson, Virginia Dept. of Motor Vehicles
	D.E. Werra, Milwaukee Police

SEMINAR

San Diego, California, The U.S. Grant Hotel
August 5 – 11, 1989

Don Kessler and Frank Ruzicka

Hughette and Jean Claude Cloutier

L/R Jerry Boyer-NICB, Unidentified, Lee Cole-LSC and Assoc., Charly Evans-NICB

San Diego Zoo, Agnes Horrigan, Joannie Pitts Marianne, Karen, Ryan, Charlie Banks.

Jim Gavigan receives AGC/IAATI Award

Past Presidents, R.McQuown #32, Rutledge #30, Pope #35, Barksdale #37, Ivkovich #34, Horrigan #16, Pike #21, Brickey #24, Zablocki #31, Van Raalte #28.

Ken MacKenzie awarded Ray Dreher Memorial Award. L to R: Van Raalte, Rutledge, AT Phillips, Ken McKenzie

San Diego Zoo, Mrs. Horrigan and Mrs. Van Raalte

H*E*A*T SHEET

TOOLS OF THE TRADE

Like skilled technicians, auto thieves rely on a variety of specialized tools to make their jobs easier — and their victims' lives miserable. Police officers confiscated the tools shown here from a thief who acquired them for the legitimate job of repossessing automobiles for creditors.

By taking a moment to familiarize yourself with the tools of the trade, you may be able to recognize and report an auto theft at work.

Collapsible athletic bags are often used to carry tools and illegal hand-held police scanners.

According to Sgt. Bruce Saller of the Michigan State Police criminal investigation section, the tools shown here would allow a thief access to most automobiles and homes.

These keys have rubberized shanks. When lubricated with a graphite solution and forcefully inserted in locks, they assume the shape of the original key and open door locks and operate ignitions of certain cars.

Thieves use common screwdrivers for a variety of purposes when entering or starting vehicles. The notched steel piece, known as a "slim jim," opens car doors by moving the internal locking mechanism.

A special wrench socket fits over and breaks the ignition key mechanism, often starting the vehicle.

Dent pullers, commonly used at collision repair shops to fix car bodies, are used to forcibly remove door locks and ignitions.

An ignition puller is used to remove the ignition key housing from an automobile's steering column. Once the key system has been bypassed, the thief is able to start the vehicle.

This bent screwdrivers unlocks the doors of certain cars by sliding into a handle opening and moving an internal locking mechanism.

1989—1990

President

L. L. Capp, Arizona Department of Public Safety

Larry was born in Dixon, Illinois but grew up in Phoenix, Arizona. Upon graduation from high school in Phoenix, Larry joined the U.S. Coast Guard and because of his attraction to police work, upon discharge started his police career in 1967 with the Phoenix Police Department. After his first few months he was assigned to the State Narcotics Bureau in 1969. Shortly, thereafter, the Narcotics Bu-

Larry Capp

reau was absorbed by the newly-created Department of Public Safety and Capp worked narcotics in the Phoenix area until 1970, which brought a transfer to Yuma. His duty there was to intercept smugglers and the drug traffickers trying to penetrate the border. Larry quotes that "those were the days".

One of his proudest achievements was a letter of commendation he received from former DPS Director Vernon Hoy after he transferred to freeway duty in July 1973, just before his promotion to Sergeant. Larry was one of the first officers with a criminal investigation background to patrol the freeway, so his expertise was a welcome to the agency.

Capp's assignments over the years have taken him to Tucson, Mohave, Phoenix and Yuma counties, until he settled in the Organized Crime Auto Theft Unit in Phoenix, 1980. At that time, the unit was a 2–man operation, but grew because of the increase in auto thefts. Car thieves from the East Coast, driven out by more intense enforcement efforts, settled in Arizona, seeing it as fertile land for their efforts.

Larry became Supervisor of the Phoenix Auto Theft Unit in 1981 and by this time DPS Auto Theft had grown to 18 commissioned officers statewide. Larry retired after 20 years with DPS in 1987.

Larry was president of the Arizona Auto Theft Investigators Association, chairman of the Arizona Automobile Theft Authority and was Treasurer of the Ari-

zona Anti Car Theft (ACT) Committee. He rose through the ranks of IAATI and became President in 1989/1990. During his tenure with IAATI, he would give seminars and exchanges technical information with other members with his expertise knowledge on vehicle theft. While holding the office President, he worked to reshape the executive board to include the addition of non-law enforcement as board officers.

Larry is currently working for Swift Transportation Company in Phoenix as Assistant Director of Security. Again, using his expertise that he gained in law enforcement, he handles and coordinates the major theft investigations at Swift, supervises their West and East Coast investigators and the background investigation unit.

Larry has been married to his lovely wife Mary for 38 years and have five beautiful grandchildren.. Following in dad's footsteps, their daughter Crista is a sergeant on the Phoenix Police Department, while their other daughter Holly is a dental hygienist.

Executive Board

1st Vice President:	P.A. Ethridge, Tennessee Department of Public Safety
2nd Vice President:	D.F. Ryan, Federal Bureau of Investigation
3rd Vice President:	J.C. Cloutier, Canadian Auto Theft Bureau
4th Vice President:	K.B. MacKenzie, Richardson, Texas Police
Treasurer:	W.G. Borman, Avis Rent A Car
Executive Director:	H. Lee Ballard, The American Road Insurance Co.
Directors:	G.M. Augusta, California Highway Patrol
	J.J. Cadigan, Federal Bureau of Investigation
	P.J. Crepeau, CARCO Group, Inc.
	D.L. Meyer, Illinois State Police
	D.W. Robertson, Virginia Dept. of Motor Vehicles
	J.L. Taylor, Cincinnati Police
	D.E. Werra, Milwaukee Police
	B. Wood, RD & L Investigations

SEMINAR

Omaha, Nebraska, Red Lion Inn
August 12 – 17, 1990

Clarence and Willie Brickey and Vivian Rutledge

Dan Ryan, Ike and Joan Ivkovich

Dick and Betty McQuown & Paul Gillilan and wife, Jan

L-R: Dan Ryan, George Wilson, and Joanie Pitts

L-R: Ziggy Zablocki and Phil Crepeau

L-R: Jim Catigan and Joanie Pitts doing the twist

L-R: Bill Johnson, Jerry Boyer, and Hector Queveva

L-R: A.T. Philips, Craig Berry, Gene Rutledge, Joannie Pitts, Ron Van Raalte, and Ken MacKenzie

1990—1991

PRESIDENT

PAT (ETHRIDGE) MITCHELL, TENNESSEE HIGHWAY PATROL

On August 16, 1990, at their annual meeting, the International Association of Auto Theft Investigators elected their first female president, Patricia Ethridge, of the Tennessee Highway Patrol, Nashville, Tenn.

Pat Ethridge opens the 39th Seminar

Pat has been a member of IAATI since 1981, when she attended a meeting of the North Central Chapter in Louisville, Kentucky. Later the same year she became a member of the Southeast Chapter at a meeting in Jackson, Mississippi. At her first southeast chapter meeting, she was elected Secretary. In August 1983, Pat was elected to the board of directors of the International, and began her climb through the chairs of office. In fact, in 1988, Pat was both the program chairperson for both the Southeast Chapters and the Internationals annual meeting, a feat that few could pull off.

Pat, a graduate of Aquinas Junior College, Nashville, where she received her degree in criminal justice, started her career with the state of Tennessee in their revenue department in 1976. She soon became an Investigator in that department's newly formed vehicle theft unit. In 1983, that unit was transferred to the authority of the Department of Public Safety, and later in 1987, the unit became a part of the Tennessee Highway Patrol, with expanded duties to include investigations of all felony crimes.

Pat has served as an instructor in interviewing techniques and evidence handling for her department.

Pat is currently assigned to the THP/Planning and Research Division and is the coordinator for the TN Watch Your Car Program. Pat is married to Jimmy Hester who is the special agent in charge of the THP/ C.I.D. unit.Pat said it was an honor and a privilege to work with IAATI over the past 22 years. Being the first female president was a challenge at times but the most rewarding of her career.

EXECUTIVE BOARD

1st Vice President:	D.F. Ryan, Federal Bureau of Investigation
2nd Vice President:	J.C. Cloutier, Canadian Auto Theft Bureau
3rd Vice President:	K.B. MacKenzie, Richardson, Texas Police
4th Vice President:	D.L. Meyer, Illinois State Police
Treasurer:	W.G. Borman, Avis Rent A Car
Executive Director:	H. Lee Ballard, Ford Motor Company
Directors:	G.M. Augusta, California Hwy. Patrol
	J.J. Cadigan, Federal Bureau of Investigation
	P.J. Crepeau, CARCO Group, Inc.
	P.J. D'Alessandro, Clarkstown, New York Police
	J. Gobby, Surete du Quebec
	J.E. Painter, National Auto Theft Bureau
	D.E. Werra, Milwaukee Police
	B. Wood, RD & L Investigations

SEMINAR

St. Paul, Minnesota, Radisson Hotel
August 18 – 23, 1991

Bo Koehler

Omaha 1990: 1st Row-Ike Ivkovich, Pat Ethridge, Larry Capp.2nd Row-Ziggy Zablocki, Lee Ballard, Dave McGillis, Gene Rutledge, Rick McQuown. 3rd Row-Ron Van Raalte, John Taylor, Greg Augusta, Dan Robertson.4th Row-Paul Gilliland, Clarence Brickey, Jerry Boyer, J.C. Cloutier, Roger Overton. 5th Row-Bill Borman, Denny Meyer, Phil Crepeau. Back Row-Ken MacKenzie, Don Werra.

39th Annual
IAATI SEMINAR
St. Paul, Minnesota

August 18-23,
1991

1991—1992

PRESIDENT

DANIEL F. RYAN, FBI (RETIRED)

Dan was one of those rare FBI Agents who worked vehicle theft cases his entire career. His investigative skills took him to New Orleans, Louisiana for the first two years then to Baltimore, Maryland for sixteen and the last eleven in San Diego. He also taught at the FBI Academy in Quantico, Virginia and taught overseas in Riga, Latvia, Warsaw, Poland and Budapest, Hungary. He also made trips to London, England and Stockholm, Sweden. He claims to have done FBI or IAATI business or monkey business in every state in the US except Alaska, Hawaii, Washington and Oregon. On escapade involved helping drive a tractor/trailer containing one million dollars of stolen Cover Girl cosmetics from Baltimore, Maryland to Los Angeles, California with a female FBI Agent.

In 1974, Clarence O. Brickey (a former IAATI President) recruited Dan to join IAATI. Dan got more involved each year first as Legislative Committee Chairman. He was involved, starting in 1976 with the National Motor Vehicle Theft Act,

Presentation of Ray Dreher Award, L to R: Ron Van Roalte, Lou Spry , Gene Rutledge, Brian Wood - Recipient, Wilheim Smith - Recipient, not pictured Ziggy Zablocki - Recipient

which was eventually signed into law by President Regan in 1984. Dan testified before the United States Congress, (along with several other IAATI members), in a successful attempt to keep the politicians from "watering down" the intent or scope of the law. He then moved on to the Executive Board, and to Seminar and Program Chairman both at the same time in 1989 in San Diego. He was elected President at the St Paul, Minnesota Seminar in 1991 and gave up the top job to J.C. Cloutier in Toronto the following year. Then he undertook the task of obtaining a firm to print and solicit advertising for the APB. After a rocky start and finding a second publisher, funds for the first time started to be deposited in our treasury. He remained as APB Committee Chairman until 1998. In 1999 at the Detroit Seminar he was selected as the recipient of the prestigious Raymond H. Dreher Award.

Dan is a native of the Chicago, Illinois area and in 1964 graduated from Marquette University in Milwaukee, Wisconsin. He was commissioned an Ensign in the U. S. Navy where he remained until he joined the FBI. His two sons, Mark and Michael both reside in Colorado. Mark is a financial analyst for a large nationwide home builder and Michael who is married, is a head chef at a restaurant in the ski country.

Dan is currently leading the "Retired Life" of a former FBI Supervisory Agent having turned in his badge in December 1996. He served twenty-nine years with the FBI, the last five as Coordinator for the San Diego County Regional Auto Theft Team (RATT). He is now working three days a week for a non-profit hospice. He hopes to keep biking through Europe and North America with his wife Karen. Karen is a speech pathologist who hopes to retire in one year after receiving her 30–year pin.

Daniel F. Ryan

EXECUTIVE BOARD

1st Vice President:	J.C. Cloutier, Canadian Auto Theft Bureau
2nd Vice President:	K.B. MacKenzie, Richardson, Texas Police
3rd Vice President:	D.L. Meyer, Illinois State Police
4th Vice President:	P.J. Crepeau, CARCO Group, Inc.
Treasurer:	W.G. Borman, Avis Rent A Car
Executive Director:	H. Lee Ballard, Ford Motor Co.
Directors:	J.J. Cadigan, Federal Bureau of Investigation
	P.J. D'Alessandro, Clarkstown, New York Police
	S.E. Gobby, Surete du Quebec
	C.D. Golemba, AAA–MI
	D.C. MacGillis, Florida Marine Patrol
	J.E. Painter, National Auto Theft Bureau
	D.E. Werra, Milwaukee Police
	B.J. Wood, RD & L Investigations
APB Editor:	Jim Spanel, Lincoln P.D.

SEMINAR

Toronto, Ontario, Regal Constellation Hotel
August 2 – 7, 1992

1992 AGC/IAATI Award

Wilheim Smih, Captain So. African Police, receives So. African Chap. Charter from past president Pat Mitchell.

L to R: Wilheim Smith - Capt So. African Police, Dan Ryan - President, Bob Springvloed - European Chapter

Jim Gavigan, ??

Dan Ryan exercises his IAATI presidency power.

Services scheduled for John F. Daniel

The Dallas Morning News, August 21, 1991

Services for former Dallas police Capt. John F. Daniel will be at 9:30 a.m. Wednesday at Laurel Land Memorial Chapel.

He died Saturday of natural causes at his home in Dallas. He was 87.

Mr. Daniel was a native of Pine Mills in East Texas. He joined the Dallas Police Department in 1929 as a bicycle patrol officer and had one of the lowest numbered badges, 14, said his wife, Geraldine "Gerry" Daniel.

He began teaching at the Dallas Police Academy in 1952 and retired from the force in 1959, Mrs. Daniel said.

Mr. Daniel had served in homicide, burglary, theft and auto theft divisions. In 1954, he was named the first president of the International Association of Auto Theft Investigators. The association invited him as its guest of honor to the 1989 convention in Galveston.

When he left the force in 1959, he became chief of security for Exchange Park Properties of Dallas. He retired from that job in 1975.

Mr. Daniel was praised in 1964 for his long-standing support of youth activities in the Dallas area by the North Dallas Chamber of Commerce.

Mr. Daniel helped start the North Dallas Chamber of Commerce Boys Baseball League, which grew to involve 1,200 youths.

He is survived by his wife; a son, John F. Daniel Jr. of Dallas; and a brother, Grady Daniel of Dallas.

C.C.Benson, John F. Daniel, Glen H. McLaughlin (IAATI Annual Conference - Galveston, TX 1988)

50 Years of History

1992–1993

President

Jean-Claude Cloutier, Insurance Crime Prevention Bureau (retired)

J.C. Cloutier, Craig Petterd

Cloutier's work career started in 1948, when he left school early in order to assist his father in the linen supply business. He completed his education by going to night school, which allowed him to eventually join the RCMP. On October 13th, 1955 he went into training in Rockliffe, Ontario, and completed his training in Regina, Sascatchuon in July of the following year. Between 1955 and 1965 he worked various assignments throughout Canada before resigning in April.

After a brief stint in real estate development, he accepted a job as a special agent for the Fire Underwriters' Investigation Bureau on January 11, 1966. In late 1966, the FUIB having started a program of sponsoring university studies for some of its Special Agents, and he was the first to volunteer and be accepted, graduating from Mc Gill University with a certificate in management in 1972.

In 1969 the Canadian Automobile Theft Bureau (CATB) was merged with the FUIB, which is when he first became interested in vehicle theft. 1972 was the year when the FUIB Head Office transferred to Toronto, where he was offered a supervisory position responsible for all investigative work done across the country, including vehicle theft. He did not stop studying and eventually obtained my Fellowship from the Insurance Institute of Canada (FIIC), with a man-

1992 Board Toronto Ontario. 1st row: John Painter-NICB Board, Connie Golemba-AA Board, Phil Crepeau 4th VP, Steve Gobby-Board, Jim Cadigan-FBI Board, Larry Capp P/P, Ken MacKenzie--2nd VP. 2nd row: Brian Wood-European Pres., Paul D'Allerandio-Board, Bill Borman-Treas, J.C. Cloutier-1st VP, Dan Ryan-Pres, Pat Mitchell P/P, Lee Ballard-Exec Sec, Harry Brady P/P, Ike Ivokvich P/P, Larry Barksdale P/P. 3rd row: Bob Suelter-Assoc Dir, G. Copeland NCRC Pres, Denny Meyer-3rd VP, Clarence Brickey P/P, Rick Buckley P/P, Don Wera-Board, Ziggy P/P, Bob Hasbrouck-North East Chapter Pres, JT Weakley-Southeast Chapter Pres.

Ruth Hart Stephens-Manhiem Auctions

Clarence Brickey

agement major, something like the CPCU designation in the USA.

In 1973, the FUIB/CATB took on a new name, becoming the Insurance Crime Prevention Bureau (ICPB). His progression through the various management levels continued and in 1982 he became General Manager of ICPB and his title was changed to President in 1984.

Shortly after moving to Toronto he had become a member of the International Association of Auto Theft Investigators. When the IAATI AGM took place in Montreal (in 1974 I believe) he was given the pleasant task of driving IAATI past president C.C. Benson and his wife to Montreal, a 6-7 hour drive. Throughout the trip, C.C. kept talking about IAATI and auto theft investigations, leading Cloutier to become more involved in IAATI activities.

In 1978 he was thrilled to be asked by his General Manager, the late Pat Collins, to attend that year's IAATI Board meeting and AGM on his behalf. The late NATB and IAATI Past President Paul W Gilliland took Cloutier under his wing and ensured that he become a member of the Board; in 1992 he was honored to be elected President of the prestigious association. Mid-way through his term he had to undergo prostate cancer surgery and was thankful to Ken Mac Kenzie who picked up his presidential tasks during his recovery. He has been cancer free since the surgery and count my blessings.

Although ill health forced him to take an early retirement in June 1997. Since retiring he and his wife, Huguette, have done quite a bit of travelling, and spend a lot more time with their four grandchildren.

EXECUTIVE BOARD

1st Vice President:	K.B. MacKenzie, Richardson, Texas Police
2nd Vice President:	D.L. Meyer, Illinois State Police
3rd Vice President:	P.J. Crepeau, CARCO Group
4th Vice President:	P.J. D'Alessandro, Clarkstown, New York Police
Treasurer:	Bill Borman, Avis Car Rental
Executive Director:	H. Lee Ballard
Directors:	R.J. Boardman, Nebraska State Police
	J.I. DeRemer, Metro Dade Florida Police
	S.E. Gobby, Surete du Quebec
	C.D. Golemba, AAA–MI
	D.C. MacGillis, Florida Marine Patrol
	J. Pitts, Hertz Rent-A-Car
	J.L. Taylor, National Insurance Crime Bureau
	B.J. Wood, RD & L Investigations
APB Editor:	Jim Spanel, Lincoln P.D.

SEMINAR

Boise, Idaho
August 1- 6, 1993

Capt. Mel Mooers-WA State Patrol

Larry Capp

A.T. Phillips Award-Glenn Wheeler, Anne Jenei-Recipient, A.T.'s daughter, Ziggy Zablocki

Bill Borman, Lee Ballard, and J.C. Cloutier

Preparing to present the Dreher Award.

Linda Young, TX ATPA

Dreher Award presented to Lee and Pat Ballard. L to R: Ron Van Raalte, Lee Ballard.

Roger Van Drew, Ziggy Zablocki, Denny Roske, Geoff Brown, Tracie Lucking, Kevin Curry, Dave Ecklund

Registration prepares to open, ??, ??, Joanie Pitts, and Marianne Finney

??, Ziggy Zablocki, Geoff Brown, Denny Roske

Denny Roske (center)

"Wild" Bill Borman

Pat Mitchell and Kenny Mash

1993—1994

President

K. MacKenzie, Richardson (TX) Police Department

Kenneth MacKenzie

Dreher Award-Harry Brady Sr.-Recipient, Joanie Pitts, Brandon Gaines, Diane Dreher-Gaines, Ron Van Raalte, Clarence Brickey-Recipient.

Award of Merit L to R: John Hanchett, Steve Gobby, David Roccaforte-Recipient, Anthony Kane, Ken MacKenzie

Ken has been with the Richardson Police Department since 1977 and has been assigned as an Auto Theft Detective since 1981. Ken was first elected to the Board of Directors in 1985 and spent four years as a Director before moving up the chairs until he was elected President at the 1993 seminar in Boise, ID. During Ken's year as President, he campaigned hard with the membership and the Chapters/Branches to make all members of Chapters/Branches, members of the International also. That year the Executive Board voted to implement the Chapter rebate program, which was later adopted by all the Chapter/Branches making members of IAATI also members of their local Chapter/Branch. This greatly increased the International membership. Ken was also heavily involved in the formation of the Australasian and Southern African Branches. Ken also served as IAATI's Exhibit Director from 1987 to 1997.

Ken is a lifetime member of the Texas Association of Vehicle Theft Investigators, where he is also a past-president and was editor of their newsletter "The Slam Hammer" for ten years. Ken has also served as the Texas Auto Theft Prevention Authority's Auto Theft Awareness Director.

Executive Board

1st Vice President:	Dennis Meyer, Illinois State Police
2nd Vice President:	Phil Crepeau, CARCO
3rd Vice President:	Steve Gobby, Surete'du Quebec
4th Vice President:	Jacques DeRemer, Metro-Dade Police
Treasurer:	Bill Borman, Avis Car Rental
Executive Director:	H. Lee Ballard
Directors:	Tom Adams
	Ron Boardman
	Bob Hasbrouck
	Nancy Kridel
	David MacGillis
	Joan Pitts
	Dennis Roske
	John Taylor
APB Editor:	Jlm Spanel, Lincoln P.D.

Seminar

Nashville, Tennessee
August 7 – 12, 1994

Steve Gobby, ??, ??, C.C. Benson, Ken MacKenzie, Denny Meyer

Denny Meyer presents Ken MacKenzie President's Plaque

Bob Springvloed, Craig Hamblin, Craig Petterd

Belinda Taylor, ??

Steve Gobby and Ken MacKenzie

Ann and Lee Ballard

Steve Gobby

Ron Van Raalte, Steve Gobby

Tommy Hansen and Nancy Kridel

Ken MacKenzie swears in new Executive Board.

Ziggy Zablocki, Neil Chamelin, Dave Ecklund

Jim Cadigan, Tommy Hansen, Kevin Curry, Ziggy Zablocki

Ziggy Zablocki and Karen Metz

John Hanchett

Kevin Curry and Diane Dreher-Gaines

Post banquet celebrations.

Charlie Banks

3M Award: Russ Suess-Recipient; Kevin Curry; Denny Meyer

1994—1995

PRESIDENT

DENNIS MEYER, ILLINOIS STATE POLICE

Prior to attending the Illinois State Police Academy, Meyer worked for a General Motors dealership and later ran his own Shell Gas Station. On April 21, 1968 he entered the Illinois State Police Academy in Springfield and began his career in law enforcement.

Dennis Meyer

EXECUTIVE BOARD

1st Vice President:	Phil Crepeau, CARCO Group
2nd Vice President:	Steve Gobby, Surete du Quebec
3rd Vice President:	Jacques DeRemer, Metro-Dade Police
4th Vice President:	Robert C. Hasbrouck, NY-NJ Port Authority
Treasurer:	Bill Borman, Avis Car Rental
Executive Director:	H. Lee Ballard
APB Editor:	Jim Spanel, Lincoln P.D.
Directors:	Norm Adams
	Tom Adams
	Howard Apple
	Ron Boardman
	Nancy Kridel
	W. Joseph Pierron
	Dennis Roske
	Roger VanDrew

SEMINAR

Orlando, Florida, Twin Towers Hotel
August 6 – 11, 1995

Swearing in officers.

In 1980 he was assigned to the Bi-State Auto Theft Unit, which was made up of officers from the Illinois and Indiana State Police and the Illinois Secretary of State Police. Three years later he became commander of the unit. In the late 80s he helped initiate formation of the Illinois Motor Vehicle Theft Prevention Council. In December 1992 he was assigned director of a new auto theft unit composed of officers from the state police and several county sheriff's agencies. He continued in this position until retirement on May 31, 1997.

Meyer was active in the North Central Regional Chapter of IAATI, serving as president in 1989-90. In 1997 he was honored with the Clyde-Oliver Award. He is presently the chairman for the LoJack Award.

He is currently retired and enjoying life with his wife, Connie.

L to R: Jack deRemer, Phil Crepeau, Denny Roske

Jack deRemer and Charlie Banks

Denny Meyer, Jack deRemer, Ziggy Zablocki

Denny Meyer and Bill Borman

President's Plaque of Recognition

AGC Award L to R: David Schwartzkopf, John Hootman, Dianna Rummel

Denny Meyer and wife

3M Award L to R: Rick Lane-Recipient, Kevin Curry, Mike Mechow

Award of Merit; D. Eastcott, J. Presley, A. Roy

116

Hughette and J.C. Cloutier

Jenny and Craig Petterd

??, Dave Ecklund

Clarence Brickey

Kiko Stewart and Terry Cook

Brad Borys and Gary Nelson

Jim and Kathy Cadigan, Ray Presley

Mrs. and Mr. Tom Marquardt

1995–1996

PRESIDENT

PHIL CREPEAU, NEW YORK CITY POLICE DEPARTMENT

Phil completed his 20 years with "New York's Finest", with the majority of his NYPD career spent as a Detective and Investigative Supervisor in the Organized Crime Control Bureau's Auto Crime Division. His most notable achievements include co-founding the NYPD Auto Crime School in 1973 and initiating the first Police Department Insurance Fraud Team in 1976. Retiring as a Lieutenant, he moved on to become a Senior Vice President with

Phillip J. Crepeau

CARCO Group, Inc., continuing his career combating auto theft and insurance fraud and affiliation with IAATI with the support of his CEO, Peter O'Neill.

Phil's first exposure to IAATI came through George Acker of the New York State Police and President of the Northeast Chapter, who recruited him to their Board of Directors in 1973. Phil continued serving NEIAATI through his presidency in 1985, when he was also elected to the International Board, serving under the guidance of President Jerry Cole. Through his years on the International Board, Phil served on many committees and was mentored by Dan Ryan, whose committee footsteps he seemed to follow. Phil served on the early APB Committee and continues troubleshooting issues affecting the magazine. As a member of the Executive Committee and President, Phil's most notable achievements include coordinating Constitution changes, which broadened our membership base and voting privileges, as well as working with Geoff Brown (grandson of our long-term Executive Director, Lee Ballard) in 1996, getting IAATI on the Internet and initiating email communications that tied our many global chapters and members much closer together.

Phil remains active on the Boards of IAATI, NEIAATI, the New York Anti-Car Theft & Fraud Association and the North American Export Committee and looks forward to one day emulating the retirement life of his IAATI mentor, Dan Ryan, without the long and grueling bicycle rides.

EXECUTIVE BOARD

1st Vice President:	Stephen Gobby, Surete du Quebec
2nd Vice President:	Jacques DeRemer, Metro-Dade Police
3rd Vice President:	Robert C. Hasbrouck, NY-NJ Port Authority Police
4th Vice President:	Dennis A. Roske, Minnesota State Police
Treasurer:	Bill Borman, Avis Car Rental
Executive Director:	H. Lee Ballard
APB Editor:	Jim Spanel, Lincoln P.D.
Directors:	Norm Adams, Toyota Motor Sales, USA
	James J. Cadigan, Federal Bureau of Investigation
	David M. Ecklund, Ft. Lauderdale Police
	Craig I. Petterd, Australian Federal Police
	W. Joseph Pierron, National Insurance Crime Bureau
	David H. Porter, CATB
	Glenn Wheeler, State Farm Insurance
	Roger VanDrew, Illinois State Police

SEMINAR

San Antonio, TX
August 4 – 9, 1996

AGC Award : Terry Lemming-Recipient and Gene Rutledge

Lo Jack Award, Jim Stevenson, David McCormick-Recipient, Peter Conner

Award of Merit, Steve Gobby and Ron Van DenHoek

Award of Merit, Steve Gobby and Kenneth Ruks

L to R: Kevin, Dennis Bielskis, Larry Fortier, Robert Greene, David Gentry

Directors Award, Roger Van Drew and Geoff Brown

??, John Hanchett

Ann and Lee Ballard, with Geoff Brown

Karen Metz, Russ Suess, Dave Ecklund, Denny Roske, Karen Roske, Tracie Lucking

Tracie Mortenson, Karen and Denny Roske, Karen Metz, Russ Suess

Geoff Brown

Jim Spanel, Jack and Sue deRemer

Koos Brandenburg

J.C. Cloutier and Craig Petterd

Steve Gilbert, Kevin Curry, Tommy Hanson, Jim Cadigan

1996—1997

President

S. Gobby, Surete du Quebec

Steve Gobby became involved in IAATI as soon as he joined the Auto Theft Section of the Crimes Against Property Squad back in 1980. He had 9 years service with the Sûreté du Québec at the time. He then spent the next 15 years of his career in the Auto Theft Section and becoming increasingly involved with IAATI. He was elected to the Board of the Northeast Chapter in 1987 and worked his way through the chairs until he was elected President of the Chapter in 1992. During these years, he

Steve Gobby

was also heavily involved in IAATI. He was elected to the IAATI Board of Directors and made his way through the chairs, being elected President in San Antonio, Texas in 1996. Part of his responsibilities during his Presidency was to ensure that the first IAATI seminar to be held outside North America went off without a hitch. Everyone will recall that wonderful seminar we had in Brisbaine, Australia. Most rewarding of all his experiences in his years with IAATI were the friendships he developed which will undoubetdly last a lifetime.

Executive Board

1st Vice President:	Jacques DeRemer, Metro-Dade Police
2nd Vice President:	Robert Hasbrouck, NY-NJ Port Authority Police
3rd Vice President:	Dennis Roske, Minnesota State Patrol
4th Vice President:	Roger VanDrew, Illinois State Police
Treasurer:	Bill Borman, Avis Car Rental
Executive Director:	Lee Ballard
APB Editor:	Jim Spanel, Lincoln P.D.
Directors:	Lester Johnson
	Joe Pierron
	Kent Mawyer
	Dave Porter
	Dave Ecklund
	Glenn Wheeler

Asst. Directors:	Craig Petterd
	Sandra Thompson
	Kevin Curry
	Karen Metz
	Linda Young

Seminar

Brisbane, Australia, Sheraton Hotel
August 3 – 8, 1997

Jim and Jill Spanel

Jack DeRemer taking boomerang lessons

Gerry Bashford and Ari Huhtinen

The guys from New South Wales

Jack and Sally de Remer, Bob Hasbrouck

Kent Mawyer, ??

Ann and Lee Ballard

Craig Petterd and Dave Ecklund

Steve Gobby

Sheep shearing at the woolshed

Steve Gobby, Roger Van Drew, Instructor

Visiting the Queensland Police Officers Club. Karen Metz, Russ Suess, Karen and Denny Roske, Kevin Curry, Max and Dave Ecklund

Dave Ecklund

Steve Gobby and Bob Hasbrouck

Dave Ecklund, Karen Metz, Ari Hutinen, Denny Roske, Russ Suess

Opening ceremonies

Jim Gavigan, Pat Clancy, ??

Queensland Police Honor Guard

Opening ceremonies

Jim Spanel, Glenn Wheeler

Kent Mawyer-Biker?

Susan Maxwell and Craig Petterd

Jill Spanel, Jim Spanel, and Pete Simet

1997–1998

PRESIDENT

J. deREMER, METRO DADE (FL) POLICE DEPARTMENT

Jack joined the Miami-Dade Police Department in 1969 and was assigned as the Commander of the Auto Theft Section in April, 1984. He soon became involved with the Florida Auto Theft Intelligence Unit (FATIU), and this led to his joining IAATI in 1986, the same year that he initiated the Miami-Dade County Auto Theft Task Force. Always a great believer in the need for inter-agency cooperation and

Jack deRemer

communication, Jack became actively involved in both IAATI and FATIU. He was elected to the Board of Directors of IAATI in 1992, and become President at the 1997 seminar in Brisbane, Australia. During his year as President IAATI continued to grow in many areas including membership, geographic representation, international recognition as the "voice" of auto theft investigators, and especially in the area of electronic communication and Internet presence. As part of this, Jack implemented a standardized electronic membership database that allowed the tracking and updating of our membership information between the chapters/branches and the international office.

Presiding over an organization as global and diverse as IAATI is both a great honor and rewarding personal challenge. The one common denominator of the Board, the chapter and local organization leadership, and the members of IAATI as a whole is an unflagging enthusiasm and dedication to the cause of the advancement of auto theft investigation and all of the related issues. Jack is grateful for having had the opportunity to contribute to

this effort, and will continue to do so. He is now retired from the Miami-Dade Police Department and is pursuing opportunities in the private sector and other areas of government service.

EXECUTIVE BOARD

1st Vice President: Robert C. Hasbrouck, NY-NJ HIDTA
2nd Vice President: Dennis A. Roske, MN State Patrol
3rd Vice President: Roger VanDrew, Illinois State Police
4th Vice President: David M. Ecklund, Ft. Lauderdale Police
Treasurer: Bill Borman, Avis Car Rental
Executive Director: H. Lee Ballard
APB Editor: Jim Spanel. Lincoln P.D.
Directors: Lester Johnson, Delaware State Police
Kent Mawyer, Texas Dept. of Public Safety
Ed Sparkman, National Insurance Crime Bureau
Craig I. Petterd, Australian Federal Police
W. Joseph Pierron, National Insurance Crime Bureau
David H. Porter, CATB
Glenn Wheeler, State Farm Insurance
Sandra Thompson, ANPAC

SEMINAR

Tulsa, Oklahoma, Double Tree Hotel
August 2 – 7, 1998

AGC Award-Genesee Co. Michgan Task Force

Sally deRemer (far right)

The Houston Crew

Lojack Award: Jim Gavigan, Mark Amos-Recipient, Dave McCormick

Rodeo in Tulsa

Bill Borman and Ron van Raalte

Don Faircloth and Harry Brady Sr.

Bill Welch, John Hanchett, Denny Meyer

Pete Simet and Steve Gobby

NE Babes: Maureen Borman, Alice Brady, Mary Hasbrouck, Arlene Sanchez, Dottie Borman

3M Award: Kevin Curry, Bill Riley-Recipient

Jim Gavigan, Mark Amos, Roger Van Drew

AGC Award-Gene Rutledge, Randy Kingler, ??

Saturday Executive Board Meeting

John Hanchett

A.T. Phillips Award-Glenn Wheeler and Tiffany Bolick-Recipient

Kent Mawyer, Kevin Curry, Dave Ecklund, Karen Metz

Calf Dressing-Missy and Roger Van Drew, ??, Jim Gavigan

Calf Dressing - Lisa Hanks, Tracie Mortenson, Denny Roske, Brad Hardin

1998—1999

President

R. Hasbrouck, New York & New Jersey Port Police

Bob was employed by The Port Authority of New York and New Jersey from August 1971 until March 1995. After completing the Port Authority Police Academy, he was assigned to JFK International Airport as a Police Officer. In addition to JFK, he worked briefly at other facilities operated by The Port Authority.

Robert Hasbrouck

In 1975, he was selected to administrate the airport's Police Impound Facility. This position required him to monitor 100,00 parking spots for stolen/abandoned vehicles, account for approx. 1,500 vehicles impounded per year, as well as identify and assure that each was returned to the rightful owner. It was during this assignment that Bob experienced the value of IAATI membership. During 1976, he was elected to the Presidency of the Port Authority Police Emerald Society.

The year 1984 brought a promotion to Detective for Bob. He was assigned to General Security duties at JFK within the Criminal Investigation Bureau. A reassignment in 1989 transferred him to the Auto Crime Unit where he served until retirement.

After retiring from the police department, Bob worked at the New York/New Jersey High Intensity Drug Trafficking Area as Program Manager for three years. Currently, he is affiliated with Meridian Management Corporation, a Department of Defense Contractor, as Information Management Officer and Special Projects.

Bob became a member of IAATI in 1971 and the Northeast Chapter in 1972. He attended his first IAATI Seminar in 1974 at Newark, DE. He served as the Chapter's Treasurer for four terms, after which he entered the Vice Presidential chairs. He served as Chapter President from 1991-92. He is a vocal supporter of the objectives and purposes of IAATI.

After serving the Northeast Chapter in positions of leadership, Bob turned to the parent organization. He was elected as a Director in 1983, and entered the Vice Presidential chairs in 1984.

After 24 years, in August of 1992, Bob retired from the New York Army National Guard as a First Sergeant. His last assignment was with the famed «Fighting 69th» Regiment.

Bob has held the unique position of President of the Hasbrouck Family Association. Most Hasbroucks in the U.S. are descended from the brothers Abraham and Jean Hasbrouck who emigrated to America in the early 1670's and established New Paltz, NY. Their original houses (as well as several others) still stand today on what is known as «The oldest Street in America with Its Original Houses.» The Hasbrouck Family Association, in conjunction with the Huguenot Historical Society, New Paltz, NY, preserves the houses for public and family viewing. He currently serves as a Vice President.

Bob and his wife Mary, reside in Plainview, NY.

Executive Board

1st Vice President:	Dennis A. Roske, MN State Patrol
2nd Vice President:	Rojer VanDrew, Illinois State Police
3rd Vice President:	David M. Ecklund, Ft. Lauderdale Police
4th Vice President:	Kent W. Mawyer, TX DPS
Treasurer:	Bill Borman, Avis Car Rental
APB Editor:	Jim Spanel, Lincoln, NE P.D.
Executive Director:	H. Lee Ballard
Directors:	David Brockman, Tulsa Police Dept.
	Ronald Giblin, Canadian Automobile Theft Bureau
	Lester Johnson, Delaware State Police
	Karen Metz, Alamo Rent-A-Car
	Ed Sparkman, National Insurance Crime Bureau
	Craig I. Petterd, Australian Federal Police
	Glenn Wheeler, State Farm Insurance
	Sandra Thompson, ANPAC
Associate Director:	John V. Abounader, NYS Dept. of Motor Vehicles
	Tracie Mortenson, 3M Corporation

Seminar

Dearborn, Michigan, Hyatt Regency Hotel
August 8 – 13, 1999

3M Award: Karen Metz, Larry Kocurek-Recipient and Kevin Curry

Directors Award, Joan Pitts-Recipient and Glen Wheeler

Lojack Award-Roger Van Drew, Mark Baillargeon-Recipient, John Nutter-Recipient and Pat Clancy

South Central Charter-Pat Bostick, Roger Van Drew, Bob Hasbrouck

3M Special Recognition Jim Holmes, Kevin Curry, Dave Ecklund

George Shemenauer, Don VonHoute, Jerry Hinton, Jim Gavigan

Jack deRemer and Tommy Hansen

Award of Merit, Tim Flynn and Steve Gobby

Award of Merit; Michael Knowlton-Recipient, Robert Rawlinson-Recipient and Steve Gobby

Incoming Executive Board

Henry Brune, Mrs. Brune, Mrs. Kocurek, Larry Kocurek

Dave Ecklund and Kevin O'Reilly-On Site Chairperson

L-R; J.C. and Hughette Cloutier

L-R; Karen Metz, Denny and Karen Roske

Russ Suess (far left)

Sandra Thompson, Bill Larocque, Tracie Mortenson, Russ Suess, Karen Metz, Ari Huhtinen, and Jack deRemer

South Central Chapter Representatives-Ken MacKenzie, Kent Mawyer, Mike Gates, Pat Bostick, Mike Ingels, Chris Malek, and Tommy Hansen

Mayor of Dearborn, MI-Michael Guido

Ronald Deziel-Dearborn Chief of Police

A.T. Phillips Award: Gilberto Bustamante-Recipient, Glenn Wheeler

Bob Hasbrouck, ??, Chief Ronald Deziel

George Schemenauer, Dave Ecklund, Kevin O' Reilly

Bob Hasbrouck, ??, Chief Ronald Deziel on right

??, Pete Simet, ??, ??

Bob Hasbrouck, Michael Guido, Dearborn Mayor, Skip Copeland

Jack deRemer, Ed Sparkman, Ron Giblin

Dan Kent, Pete Simet, ??, Ronnie Van Den Hoek

Dreher Award: L to R-Dave Ecklund, Dan Ryan-Recipient, Ron Van Raalte

1999–2000

PRESIDENT

D. ROSKE, MINNESOTA STATE PATROL

It was Denny Roske's pleasure to represent IAATI as its President for 1999-2000 as we traveled into the new millennium. As we crossed the bridge into the new century, IAATI was reaching for an all time high membership of nearly 3,000. Our Annual Seminar attendance in Vancouver was at 455. It had been

Denny Roske

eight years since we held the International Seminar in the great country of Canada. The long wait was well worth it. The On-site Committee did a wonderful job in putting on a fantastic seminar. Things were looking great.

However, IAATI was also faced with new challenges not addressed in the past. There were concerns over the European Branch. An oversight committee was formed to review the concerns of its members. The geographical area and language barriers made the business end of the European Branch exceedingly difficult. This situation at first looked rather gloomy, but out of the gloom came a bit of light, and then after many months, the sun came shinning through. The oversite committee recommended to the Board of Directors that the European Branch be dissolved, and that the United Kingdom and the European continent apply for charters and become separate IAATI Branches. The Board concurred, and the European Branch was dissolved. The United Kingdom and the European countries went to work reorganizing and applied for new branch charters of IAATI. This did become a reality the following year. So from the demise of one branch, IAATI bounced back with two new branches. Once again came back stronger than ever.

Denny's final message to the membership as President in the APB was: " I wish to thank all of the members of IAATI for the privilege of serving as your President this past year. It's been a wonderful year

meeting with many of you at the various chapter / branch seminars. It is truly a time in my life and career that my wife Karen and I shall remember fondly."

Denny retired on Jan. 29, 2002 after serving for 31 years with the Minnesota State Patrol. The last 18 years of that time was spent working vehicle theft. Denny intends to attend seminars and remain active with IAATI.

EXECUTIVE BOARD

1st Vice President:	Roger VanDrew, Illinois State Police
2nd Vice President:	David M. Ecklund, Ft. Lauderdale Police
3rd Vice President:	Kent Mawyer, Texas Department of Public Safety
4th Vice President:	Craig I. Petterd
Treasurer:	Bill Borman, Avis Rental Cars
APB Editor:	Jim Spanel, Lincoln, NE P.D.
Executive Director:	H. Lee Ballard
Directors:	Lester Johnson, Office of the Attorney General
	John Abounader, New York Dept. of Motor Vehicles
	Ed Sparkman, National Insurance Crime Bureau
	Ronald VanDen Hoeck, Belgian Gendarmerie Antwerp
	Karen Metz, Alamo Car Rental
	Ronald J. Giblin, Insurance Crime Prevention Bureau
	Glenn Wheeler, State Farm Insurance
	Sandra Thompson, ANPAC

Director of Marketing: Tracie Mortenson, 3M

SEMINAR

Vancouver, British Columbia,
Best Western Richmond Inn
July 31 – August 4, 2000

AGC Award L to R: AGC Seattle Chapter Rep. Henry Brune, Sgt Jimmy Towe-Recipient, Gene Rutledge, Dennis Roske

LoJack Award, L to R: Roger Van Drew, Robert Binder-Recipient, Kenneth Hawkins-Recipient and Pat Clancey

Presidents Award Gene Rutledge and Dennis Roske

AT Phillips, Fred Williams-Recipient and Glenn Wheeler

Directors Award, Bo Kohler and Glenn Wheeler

3M Award L to R: Robert Hart, Steven Troyd, Karen Metz, Michael Mechow, Tracie Mortenson, Martin Finn-Recipient

L to R: Tim Flynn, Mark Barkley and Ron Giblin

Newly appointed Executive Board

Lisa Hanks and Ron van Raalte

Vancouver B.C. City P.D. Pipe and Drum band

Kent Mawyer

Bo Kohler and Glenn Wheeler

Kent Mawyer and Denny Roske

Glenn and Sandy Wheeler, JIll Spanel

Opening ceremonies

Darrell Ehlers, Carol Van Natter, Bill Larocque, Jerry Boyer, T.J. Kistner-WRC Officer of the Year, Joan Pitts-WRC President, Marianne Finney,Cliff Chezunn

??, Roger Van Drew, ??, Tommy Hansen, Charlie Banks

Denny Roske swears in Roger Van Drew

Mike Petroski, Tracie Mortenson, Vancouver City P.D., Karen Metz, John Abounader

President's Reception

Vic and Sherri Johnston (Lo Jack)

President's Reception

Mrs. Spanel violating Canadian law.

2000—2001

PRESIDENT

ROGER VAN DREW, ILLINOIS STATE POLICE

A native of Sterling, IL, Roger graduated from high school in 1965, then enlisted in the U.S. Navy two years later, where he spent four years in naval aviation in a transport squadron as an Aviation Metal and Hydraulic Specialist. After additional study and training, he earned aircrew wings as a loadmaster

Roger Van Drew

for three different aircraft. He was certified as a loadmaster instructor for the squadron, where his love of teaching began.

Upon release from military duty he returned home and worked a few jobs. At a wedding reception, he was introduced to the Operations Lieutenant for the Illinois State Police. After their conversation and a two–year period of testing and waiting he found himself joining the Illinois State Police in 1971.

Roger Van Drew, Dave Ecklund, Kent Mawyer, Wayne Burr, Sean Burke

He worked as a patrol officer, and later a Field Training Officer and member of the Riot Control Training Team. Then, in 1983, he became a Vehicle Investigation Officer and joined both IAATI and the NCRC. Through the next 18 years to continued to instruct in many areas of vehicle theft and fraud related matters at many levels.

Through his association with IAATI and NCRC, he has served in many positions on both boards. He was honored to be the 1994–95 NCRC President and 2000–01 IAATI President. In July 2001, he retired with 30 years of service to the Illinois State Police, but plans to maintain his relationship with both associations.

EXECUTIVE BOARD

1st Vice President:	David M. Ecklund, Ft. Lauderdale Police
2nd Vice President:	Kent W. Mawyer, Texas Dept. of Public Safety
3rd Vice President:	Craig I. Petterd, Australian Federal Police
4th Vice President:	Karen Metz, ANC Rental Corp.
Treasurer:	Bill Borman, Avis Rental Cars
APB Editor:	Jim Spanel, Lincoln, NE P.D.
Executive Director:	H. Lee Ballard, Ford Motor Co.
Directors:	Tommy Hansen, Galveston County Sheriff, Texas
	Bill Larocque, Alberta Motor Assn. Insurance Co.
	Kevin McHugh, Braintree, Massachusetts Police
	Ronald VanDen Hoeck, De Vaderlandsche Insurance
	James D. Holmes, D.C. Metro Transit Police
	Ronald J. Giblin, Insurance Crime Prevention Bureau
	Glenn Wheeler, State Farm Insurance
	Russell Suess, Ft. Lauderdale Police
Director of Exhibits:	Sandra Thompson, ANPAC
Director of Marketing:	Tracie Mortenson, 3M

SEMINAR

Virginia Beach, Virginia, Doubletree Hotel
August 5 – 10, 2001

A.T. Phillips Award, Glenn Wheeler and Linda Gunderson-Recipient

Award of Merit, Bob Hasbrouck and Det. Michael Lapasnick

AGC Award, Henry Brune, Stu Megan and John Abounader-Recipient

LoJack Award (L to R): Joe Rainone, Det. Cliff Bieder-Recipient and Roger Van Drew

Bob Sutherland, Phil Crepeau, Bob Hasbrouck, Harry Brady Sr., Bill Borman, Kevin McHugh, Kevin Cook

IAATI Chapter and Branch Presidents (L to R) Larry Barzynski-NCRC, Tony Simms-UK, Bob Suthard-NERC, Bill Larocque-Western, John O'Byrne-Australia, Ron Van Den Hoeck-European, Chris Malek-SCRC, Sean Burke-SERC

Directors Award (L to R) Glen Wheeler, Kevin Curry-Recipient and Wayne Burr

Presidents Award, R.Van Drew presents to Lee Ballard

Opening ceremonies

Wayne Burr and wife, Sean Burke, VA Beach Chaplain

S.E. Chapter Attendees

UK Charter Presentation-Dave Ecklund, Tony Simms, Alan Taylor

3M Award L to R: Jerry Smith, Rob Turano, Tom Dupczak, Greg Klees, Tracie Mortenson, Jim Holmes-Recipient, Karen Metz, Pride Rivers, Robin Russell

Roger Van Drew swears in Dave Ecklund as President

Sean Burke (incoming S.E. President) congratulates Past President Wayne Burr

Incoming Executive Board

2002 Albquerque On-Site Committee

Bill Webb, Elizabeth and John Sids

2001–2002

PRESIDENT

DAVID ECKLUND, FT. LAUDERDALE (FL) POLICE DEPARTMENT

Captain Dave Ecklund is President of the International Association of Auto Theft Investigators for 2001-2002. IAATI is an International Organization with Eight Chapters world-wide. Membership includes approximately 3,500 members from 42 Countries.

David Ecklund

Serving Fort Lauderdale since 1974 and receiving his BAA from Florida Atlantic University, Dave is presently assigned to the Operations Division. Dave headed the Auto Theft Unit from 1988 until 1998. He is Past President of the Florida Auto Theft Intelligence.

Dave has developed and provides instruction in the field of Auto Theft Investigation and Prevention at the local, state, and federal level. He has provided in-service training to auto theft investigators at the FBI Academy, Quantico, Virginia. He conducts training for the Federal Bureau of Investigation in foreign countries for International Training Initiative and he conducts training for the International Association of Auto Theft Investigators at their annual training seminar.

Dave is very honored by being elected IAATI's 50th president and will always have great memories. He has found dealing directly with auto theft professionals world wide to be very gratifying.

He is very proud of IAATI, its members, and his association with them.

EXECUTIVE BOARD

1st Vice President:	Kent W. Mawyer, Texas Department of Public Safety
2nd Vice President:	Craig I. Petterd, Australian Federal Police
3rd Vice President:	Karen Metz, Ft. Lauderdale Police (ret)
4th Vice President:	Kevin McHugh, Braintree Police
Treasurer:	Bill Borman, Avis Rental Cars
Executive Director:	John V. Abounader, New York Dept. of Motor Vehicles
Directors:	Ronald J. Giblin, Insurance Crime Prevention Bureau
	Tommy Hansen, Galveston County Sheriff, Texas
	James D. Holmes, D.C. Metro Transit Police
	Bill Larocuqe, Alberta Motor Assn. Insurance Co. (RCMP Retired)
	Mikel Longman, Arizona Dept. of Public Safety
	Russell Suess, Ft. Lauderdale Police
	Ronald VanDen Hoeck, De Vaderlandsche Insurance
	Glenn Wheeler, State Farm Insurance
Director of Exhibits:	Carol Vannatter, AAA Southern CA
Director of Marketing:	Tracie Mortenson, 3M
APB Editor:	Jim Spanel, Lincoln, NE P.D.

SEMINAR

Albuquerque, New Mexico, Crowne Plaza Pyramid
August 4–9, 2002

Seminar On-Site Committee Front Row (L-R): Elizabeth Sides, Belinda Garland, Pam Moreno, Mike Sandoval, Bev Sandoval, Angelique Dear, Ellen Joas, Back Row (L-R): John Sides, Albert Franch, Karen Franch, Bill Webb, Mary LeRoy, Joe Byers, Laura Tinagero, Cynthia McVay, Marty Trujillo, Robert Radosevich, John Dear, Gerard Barela

North Central Regional Chapter-Back Row (L-R): Emmett Moneyhun-Kane Co. Auto Theft, Mark Eaton-Kane Auto Theft, Bill Cameron-Insurance Bureau of Canada, Roger van Drew-IL State Police, Denny Meyer-IL State Police, Neal R. Wisner-National Insurance Crime Bureau, Kevin Curry-3M, Steve Duvall-IN State Police, John Pavlenic-Kane Co. Auto Theft, Val Vitols-MI ATPA, John Nichol-State Farm, Bloomington, IL, Robert Ross-State Farm Ins. 2nd Row (L-R): Guillermo Trujillo-Kane Co. Auto Theft, Jim Spanel-Lincoln, NE P.D., Barry G. Ward-Manituba Public Ins., Melissa van Drew-IL State Police, H. Lee Ballard-Ford Motor Co., Jim Gray-St. Paul Police, Tom Bergren-St. Paul Police, Dave Tuepkema-MI ATPA, Chuck Padget-IN State Police, Glenn R. Wheeler-State Farm Ins., Wayne Johnson-MPLS Police, Ed Shepherd-Burnsville P.D., Front Row (L-R): Maureen Tholen-3M, Denny Roske-MN State Police, Nicole Frearicks-Dakota Co. MN, Ed Sparkman-NICB, Steve Stelter-DuPage CO. Auto Theft TaskforceNewt Shoup-MI ATPA, Tracie Mortenson-3M, Bentley Jackson-Burnsville MN P.D., Dave Robinson-Ontario Prov. Police, Linda Baumann-NE State Police

Australasian Branch (L-R): John O'Byrne, Troy Hogarth, Serena Burton, Craig Petterd

United Kingdom & European Branch-L-R: Ton van der Lee, Leif Bjorkland, Tony Simms, Ronnie van den Hoeck, Cees Feenstra, David Raban, Ari Huhtinen, Alain Barbier, Brian Wood, Gerry Wood

South Central Regional Chapter-5th Row (L-R): David Mendenhall, Kyle Edwards, Charles Woods, Kent Mawyer, Larry Kocurek, John P. Slater, John Nicholes, Tim "X" Files, Eddie Evans, Joey Canady, Rob Emmons, Christopher Malek, Wallace E. Hood, Jr., Larry Swinford, Sherry Anderson, Darryl Norris, David Page. 4th Row (L-R): Rick Zimmer, Bill Beall, Oscar Martinez, Lee DeVaney, Harold Stech, Tim Goodwin, Henry H. Brune Jr., Mike Oglesby, ??, Roger Perry, Larry Oliver, John Wise, Dennis J. Damer, John D. Sides, Tracy Utsey, Elias Camacho, Walt S. West, Bill Skinner, John W. Alexander. 3rd Row (L-R): ??, Dna Wickland, Doug Triplett, Ron Campos, Gary Horne, Todd Hester, Gary Keiser, Antonio Sanchez, Joel Garcia, Clifford Smith, Darrell Adams, Tommy Hansen, Robin A. Leach, Victor Boudreaux, Landis J. Cravens, Johnny Burks, Bruce Jackson, Emzla Pitts, Leonard McFadden. 2nd Row (L-R): Bob Harshaw, Pat Wilkerson, Rusty (John) Alentine, Alan Rousseau, Armando Fuentes Jr., Mark Collins, Jackie Deane, David Ramos, Wayne Hewett, Mac Tristan, David Jimenez, James Burson Sr., Ellen Joas, Kelly Roberts, Tommy Roach, Don Martin, David Dickerson. 1st Row (L-R): Laura L. Tinagero, Bill Webb, Pam Moizeno, Linda Mendoza, Michelle, Kleiss, Susan Sampson, Jose M. Morales, Michael A. Gates, Belinda Garland, John Dear, Don Faircloth, Ken Mac Kenzie, Cynthia G. McVay.

Western Regional Chapter 5th Row (L-R): Dave Smith, Jim Delashmutt, Mike Miller, Mikel Longmar, Brian R. Salata, Ruben C. Saavedra. 4th Row (L-R): Charlie Bubar, ??, ??, Eric Wiseman, ??, Jim Rudisey, Frank Gaber, Marcia Hancock, Tom Vickers, Frank Zangar. 3rd Row (L-R): Wally Duperon, George Green, Darrel Ehlers, Howard Johnson, Fred Bamonte, Rich Bathal, Joe Brosius, Tony Bogacz, Bobby Owens, John Gantt. 2nd Row (L-R): Susan L. Luder, Marc Micciche, Jim Kautz, Gary Labb, Gene Rutledge, Jerry Boyer, Michael Soelberg, Scott Green, Mary E. LeRoy, John Gantt. Front Row (L-R): Bill Larocque, Carol Van Natter, Joanie Pitts, Chuck Wright, Michael Vanorski, George A. Hoke, Alfonso Novoa N.

Northeast Regional Chapter Standing (L-R): Kevin Cook, Bill Borman, Mike Petroski, Lyle Parker, Bob Hasbrouck, Kevin Rowayne, Carl Stowell, Bob Southard. Kneeling (L-R): Steve Renaldi, Eileen Langer. Laying Down: John Abounader.

Southeast Regional Chapter Back Row (L-R): Mark Lewis, Mark Eastman, Joe Stasio, Richard Penton, Gene Hass, Tom Morton, Ronnie Dean, H. Lee Ballard, Gary Nelson. Middle Row (L-R): Deb Mazyck, Charlie Banks, Rusty Russell, Bobby Brantley, Pete Chrisley, Sean Burke, Pat Hester, Patrick Gough, Russell Suess. Front Row (L-R): Bob Jagoe, JIm Cadigan, JIm Hester, Chris McDonald, Diane Mandeville.

Past Presidents in Attendance - Seated (L-R): Glen McLaughlin, Mrs. Daniel (representing John Daniel). Standing (L-R): Denny Roske, Rob Hasbrouck, Clarence Brickey, Ken MacKenzie, Denny Meyer, Roger van Drew, Gerry Cole, Ziggy Zablocki, Dave Ecklund, Dan Ryan, Steve Gobby, Pat Hester, Ron Van Raalte, Gene Rutledge.

Kent Mawyer, Mrs. John Daniel, Glen MacLaughlin, Ken MacKenzie

LoJack Award (L-R): Pat Clancy, Terry Kelly, Mark Foraker-Recipient, Roger Van Drew

3M Award (L-R): Kevin Curry, Maureen Tholan, Patrolman Greg Rule-Recipient, Tracie Mortenson

Director's Award (L-R): Glenn Wheeler, Brian Wood-Recipient

A.T. Phillips Award (L-R): Bill Wheeler, Tom Calandrillo-Recipient

Raymond H. Dreher Award; Ziggy Zablocki and Tracie Mortenson-Recipient

Raymond H. Dreher Award-Ziggy Zablocki presenting to (L-R): Mrs. Daniel, John Daniel Jr-accepting in honor of John Daniel Sr.; Glen MacLaughlin-Recipient, Susan (Glen's daughter), Ken MacKenzie.

Raymond H.Dreher Award-Presented by Ken MacKenzie (L) and Bill Skinner (R) to C.C. Benson (center) at his Dallas home office after the 50th seminar.

AGC Award (L-R): Harry Brune, AGC Rep, AGC Rep, Sgt. Gary Horne-Recipient

Award of Merit (L-R): Bob Hasbrouck, Recipients-Det. Lt. Barry Barber, Det. Sean Burke, Det. Sgt. RObert Jagoe, Det. Chris McDonald

3M recognized for sponsoring Fiesta Night-(L-R): Elizabeth Sides, John Sides, Tracie Mortenson, Kevin Curry, Maureen Tholen, Dave Ecklund, Karen Metz.

Fiesta Entertainment

Guests were escorted to the Fiesta. (L Isle) Jenny Petterd, Bill Laroque, Kevin Curry, Kent Mawyer (R Isle) Carol Vannatter, Denny Roske

A variety of Spanish and BBQ food was served

Pitch and Putt golf contest

The Van Drew Family

Motor Escort to the Fiesta

John Sides and Bill Webb coordinate escort to the Fiesta

Fireworks

THE FIESTA ENABLED GUESTS TO
FULFILL THEIR WILD WILD WEST
FANTASIES

Steve Gobby and Vickie in "authentic" western wear

Arizona Auto Theft Prevention Authority-Left to Right: Ruben Saavedra, Carlos Vega, Jr., Mikel Longman, Alfonso Navoa, Tracie Mortenson, George Hoke

Mike Petrowski

Karen Metz and Antonio Montanaro

John O'Byrne, Samantha Batchelor, Serena Buxton

Exhibit and Break Area

IAATI Merchandise Sales Professionals Mike Petrowski and Bill Larocque

Catching up

Tommy Hanson

Catching up

John Aboumader and Mike Petrowski

The Galveston County Auto Crimes Task Force crew styles again!

NE Chapter Hospitality Hosted by NE Past Presidents

"Where is my class?" Neil Wisner.

*Avid pin collectors
Ron Van Raalte and Joanie Pitts*

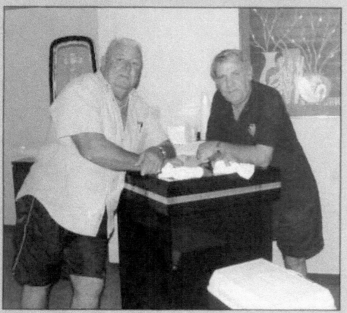

Ziggy and Charlie do a gret job hosting the "information exchange" rooms, THANKS TO LOJACK!

Opening ceremonies

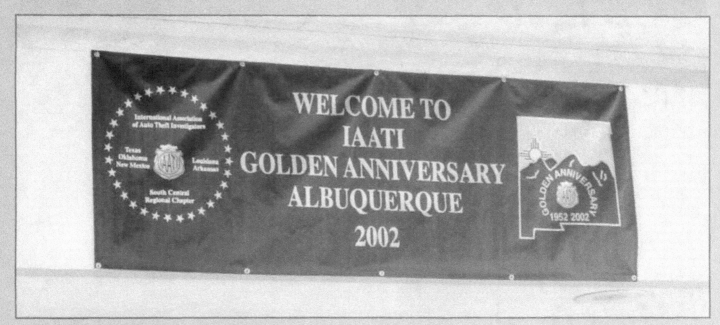

PRESIDENT'S RECEPTION

President Ecklund welcomes seminar attendees

??, Ari Huhtinen

Recognition of seminar sponsors

Mike Gates, Henry Brune, Bill Skinner, Linda Mendoza

Jim Spanel, Barry Barber, Sean Burke, Pete Chrisley

Charlie Bubar, Jerry Boyer, Wally Duperon

PRESIDENT'S RECEPTION

Willy and Clarence Brickey

John O'Byrne, Serena Buxton, Craig Petterd

Ronnie Van den Hoeck and Ton Van der Lee

Russ Suess and Kim Temple

Western Chapter Delegates (L-R): ?? Johnson, Virginia Johnson, Colleen Boyer, Minnie Kessler, Jerry Boyer, Don Kessler

3M's IAATI Members (L-R): Kevin Curry, Maureen Tholen, Tracie Mortenson

ANNUAL BANQUET

David and Cathy Robinson with Jenny and Craig Petterd

Kevin Ronayne, Carl Stowell, Steve Rinaldi, Bob Southard

Pam Moreno, Bill Webb, Laura Tenagero

Jim and Pat Hester with Jim Cadigan

SCRC Host Chapter President addresses attendees. (L-R) Max Ecklund, Mike Gates, Karen Metz

John Sides, On-Site Committee Chair, thanks attendees

ANNUAL BANQUET

Dave Ecklund passes the gavel to incoming president, Kent Mawyer

Kent Mawyer

2002-2003 Chapter/Branch Presidents
Dave Robinson, Kevin Cook, Ton van der Lee, Tony Simms, Bill Larocque, John O'Byrne, Mike Gates

2002-2003 IAATI Executive Board
Seated (L-R): Bill Laroque, Director; Ron van den Hoeck, Director; Sean Burke, Director; Carol Vannatter, Director of Exhibits; Karen Metz, 2nd VP; Tracie Mortenson, Director of Marketing. Standig (L-R): Mike Gates, SCRC President; Ed Sparkman, Assoc. Director; Henry Brune, Assoc. Director; Tony Simms, Director; Glenn Wheeler, Director; Mike Longman, Director; Tommy Hansen, 4th VP; Russ Suess, Director; Bill Borman, Treasurer; Kevin McHugh, 3rd VP; John Abounader, Executive Director; Craig Petterd, 1st VP; Kent Mawyer, President.

CHIEF

OFFICIAL USE ONLY

Past President, Jerry Cole in lockup, Galveston, TX Seminar

AUSTRALASIAN BRANCH HISTORY

The original idea for the formation of an Australasian Branch came about during a discussion at the hospitality room at the 1992 International Seminar in Toronto, Canada. Following this, interested parties in Australia and New Zealand were invited to a formation meeting in May 1993, in Canberra, Australia. People in attendance agreed to establish the Branch.

An interim Committee was elected at that meeting, as follows:

President:	Craig Petterd
Vice-President:	Susan Maxwell
Secretary:	Eddie Challenger
Treasurer:	Russell Rowell

In September 1993 the first Branch meeting was held, again in Canberra. We were fortunate to have the International President of IAATI, Mr. Jean-Claude Cloutier, in attendance. Branch member Mr. John Bennett was appointed as the first Editor of the Branch Newsletter (subsequently named the *Vehicle Investigator News*)

In 1994 the Branch held its first Annual Training Seminar, in Sydney. Then International President Mr. Ken MacKenzie officially presented the Branch with its Charter document.

Subsequent annual Seminars were held in the following locations:

1995	Melbourne
1996	Adelaide
1997	Brisbane
1998	Sydney
1999	Canberra
2000	Gold Coast
2001	Melbourne
2002	Adelaide

The 1997 Seminar in Brisbane was particularly notable, as the Branch hosted the International Seminar. This marked the first occasion in IAATI's history that their annual Seminar had been held outside North America. Two hundred delegates and sixty companions attended the meeting.

AUSTRALIAN BRANCH PAST PRESIDENTS:

1993–1997	Craig Petterd
1997–2000	Tony Ward
2000–current	John O'Byrne

Membership is made up of representatives from police services (investigators, analysts, and forensic

staff), insurers, private investigators, vehicle registration authorities, vehicle manufacturers and others with a legitimate interest in vehicle theft investigation, prevention and education. As well as regular regional meetings, the Australasian Branch conducts an Annual Training Seminar to help members keep abreast of the latest trends, issues, products and initiatives throughout Australasia and the world. The 2002 Training Seminar is the 9th such Seminar and promises to be of benefit to anybody with an interest in reducing the problem of motor vehicle theft.

Attendees visit Toyota Altona Plant

L-R: Roger van Drew, Gerry Bashford, Troy Hogarth, John O'Byrne, Dennis Conner, Paul Thomas, Terry Moore, Craig Petterd, Ian Gunthorpe

Tony Ward welcomes Roger VanDrew, IAATI president

L-R: Craig Petterd, Jean-Claude Cloutier, Susan Maxwell, and Eddie Challenger

EUROPEAN BRANCH HISTORY

In June 1984 the first steps for IAATI in Europe were taken by Brian Wood, together with Hugh Ashton and a couple of other people from the United Kingdom.

A seminar was organized at the Post House Hotel, Heathrow, London which was attended by 104 delegates.

In April 1987, the same committee organized a second three days seminar, this time at Leicester Polytechnic. This event attracted over 130 delegates. A feature of this event were visits on the third day to the factories of Jaguar, Land Rover, Rover and JCB.

Because no European Branch existed at that time the initial costs were paid by Brian Wood. His Bank Manager was anxiously watching his account during that period.

While travelling to the IAATI seminar at San Diego in 1989, Gene Rutledge and Brian Wood discussed the possibility of forming a European Branch. At that time there were about 30 European members and it was thought that the formation of a European Branch would be one way to increase membership.

During the 1989 International seminar Brian Wood called together those that had come over from Europe, Bob Springvloed (The Netherlands), Bo Kohler (Sweden), John Hanchett (UK) and Kenneth Russell (UK). Also present was Gene Rutledge (USA). The idea was strongly supported and an approach was then made to the Executive Board to carry the idea forward.

On arrival back in England Brian Wood contacted other UK members who expressed their interest and arrangements were made for a preliminary meeting of all members. The inaugural meeting of the European Branch was held on Sunday, 18th November 1990 at the Metropolitan Police Sports and Social Club, Imber Court on the outskirts of London.

Here nine members of IAATI were elected as Officers of the Chapter which later became known as the European Branch. Brian Wood became the first President and Hugh Ashton the Secretary, a position which he should held for nine years.

From L to R: Harry Van Bree, Giles Desbos, Bob Springvloed, Walter Van Vlasselaer, Barry Hancock, Ton Vander Lee, Robert Nicol, Ari Huhtinen, Vlastimil Fric. Squatting L to R: Ronald Van den Hoeck, Vito Bivacco

Nominations for the Officers of the proposed new Branch were obtained and elections were arranged. Brian Wood, with the help of J.C. Cloutier of Canada drafted the new Constitution and Rules for the proposed European Branch. These were then submitted to the Executive in the USA who subsequently approved them.

The European Committee was approved by the USA Executive and the Charter granted later that year. The European Branch was born.

In 1991 Bob Springvloed , Police Officer from the Netherlands was elected as second President of the Branch, a position which he held till 1996. On the Madrid Seminar Ronald Van den Hoeck, Chief of the Stolen Vehicle Squad from the Belgian State Police in Antwerp took over the Presidency till November 2001.

At the Lyon Seminar in November 2001, which was organized in conjunction with the Interpol Headquarters Secretariat General in Lyon, Ton Van der Lee, Police Officer from the Netherlands Police was elected as the fourth President of the European Branch.

In 2000 The European Branch was invited to participate in the Interpol Project STORE-STOCAR (**STO**p **RE**gistration of **STO**len **CAR**s). This ambitious project has 5 working groups : ASF-SMV, Wrecks, Registration, Import-Export and VIN-Assist. For this last working group IAATI is strongly involved to create a European VIN-Assist system similar to the Northern America VIN-Assist.

Successful seminars were held in Paris, Madrid, Coventry, Budapest, Luton, Lausanne, Antwerp, Amsterdam, Helsinki.

At the end of 2001 there were 245 European members from 20 different countries. Thanks to successful annual seminars the membership is still growing.

There is a partnership with ACEA – the European Car Manufacturer Association – for the annual ACEA/IAATI Award for outstanding contribution to car theft investigation.

Hugh Ashton received in 2001 the European Directors Award for his outstanding work for IAATI in Europe. Bo Kohler from Sweden received the international Directors Award at the Vancouver Seminar in 2000.

The European Branch is proud to welcome all IAATI members on the 52nd International Seminar which will be held in Antwerp in August 2004.

Past Presidents from the European Branch:
Ronald Van den Hoeck (B)
Brian Wood (UK)
Dave Ecklund (International President IAATI 2002)
Ton Van der Lee (NL)
Bob Springvloed (NL)

European Contingent with J.C. Cloutier and Chris Hotsson

Past Presidents from European Branch (L-R): Ronald Van den Hoeck (B), Brian Wood (UK), Dave Ecklund (International President IAATI 2002), Ton Van der Lee (NL), and Bob Springvloed (NL)

The ACEA-IAATI Award 2002 - Winner Prague Police Department - Czech Republic

Dave Ecklund and Ronnie Van Den Hoeck

NORTH CENTRAL REGIONAL CHAPTER (NORTH AMERICA)

Illinois
Iowa
Indiana
Kansas
Kentucky
Manitoba, Canada
Michigan
Minnesota
Missouri
Nebraska
North Dakota
Ohio
Ontario, Canada
South Dakota
Wisconsin

PRESIDENTS

1972–74	Ben Covey, Illinois State Police
1974–75	Ronald Voelker, Harvey IL Police Dept.
1975–76	Harold Westbrock, St. Louis Police Dept.
1976–77	Wayne Schrage, Southern Illinois University Police
1977–78	John Cardwell, Kokomo, IN Police
1978–79	Russell Clemmons, Kankakee IL Police
1979–80	Vladimir Ivkovich, Illinois Secretary of State Police
1980–81	Thomas Febash, Illinois State Police
1981–82	Edward Lloyd, Illinois State Police
1982–83	John Kelly, Iowa Dept. of Transportation
1983–84	William Kimball, Chicago Police
1984–85	Robert Rosenbaum, Kokomo, IN Police
1985–86	Paul Seiler, Chicago Police
1986–87	Jack Townsend, Illinois State Police
1987–88	Donald Werra, Milwaukee Police
1988–89	Dennis Serafini, Illinois Secretary of State Police
1989–90	Dennis Meyer, Illinois State Police
1990–91	Frank Barabas, Novi MI Police

While 2002 marks the 30th Anniversary of the granting of an IAATI charter to the North Central Regional Chapter, the founding membership had been active in auto theft instruction and investigation for more than ten years prior!

Illinois State Police Captain Clyde Oliver initiated the Annual Midwest Motor Vehicle Theft Conference in 1962. Originally this conference was restricted only to members of ISP Vehicle Identification Bureau. As word of the conference and its' educational value got out, other police agencies from the Midwest requested to attend. What started out as a small group of Illinois State Police Officers grew until it became too difficult for one agency to host the conference each year.

With the encouragement and guidance of Captain Oliver, a group of officers petitioned the International Association of Auto Theft Investigators for permission to charter a new chapter to meet the needs of law enforcement officers from the Midwest. On January 1, 1972, the North Central Regional Chapter was born.

With more than a thousand active members, the chapter trains law enforcement and insurance investigators from the states of Illinois, Indiana, Iowa, Kansas, Kentucky, Michigan, Minnesota, Missouri, Nebraska, North Dakota, Ohio, South Dakota, Wisconsin, and the Canadian Provinces of Manitoba and Ontario.

Published quarterly, **RECOVER** is the official publication of the NCRC. It contains an announcement of upcoming training programs, investigative tips and news of recently completed criminal cases.

Each year the chapter continues to host the Annual Midwest Motor Vehicle Theft Conference. Featured at the conference are cutting edge training and technologies as well as the opportunities to reach out to other chapter members for assistance and the sharing of ideas. The Annual Business Meeting and election of officers is held during the conference.

1991–92	G.J. Copeland, Marion Co. IN Sheriff's Dept.
1992–93	Billy Hacker, Milwaukee Police
1993–94	Nigel Norris, Ontario CA Provincial Police
1994–95	Roger VanDrew, Illinois State Police
1995–96	Thomas Marquardt, FBI, Madison WI
1996–97	Kenneth Schimnoski, Michigan State Police
1997–98	Peter Simet, Milwaukee Police
1998–99	G.J. Copeland, Marion Co. IN Sheriff's Dept.
1999–2000	Kenneth Colby, Kalamazoo County MI Sheriff's Dept.
2000–01	George Schemenauer, Berrien Co. MI Sheriff's Dept.
2001–02	Laurance Burzynski, WI State Patrol
2002–03	Dave Robinson, Ontario CA Provincial Police

Pete Simet receives Clyde Oliver Award

Don Werra and Paul Seiler

Jack Townsend and Paul Seiler

2001 Seminar - Des Moines, IA, Barb Rambo (right)

L-R: Kirk Sayles, Dave Robinson, Ken Hawkott, John Talbot, Bill Sirnus

L-R: Jeff Pfoteneuor, Barb Rambo, ??, Mike Schlomas

L-R: Ron Van Raalte, Ron Powell, Dan Greene, Mary Look, Robert Ennis

Cheryl Zofkie, Tracie Mortenson, Barb Rambo

Indy 500 Race Track-2001

Ken Hawcott and Skip Copeland

Indy 500 Race Track

NORTHEAST REGIONAL CHAPTER

Connecticut
Maine
Massachusetts
New Brunswick, Canada
New Hampshire
New Jersey
New York
Newfoundland, Canada
Pennsylvania
Quebec, Canada
Rhode Island
Vermont
Prince Edward Island, Canada

PRESIDENTS

1972–73	Harry J. Brady, Sr.
1973–74	George Acker
1974–75	Louis W. Spry
1975–76	Edward T. Cox
1976–77	Herbert L. Burr
1977–78	Vincent Mendillo
1979–80	John W. Staudt
1980–81	Erwin H. Moore
1981–82	Frank J. DeMartino
1982–83	Donald St. Amand
1983–84	Norman O. Bureau
1984–85	Howard H. Fronk
1985–86	Philip J. Crepeau
1986–87	Harry S. Fox
1987–88	Michael A. Caulfield
1988–89	Harry J. Brady, Jr.
1989–90	Paul J. D'Alessandro
1990–91	Roger D. Overton
1991–92	Robert C. Hasbrouck
1992–93	Charles Kelly
1993–94	Stephen Gobby
1994–95	Craig W. Hamblin
1995–96	William G. Borman
1996–97	Frank A. Ruzicka
1997–98	Robert Crepeau
1998–99	Donald Weber
1999–00	Bruce Saville
2000–01	Kevin McHugh
2001-02	Robert Sutherland
2002-03	Kevin Cook

The NE-IAATI was formed and received its charter from IAATI in 1972. The founding charter members in their wisdom saw the present and future need of an organization, which would serve those persons involved in the field of vehicle theft investigation in the northeastern USA, and the eastern part of Canada. The high population density and the proximity of the Canadian border dictated the need for the setting up of a separate chapter to handle the unique problems prevalent in this geographical area of the North American continent.

The concept, based on the philosophy of IAATI, is to provide unhindered assistance expeditiously by a group of well-trained, dedicated vehicle theft investigators regardless of location in any state or on either side of the border.

Our continuing gratitude must be given to these far-sighted individuals who have continued to provide a steadfastness of purpose to our organization. Indeed their names should be noted. The charter members of the NE-IAATI are:

Harry J. Brady, Sr.
George J. Acker (deceased)
Herbert L. Burr
Angelo J. Carcaci
Joseph M. Carroll (deceased)
Carl J. Catalano (deceased)
Edward T. Cox
John J. Scarisbrick, Jr. (deceased)
William D. Schauman
Lawrence J. Troiano

This is the basic philosophy that has been carried through consistently since that time and it is the philosophy that can carry this association into the future.

Since receiving its Charter, four of its Past Presidents have gone on to serve as President of the International Association of Auto Theft Investigators: Harry J. Brady, Sr.; Philip J. Crepeau; Stephen E. Gobby; and Robert C. Hasbrouck. Additionally, two members of the Northeast Chapter have served as International President, Louis Spry and Jean Claude Cloutier.

Quebec Provincial Police donated NE flag

1988-NE Pres. presents John J. Scarisbrick Award. (L-R): Alice Brady, Harry Brady, Sr. - Recipient, Harry Brady, Jr., Bill Borman

Montreal

Kevin Cook, Robert Southard, Kevin McHugh, Kevin Ronayne

Harry Brady Sr. and Harry Brady Jr.

Roger Overton-new award

George Vasquez

NE Past President (L-R): Harry Brady Sr., Steve Gobby, Dan Weber,Phil Crepeau, Bob Crepeau, Bill Borman, Norman Bureau, Frank DeMartino, Harry Brady Jr., Howie Fronk, Bob Hasbrauck, Herb Burr, Frank Ruzcka, Ed Cox

NE Presidents Back Row (L-R): Harry Fox, John Staudt, Howie Fronk, Phil Crepeau. Front Row (L-R): Herb Burr, George Acker, Harry Brady, Frank DeMartino, Ed Cox

NE award George Acker, Harry Brady Sr

Frank Ruzicka and Bruce Saville

Kevin Cook

North Eastern Chapter Founders - Back row (L to R) Angelo J. Carcaci, Pennsylvania State Police; Joseph M. Carroll, National Automobile Theft Bureau; Carl J. Catalano, Massachusetts Registry of Motor Vehicles; Lawrence J. Troiano, Suffolk County (NY) Police Department. Front row (L to R) Harry J. Brady, Sr., The Port Authority of New York and New Jersey Police Department; George J. Acker, New York State Police; William D. Schauman, New Jersey State Police; John J. Scarisbrick, Jr., Avis Rent A Car. Not pictured - Edward T. Cox, Hempstead (NY) Police Department, Herbert L. Burr, Massachusetts Registry of Motor Vehicles.

SOUTHEAST REGIONAL CHAPTER

In spring 1975, Thomas Horrigan roughed out the Constitution/Bylaws for the Southeast Chapter-IAATI. Assistance was rendered by Clarence Brickey, Lloyd Letterman and Robert Pruett in getting the SEC moving. The SEC had their first seminar in Raliegh, N.C., in the spring of 1976, with Lloyd Letterman and his friends providing a very successful seminar. W.S. (Sonny) Plowden was elected the first SEC-IAATI President.

The SEC IAATI has held a seminar every year since 1976 and several joint seminars with the parent IAATI. Lloyd Letterman, the original elected treasurer, held office from 1976 until the early 1990's, when he retired from that position. Letterman is the only person in the SEC who was given a life membership. In 1985, Clarence Brickey, a past-president, was elected secretary of the SEC and held that position until 2000 when he left for health reasons. During his tenure in the late 1990's membership increased to over 900 members per year.

SEC seminars have been held in every southeastern state in the U.S. Louisiana was ceded to the South Central IAATI Chapter several years ago for geographical reasons. Every seminar was successful.

During the 1999 Asheville, N.C., seminar, the SEC adopted an investigator certification project. Level I and Level II processes were developed in this project. A Level III process is being developed for advanced certification. The parent IAATI has adopted the SEC project and IAATI will finalize the project and continue the program for international certification.

Alabama
Delaware
Georgia
Florida
Maryland
Mississippi
North Carolina
South Carolina
Tennessee
Virginia
West Virginia

PRESIDENTS

1974–75	W.S. Plowden, S.C. Law Enforcement Division, SC (Deceased)
1975–76	Thomas J. Horrigan, Metropolitan Police Dept., Washington, D.C. (Retired)
1976–77	J. Guy Hall, Anne Arundel Co. Police Dept., Glen Burnie, MD. (Retired)
1977–78	Ralph G. Beasley, Alabama Bureau of Investigation, Montgomery, AL (Retired)
1978–79	Troy R. Smith, Cobb County Police, Marietta, GA (Retired)
1979–80	Robert A. Pruett, North Carolina Division of Motor Vehicles, Raleigh, NC
1980–81	Clarence O. Brickey, Maryland State Police, Pikesville, MD (Retired)
1981–82	Virgil Luke, National Insurance Crime Bureau, Pearl, MS
1982–83	Charles D. Banks, Ft. Lauderdale Police Dept., FL (Retired)
1983–84	Kenneth W. Combs, Alabama Bureau of Investigation, Gurley, AL (Retired)
1984–85	Harry E. Harper, Baltimore Police Dept., Columbia, MD (Deceased)
1985–86	Lloyd D. Moree, Jr., Tennessee Highway Patrol, Nashville, TN.
1986–87	Ralph V. Crow, Virginia State Police, Richmond, VA (Retired)
1987–88	James D. Holmes, Metro Transit Police, Washington, DC.
1988–89	Gerard E. Schad, Delaware State Police, Odessa, DE (Retired)
1989–90	Patricia A. Mitchell, Tennessee Highway Patrol, Nashville, TN
1990–91	David C. MacGillis, Florida Marine Patrol, Tallahassee, Fl

Pat Hester

1991–92	James T. Weakley, Virginia State Police, Chesapeake, VA (Retired)
1992–93	James L. Stewart, Orange Co. Sheriff's Office, Orlando, FL
1993–94	Thomas R. Morton, National Insurance Crime Bureau, Lithonia, GA
1994–95	Gary L. Nelson, Virginia Beach Police Department, Virginia Beach, VA
1995–96	William E. Ausley, Great American Insurance Company, Raleigh, NC
1996–97	Lester E. Johnson, Delaware State Police, Odessa, DE (Retired)
1997–98	Stephen W. Cook, Orange County Sheriff's Office, Orlando, FL
1998–99	Dennis W. Midgette, Jr., Virginia Police Dept., Chesapeake, VA (Retired)
1999–00	Ronnie Dean, National Insurance Crime Bureau, Charlotte, NC
2000–01	C. Wayne Burr, SC Law Enforcement Division Columbia, SC
2001–02	Sean P. Burke, Baltimore County Police Dept., Towson, MD

LIFETIME MEMBER

Lloyd Letterman   North Carolina Division of Motor Vehicles, Raleigh, NC (Deceased)

Past presidents Jim Holmes, Ralph Crow, Charles Banks

SEC IAATI 1991 Letterman recieving thanks for membership as original treasurer retiring.

Attending classes SEC 6-97 Seminar

Three past presidents and one life membership. David MacGillis, Clarence Brickey, Charles Banks, Lloyd Letterman

SEC-IAATI Myrtle Beach Seminar Banquet

SEC IAATI opening ceremonies-Bill Ausley and Steve Cook

Robert Pruett, Mos Hooper, Harry Harper (deceased), Paula MacGillis, David MacGillis

SEC IAATI Banquet Paula MacGillis, David MacGillis

SEC Banquet headtable (R-L): Willie Brickey, Libby Ausley, Bill Ausley, Sue Midgette, Dennis Midgette, Terry Cook, Steve Cook

SEC Seminar Clarence Brickey and Virgil Luke

Classes well attended

Lloyd Letterman

Exchanging office Dennis Midgette and Steve Cook

SEC IAATI Class examining vehicles for ID

177

Karen Roske, Denny Roske, ??-2000 Southeast Chapter Seminar Charleston, SC. Aboard U.S.S. Yorktown

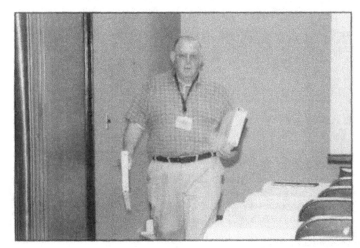

SOUTH CENTRAL REGIONAL CHAPTER

Arkansas
Louisiana
Oklahoma
Texas
New Mexico

History of TAVTI and the South Central Regional Chapter

The Texas Association of Vehicle Theft Investigators (TAVTI) was founded in 1975 by 28 police representatives who were concerned about the high rise in auto theft. Worth Seaman was appointed first president.

In 1976, TAVTI sponsored legislation requiring salvage yards to keep records. In 1977 they called for the standardization of CVINS. This was the beginning of many laws and regulations that TAVTI has sponsored and supported throughout the years.

In 1991, TAVTI sponsored the Auto Theft Prevention Authority. This program allowed the state to use grant money to support auto theft task forces throughout the state of Texas. It also supports crime prevention programs throughout the state.

In 1996, TAVTI helped host the IAATI Conference in San Antonio, and in 1999 voted to become a member of IAATI to be affiliated with the South Central Chapter, which also includes New Mexico, Oklahoma, Louisiana and Arkansas.

TAVTI PRESIDENTS

1975	Worth Seaman
1976	Edward D. Sanders
1978	Sam Gonzales
1979–80	James Cumby
1980–81	Henry Lipe
1981–82	Tommy May
1982–83	Bryan Clark
1983–84	Harold Moe
1984–85	Tommy Hansen
1985–86	Roy Newman
1986–87	Gary Pinkston
1987–88	Dale Hill
1988–89	Henry Brune, Jr.
1989–90	Ken McKenzie
1990–91	David Luther
1991–92	Frank Malinak III
1992–93	George Gandy
1993–94	Kenny Schull
1994–95	Cliff Babbitt
1995–96	Rick Darby
1996–97	Brad Keefer
1997–98	Kent Mawyer
1998–99	David Turner

SCRC PRESIDENTS

1999–00	Pat Bostick
2000–01	Mike Ingels
2001–02	Chris Malek
2002–03	Mike Gates

C.C. Benson 1975

Swearing in 2001-2002 SCRC Board.(L to R) Chris Malek, Mike Gates, Larry Kocurek, Frank Ramirez, Elliot Rousseau and Bill Skinner

IAATI President Dave Ecklund addresses the crowd.

L-R: Henry Brune, Judy Blando, Ann Wyatt, Chris Malek, Mike Gates, Mike Ingels

BBQ greeters Roger Van Drew, Larry Kocurok, Tracie Mortenson, Kent Mawyer, Mike McClain, Tommy Hansen

L-R: Chris Malek, George Rick, Gary Darby, Ken MacKenzie, Tommy Hansen, Kent Mawyer, Henry Brune, Tommy May, Henry Lipe, Mike Ingels, Kenny Schull

2002 SCRC Training Seminar Attendees

Texas Region I-Dale Binkert, Royce Jordan, Roy Pierce, Bill Beall, Ken MacKenzie, Jackie Deane, Pat McGrail, Wallace Hood, Daniel Pearson, Rick Hernandez, Brain Johnson, Antonia Rodrihuez, Rick Darby, Larry Lunsford, Frank Vanek, Johnny Hicks, Frank Ramirez, Ron McLeon, Steve Aulbaugh, David Wallace, Jerry Sadler, Doug Shelley, H.L. Ratcliff, George Gandy, Bill Skinner, Paul Figueroa, Dave Nails

Texas Region II-Keith Kucifer, Jim Woods, TJ Salazar, Chris Zermenu, Kevin Moneyhun, Ken Miller, Jim Dodson, Tommy Hansen, Danny Sheppard, Mike Mize, Joitar Bedinfeld, David Graham, Red Lehman, Mike Woychesin, Joe Munoz, Ray Dupont, Roger Barker, Alan Rousseau, Rob Emmons, Mike Ingels, Chris Malek

Texas Region III-Henry Brune, Pete Garza, Tony Yzaguirre, Joe Mireles, Victor Alvarado, David Brosh, Ray Dustin, Tom Maurice, Kelly Gleason, Marty Jassu, Michael Gates, Michael Ilse, Frank Elizondo, Orlando Juarez, Archie Harben, John Bailey, Harold Stech, Jose Sauceda, Kenny Schull

Texas Region IV-Pat Bostick, Sammy Prieto, Randy Swick, Grabb Davis, Johnny Munoz, Rene Cardona, Bobby L. Vargas, Jesus Becerra

Texas Region V-Louis Cardinal, Kat Anderson, Doug Triplett, Terry Morgan, Ann Wyatt

Texas Region VI-Joey Canady, Brad Haddin, John Vigel, Steven Taylor, Jeff Seahoh, Mike Roberts, Bob Buck, Chris Rowland, Mark Zimmerhanzel, Tom Peters, A.J. Wahl, Stan Roper, Bobby Bailey, Jeff Fudge, Bruce Spence, Cody Toppel, Rudy Woods, Bob Hagan, Gil Hernandez, Kent Mawyer

Louisiana-Brandon Ortiz Sr., Bill Bobbitt, Jimmy Jeter, Peter Perrin, Rick Thigpen

CHAPTERS & BRANCHES

SOUTHERN AFRICA BRANCH

The decision for the South African Police, which is a national force, to join the IAATI was taken by the SAP executive, after the late Colonel Willem C Smith attended the 36th Annual meeting in Galveston, Texas. This meeting was also attended by the then Chief of the Criminal Investigation Department, Lieutenant General Stan Schutte, who realized the worth of being a member of the organization would hold for not only the SAP, but the newly established SAP Vehicle Theft Unit in particular.

On 28 November 1988 Willem C Smith was elected as the Regional Representative for IAATI Southern Africa.

The second IAATI meeting to be held outside the USA, was held in Cape Town South Africa at a midyear Conference from 24-28 March 1991. This meeting was attended by Jean Rutledge Larry Capp, and Ken Mac Kenzie from the USA and Brian Woods from the UK and Bob Springvloed from Holland to name a few. It was at this meeting that the Southern Africa Branch was established as a fully-fledged branch, with Willem C Smith elected as the first president.

During the years 1992 and 1993 local training seminars were held for the Vehicle Theft Unit at which time IAATI Training was incorporated in to the Seminar.

An internationally flavored training seminar was held at the SA Police Holiday Resort at Nylstroom in the Northern Province of South Africa, which was attended by the then president of IAATI, Ken Mac Kenzie.

A second training seminar was held at the same venue during 1995, but due to the South African political situation at the time, was not attended by any IAATI board members. It was shortly after this time, and as a result of the new political order in the country and the change in S A Police policy and a rapid decline in membership, that the remaining Southern African board consisting of WC Smith past president, Tinus Odendal past president and Gerald Davis last elected president, decided that the SAB should be suspended as a branch until the situation had stabilized.

We are now entering what appears to be a stable phase and we are currently trying to resurrect the old branch again

L-R: Wilheim Smith, Brook Schaub, Tinnus Odendal, Ken MacKenzie

UNITED KINGDOM BRANCH

For many years IAATI International had a number of United Kingdom members, two of which come immediately to mind: Brian Wood, a former past president and John Hanchett, a director of the European Branch. In November 1990, at a meeting held at the Metropolitan Police Sports Club, Imber Court, London, the European Branch was created and ran successfully for the next nine years. To strengthen IAATI's representation abroad it was decided to have a separate United Kingdom Branch, which was approved by the International Committee on January 1, 2001.

The International President, David Ecklund, present the Regional Charter to the UK Branch in a special ceremony at the annual seminar in Virginia Beach, in August 2001.

The UK Branch has gone from strength to strength since its inauguration with its first successful seminar held at the Metropolitan Police Sports Club, Bushey, London, in September 2001, plus an extensive training session held in conjunction with the Avon & Somerset Police.

The following are the elected members of the UK Branch Board for the year 2002:

President:	Tony Simms, Metropolitan Police/ABI, Retired
1st Vice President:	Alan Taylor, Kent Police, Retired
2nd Vice President:	Bryan Sheppard, Avon & Somerset Police
Secretary:	BryanKing-Williams, Merseyside Police Retired, Ins. Investigator
Treasurer:	Ken Howard, Metropolitan Police, Retired, Ins. Investigator
Director:	Dr. Ken German, Stolen Vehicle Squad, New Scotland Yard
Director:	Mark Jones, Fraud Manager, Direct Line Insurance
Director:	Roger Elliot, Chief of Police, Tilbury Port Police
Director:	Michael Hinchliffe, External Affairs, Retaingroup
Director:	Andy Bird, Criminal Intelligence Bureau, Essex Police
Director:	Allie Burgess, Asst. Director, Fraud & Police Liaison, CIFAS
Director:	Ian McKinlay, Intelligence Liaison Officer, Strathclyde Police
Director:	Peter Scott, Force Intelligence Bureau, Hertfordshire Police

KEITH ENGLISH AWARD

The Keith English Award is presented each year to an individual, department or organization that distinguished themselves in the area of vehicle theft, investigation or prevention. Keith was a long-serving member of IAATI and a founder member of the European Branch, but sadly was killed in a road accident in 1992.

The International President, David Ecklund, presented the award to Mr. Andrew Kaye, representing the PATSY Group (Port Anti–Theft System) at the Annual Seminar at Bushey in September 2001.

Dave Ecklund 2001 International IAATI President presents Tony Simms with our new United Kingdom Charter at the International Seminar at Virginia Beach August 9, 2001.

Dave Ecklund presents Keith English Award to Andrew Kaye (Rose Bowl) Senne Bushey, September 2001.

United Kingdom Board 2001. Front (R to L) Andy Bird, Jim McNurty, Tony Simms, Michael Hinchliffe, John Hanchett. Rear (R to L) Ken German, Ken Howard, Bryan King-Williams, Roger Elliot, Alan Taylor, Bryan Sheppard, Roger Durrant, Mark Jones.

The UK Board were honored to have the International President David Ecklund visit the branch for a few days, which included an excellent presentation at our first seminar on motorcycle crime in the U.S. Dave, who is a serving car squad officer in the State of Florida, was delighted to have had the opportunity to visit an operational squad at New Scotland Yard to see at first hand how vehicle crime was being tackled in the United Kingdom. Here is Dave with Detective Steve Wim Penny.

WESTERN REGIONAL CHAPTER

Alaska
Alberta, Canada
Arizona
British Columbia, Canada
California
Colorado
Hawaii
Idaho
Montana
Nevada
Oregon
Saskatchewan
Utah
Washington
Wyoming

The idea of forming a Western Regional Chapter of IAATI had been discussed many times by auto theft investigators in the West for many years. The idea surfaced again at the IAATI Seminar held in Salt Lake City, Utah in 1987. John Jones of the Utah Dept. of Public Safety organized a group of interested parties and the formation of a Western Regional Chapter began. Initially there was some opposition and skepticism to the formation of the WRC. It was felt in some quarters that the formation of a WRC would harm the International. As well there were several local auto theft organizations already in existence and working well in the West and in some cases had been for the previous 40 years!. Some of these organizations at the time were IATFI, CATI, WSATI, SNARE and AATIA. The organizers of the new WRC had no desire to infringe on them, but rather to enhance them by having a delegate sit on the Board of the International. Other IAATI Chapters enjoyed this benefit so John Jones (JJ) and his committee polled the various Auto Theft Associations in the West and determined that an overwhelming number were supportive of the formation of a Western Regional Chapter. A Board was formed consisting of a President and four (4) Vice-Presidents and 10 Directors. All Board members were executive members and representatives of the independent auto theft associations from the Western States and Canada. In March of 1988, JJ attended the mid-year meeting of the IAATI Board in Chicago, Illinois and subsequent approval to form a Western Regional Chapter was given by IAATI President Paul Gilliland and the IAATI Board. JJ and his "appointed" Board subsequently met in Reno, Nevada in May of 1988 and formalized the Western Regional Chapter. A constitution was drafted, the first "official" Board of Directors was elected, and a membership roster was completed. As well it was agreed that the Board of Directors would be comprised of the presidents of the Independent Auto Theft Associations within the Western Region a fact that exists to this day. The stated objective of the West-

ern Regional Chapter was to support regional training provided by the Independent Auto Theft Associations and not to develop a separate Western States Training Seminar. The training seminar provided by IAATI on an annual basis would receive the full focus and support of the WRC. As a result of this stated objective the Western Regional Chapter became officially known as the "paper chapter" as, unlike the other Regional Chapters within IAATI, no yearly training seminar would be held so as not to conflict with the Independent Auto Theft Associations. This objective remains in place even today. In the fall of 1988 at the 36th Annual IAATI Training Seminar held at Galveston, Texas the Western Regional Chapter, commonly referred to as the "paper chapter", was given life and its charter and officially welcomed into the IAATI family. The first elected President of the WRC was John H. Jones. With the exception of a few "lean" years the WRC continues to grow and prosper. Several of those who have served as Presidents in the past have been Frank Zangar, Jerry Boyer, Darrell Ehlers, Joanie Pitts, Cliff Chezum and Bill Larocque. Space does not permit the naming of all those who have contributed in so many ways with the formation and ongoing support of the WRC. The WRC continues to serve the Western United States including Alaska and Hawaii along with the Western Canadian Provinces of Alberta, Saskatchewan and British Columbia.

PAST PRESIDENTS

John Jones
Jerry Boyer
Brian Flaherty
John Gant
Frank Zanger
Daryl Elhers
Joanie Pitts
Cliff Chezum
Bill Larocque

Western Regional Chapter Charter

Opening ceremonies

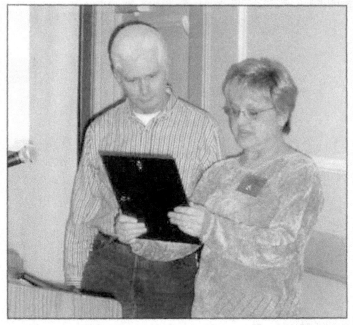

Terry Cramer and Carol Vannatter

Terry Cramer and Lou Kovin

Gerry Boyer, Roger Van Drew, Joanie Pitts, and Carol Vannetter

Joan Pitts, Carol Van Natter, Jerry Boyer, Bill Larocque, Howard Johnson at WRC-AOM Palm Springs 2001

Diana Rummel

Seminar Opening Ceremonies

Boat identification training

Randy Ballin with VIN-nie Bob

Gary Labb and Marianne Finney

Marianne Finney and Carol Vannatter buying that last chance to win!

IAATI AWARDS

RAYMOND H. DREHER MEMORIAL AWARD

Dreher Award Recipients Present at 50th Seminar (L-R): H. Lee Ballard, Bill Borman, Tracie Mortenson, Charlie Banks, Clarence Brickey, Glen MacLaughlin, Gene Rutledge, Joanie Pitts, Ron Van Raalte, Dan Ryan, Mrs. John Daniel (for John Daniel), Ziggy Zablocki, Ken MacKenzie, John Daniel, Jr. (for John Daniel Sr.)

The most prestigious award of the Association. The award is named in honor of the late Raymond H. Dreher of the Missouri Highway Patrol. The award is given to Association members who have distinguished themselves by service to the Association, or for other outstanding acts in the vehicle theft field. Candidates shall be selected based upon extraordinary service to the Association and not those services normally required of the Association members, or for other significant acts bringing favorable credit to the Association or it's members.

RECIPIENTS:

1984	Ron Van Raalte, Arlington Heights (IL) PD
1985	Gene Rutledge, California Hwy Patrol
1987	Charlie Banks, Ft. Lauderdale (FL) PD
1987	Tom Horrigan, Metropolitan Police of Washington, DC
1988	A.T. Phillips, State Farm Insurance Co.
1989	Ken MacKenzie, Richardson (TX) PD
1990	Joan Pitts, Hertz Corporation
1992	Willem Smith, Police of South Africa
1992	Ziggy Zablocki, Broward County (FL) Sheriff Dept.
1992	Brian Wood, Metropolitan Police of London
1993	Lee and Pat Ballard, Ford Motor Company
1994	Harry Brady, Sr., Port Authority of New York & New Jersey
1994	Clarence Brickey, Maryland State Police
1998	William Borman, New York City PD
1999	Dan Ryan, FBI
2002	The Founding Fathers of IAATI: John F. Daniel-Dallas, TX PD; Glen MacLaughlin-Texas DPS; C.C. Benson-NATB Dallas, TX
2002	Tracie Mortenson-3M Company

A.T. Phillips

In the early 80's, A T who was then a consultant with State Farm was charged with first developing a fraud awareness program to be presented to State Farm personnel across the United States and Canada The subsequent challenge would be to develop a curriculum to train prospective SIU Personnel. In those early years, SIU's were evolving in the insurance industry. Because auto theft is so pervasive and because it is easy to identify on the front end, it was logical for A T to focus his efforts there. Then came the challenge of where he would find the information he needed to accomplish his goals. He turned to IAATI. A T became a member of IAATI and began calling on its' members to help him develop his programs. The IAATI teachers began teaching and that effort resulted in one of the best awareness and training programs in the insurance industry.

In 1990 at the annual IAATI seminar in Omaha, Nebraska A T became the first non law enforcement member to be appointed to an IAATI board position. That general assembly should go down in story as an example of the democratic process exercised within IAATI. Up to this point in his affiliation with IAATI, A T had served on and chaired a number of committees and ushered IAATI into the electronic world by arranging the donation of our very first computer.

In 1991, having just returned from his annual physical and given a clean bill of health, A T succumbed to a massive heart attack and died instantly.

In an effort to recognize the many contributions he had made to IAATI and to preserve that recognition, IAATI asked State Farm Insurance Company to co-sponsor the A T Phillips award to recognize the SIU individual or unit who has demonstrated the most exceptional investigation of an auto theft and/or related crimes. The first award was presented in 1992 at the annual seminar in Boise, Idaho.

RECIPIENTS:

1993	Anne Jenei
1998	Tiffany Bolick
1999	Gilberto Bustamante
2000	Frederick Williams
2001	Linda Gunderson
2002	Tom Calandrillo

AGC / IAATI Award

This award was created as a joint venture between the Associated General Contractors of America and the Association. It is intended to honor any person possessing the qualifications of an active member of the Association, although membership is not a prerequisite, who has in some way distinguished themselves in the field of offroad (farm & construction) equipment investigation/recovery. It is not intended to be awarded to anyone other than actual field investigators or first-line supervisors of field investigators.

RECIPIENTS:

1989 – Jim Gavigan
1992 – Unidentified – photo page 105
1995 – David Schwartzfopf, John Huotman, Dianna Rummel
1996 – Terry Lemming
1998 – Randy Kugler
2000 – Jimmy Towe - Texas
2001 – John Abounader, NY State DMV
2002 – Gary Horne, TX DPS

AGC/IAATI Award

The Associated General Contractors of America
and
The International Association of
Auto Theft Investigators

Proudly Presents This Award To

JIMMY C. TOWE
Texas Department of Public Safety

For your devoted Public Service and
Exceptional Achievement in the Investigation
and Recovery of Stolen Construction
and Farm Machinery.

JULY 2000

IAATI Awards

IAATI Award of Merit

This award was created to honor a person, group, department or company for outstanding contribution in the area of vehicle theft investigation or prevention.

RECIPIENTS:

1993
Winner of the Award of Merit
Anthony Kane – NICB (USA)
Interstate Theft Unit – FBI (USA)

1994
Winner of the Award of Merit
Sergeant David Roccaforte - San Francisco Police Department (USA)

1995
Winner of the Award of Merit
Edmonton Integrated Intelligence Unit and Sûreté du Québec (Canada)

1996
Winner of the Award of Merit
Gendarmrie Antwerp, Belgian Stolen Vehicle Squad
Ron van den Hoeck, Kenneth Ruks

1997
Winners of the Award of Merit
Ontario Provincial Auto Theft Team (P.A.T.T.) - Project No-Nam (Canada)
Winners of the Certificate of Merit
Lake Worth/Palm Beach County Auto Theft Force (USA)
Tulsa Police Department (USA)
Port of Tilbury Police (UK)

1998
Winner of the Award of Merit
Detective Peter Simet - Milwaukee Police Department (USA)
Winners of the Certificate of Merit
Agent John D. Sides - New Mexico State Police (USA)
Auto Theft Unit - Tulsa Police Department (USA)

1999
Winners of the Award of Merit
Detectives Robert Rawlinson and Michael Knowlton - Pine Bluff Police Department (USA)
Tim Flynn - Co-operators Insurance Company (Canada)

2001
Winners of the Certificate of Merit
Cumberland County Pennsylvania Auto Theft Unit

2002
Winner of the Award of Merit
Baltimore Regional Auto Theft Team

IAATI Awards

3M Vehicle Theft Investigators Award

This award was created in 1988 as a joint venture between 3M and the Association. The award is open to any person or unit possessing the qualifications of an active member of IAATI, although membership is not a prerequisite. It is intended to honor any person (or unit/team) who has in some way distinguished his or herself in a vehicle theft investigation where component part labels carrying the 17 character VIN played a significant part in the success of the investigation.

Recipients:

2002 - Patrolman Greg Rule - South Brunswick Township Police Dept.
2001 - United States vs Theodore Dizelos
2000 - Joint FBI/New York City PD. Auto Larceny Task Force
1999 - Sgt Larry Kocurek, Texas Department of Public Safety
1998 - Detective Bill Riley, Kentucky State Police
1997 - Detective John Pierce, Metro- Dage Police Dept., Multi-Agency Auto Theft Task Force
1996 - MI State Police, Western Wayne Auto Theft Section
1995 - FBI Joint Auto Larceny Task Force
1994 - Detective Russell Suess, Ft. Lauderdale Police Dept.
1993 - Detective Dennis Hossfeld, Seattle Police Dept.
1992 - New York City Police Department, Auto Crime Division
1991 - Detective Joseph Dejanovich, Chicago Police Dept.
1990 - Detective Peter Simet, Milwaukee Police Dept.
1989 - Trooper Tim Dumas, Connecticut State Police

IAATI / LoJack Award

This award was created in 1993 to honor law enforcement officers whose efforts, in conjunction with the use of any electronic tracking device, make the most significant impact on the recovery(s) of stolen vehicle(s).

RECIPIENTS:

2002 - Detective Mark Foraker, Delaware State Police
2001 - Detective Cliff Bieder, New York Police Department, Auto Crime Division
2000 - Detective Robert Binder, LAPD & Officer Kenneth Hawkes, LA Port Police
1999 - Trooper John Nutter-MA State Police; Sgt Thomas Charette & Officer Mark Baillargeon-Chicopee, MA PD
1998 - Officer Mark Amos, Detroit PD
1996 - Officer David McCormick, Southfield MI PD
1995 - Officer Ray Bedal, Metro-Dade PD

AUSTRALIA

ADRIAN J. NELSON, NSW
ALAN J. BEDDALL, NSW
ALEXANDER ELLIOTT, WA POLICE SERVICE, WA
ANDREW CARRUTHERS, NSW
ANDREW G. BOSLEY, SOUTH POLICE
ANDREW P. LENNON, ALLIANZ INS LTD, NSW
ANTHONY M. MARMONT, N FEDERAL POLICE, ACT
BARRY CRAIG, NSW
BARRY HAYLOCK, BONILLO Pty, QLD
BARRY PHILLIPS, RTA, NSW
BLAYNE WEBB, WEBBSOLO Pty Ltd, NSW
BOB B. MCKAY, R & J MCKAY INVESTIGATIONS
BRETT FORWARD, FORENSICS LOCKSMITHS, VIC
BRETT JUDD, FREELANCE INVESTIGATIONS, SA
BRIAN PERRY, REPELLAR CAR ALARM, NSW
BRUCE RICHARD TRITTON, PROBE INVESTIGA-
TIONS, VICTORIA
CAROLYN BOYLE, WA
CATHERINE V. BROWN, QUEENSLAND POLICE SER-
VICE, QLD
CHRIS J. HUDSON, HUDSONS, ACT
CHRISTOPHER J. HACKETT, SA
CHRISTOPHER J. PAYNE, NSW
CLIVE BRUSHETT, NSW
CORALEA CAMERON, NRMA INSURANCE, QLD
CRAIG I PETTERD, ACT
DAVID ROGERS, TRANSPORT SA, SA
DEAN PETERS, TRANSPORT SA, SA
DEITH BURY, TORQUE MATIC
DENNIS CONNOR, SOUTH N POLICE, SA
DEREK BURLING, CGU INS, WA
DOMINIC CAMBARERI, VIC
FRANCIS P. KERRIGAN
FRANK HUCKSTEPP, RCAV GENERAL INS, VIC
GEOFFREY J. CASEY
GEORGE DE LUCA, IMA INS, VIC
GEORGE GEORGIOU, CGU INS, SA
GERRY NULL BASHFORD, VIC
GLEN E. WALKER, WA
GRAHAM BATH, SA ATTORNEY GENERALS DEPT, SA
GRAHAM J. KAYLER-THOMSON, GEELONG ASSES-
SORS, VIC
GRAHAM K. WEST, BARRINGTON GROUP, NSW
GREG HILL, VIC
GREGORY D. NOKE, L.J. McCLEMENTS & ASSOC,
NSW
GREGORY W. BOLLEMEYER, INVESTIGATION SER-
VICES, SA
GRETTA SELLARS, NSW
HARRY RAKINTZIS, AAMI INS, VIC
IAN C. GUNTHORPE, QUEENSLAND POLICE SER-
VICE, QLD
IAN J. PAKES, VIC
IAN R. MILLER, CIBEX PTY LTD, NSW
ILIANNA SKORDOS, NRMA INS, NSW
JAMES A. COOK, INS MANAGEMENT SERVICES AU
P/L, WA
JAMES DARCY, R A C INS, WA
JASON MILLS, WA
JERRY GORDON HOLMES, RACO INSURANCE
JOHN BARTON, NSW
JOHN BELL, J.D. BELL & ASSOCIATES, ACT
JOHN M. MARSHALL, FORENSIC CONSULTING SER-
VICE PTY LTD
JOHN MANGOS, VIC
JOHN NETTLEBECK, TRANSPORT SA, SA
JOHN P. O'BYRNE, NRMA INSURANCE LTD, QLD
JOHN PANOZZO, TOYOTA
JOSEPH MOSKWA, RACQ INSURANCE, QLD
JOSHUA G.B. RAYNER, QUEENSLAND POLICE SER-
VICE, QLD
KAYLENE ARNELL, STREET LEGAL INCORPORATED,
SA
KEITH T. SCHMIDT, QLD POLICE SERVICE, QLD
KRISTIN ZEMEN, SA ATTORNEY GENERALS DEPT, SA
KYM T. CHILTON, NT
LARRY JAMES CANTWELL, RACO INSURANCE, QLD
LESLIE CLIMO, NSW
LESLIE M. FULLER, NSW
LISA YOUNG, NSW POLICE, NSW
MARK BENNEDICK, QLD
MARK BORLACE, ROYAL AUTO ASSOC OF SOUTH,
SA
MARK POLLARD, CGU INS, SA
MARK SCULTHORPE, FORENSIC ACCIDENT RECON-
STRUCTION, NSW
MARK SHEARAN, LYONS TAYLOR & ASSOCIATES,
NSW
MARTIN R. GREEN, CGU INS, NSW
MARTIN R. WEBB, ZURICH N INS
MICHAEL JAMES BAILEY, RAC INSURANCE, WA
MICHAEL SEIDL, NSW
MICHAEL WILLIAM HAYMAN, NSW
MIKE MAXWELL, TASMANIA POLICE SERVICE, TAS
NEIL R. YEOMANS, CGU INSURANCE
NICHOLAS GRANT, BYRANT CORP/ACATA-ASIAL,
NSW
PAUL D. THOMAS, SOUTH AG OFFICE, SA

PAUL JOSEF, BMW, VIC
PAUL MURRIHY, VIC
PETER BROWN, NSW
PETER BUTTS, N TRANSPORT INVESTIGATION, VIC
PETER HISCOCK, PETER HISCOCK & PARTNER Pty
Ltd, VIC
PETER J. FORBES, PJ. FORBES CONSULTING SER, SA
PETER McBEAN, RACO INSURANCE, OLD
PHILLIP JOHN CLOHESY, RACO INSURANCE, OLD
QUENTIN D. MILLS, VIC
RENEE HOUSE, CLMS INVESTIGATIONS & ASSESS-
MENT, OLD
RICHARD SCOTT BUBNER, TRANSPORT SA, SA
ROBERT J. HENNIG, N CORPORATE SECURITY, VIC
ROBERT J. KING, J & D.B. THOMAS & ASSOCIATES,
NSW
ROBERT MUIR, ACT
ROBERT POTTER, SA ATTORNEY GENERAL'S DEPT,
SA
ROBERT TAYLOR, CGU INS, SA
RODNEY MOORE, QUEENSLAND
RON C. DOLLIVER, R A C INS, WA
RONALD E. SCOTT, NSW
ROSS A. MORSON, R.A. MORSON & ASSOC Pty Ltd,
NSW
ROSS D. SQUIRE, ABC FORENSIC, NSW
RUSSELL PARKINS, ROAD TRANSPORT ENFORCE-
MENT, SA
SERENA A. BUXTON, N FEDERAL POLICE, ACT
SHANE ILLMAN, CGU INS, VIC
TED HOMEYER, NSW
TERRY MOORE, AUSTROADS, NSW
TONY WARD, NSW
TRACEY MARGARET YOUNG, N FEDERAL POLICE,
ACT
TREVOR L. CARE, NSW
TROY HOGARTH, IMA INS, NSW
TROY R. RUSSELL, NSW POLICE SERVICE, NSW
WARREN FLETCHER, NSW
WAYNE A. RASSMUSSEN, QUEENSLAND POLICE
SERVICE, QLD
WILLIAM JOHN MERIFIELD, ROADS AND TRAFFIC
AUTHORITY, NSW
WILLIAM NOEL DE SAIR, VIC

BAHAMAS

ELSWORTH A. MOSS, RBPF CRIMINAL INVESTIGA-
TION DEPT, GB

BELGIUM

ALFONS BASTIAENSENS, ANTWERP (BE) POLICE
DEPARTMENT
BERNARD BELLEMANS
BRUNO VAN DE VYVERE, AXA INSURANCE
CARLOS BARRETO, CAR RECOVERY SERVICE
CARLOS LOWIE
CHRISTOPHE SERGEANT
CLAUDE GAUMIER, ANTWERP POLICE DEPT.
DANIEL GOFFIN
DANIEL THIRY
DANY DONNEN, GOCA AUTOMOBILE INSPECTION
DIDIER DEVILLERS, FEDERAL POLICE G FORM
DIRK ROMBOUTS, ANTWERP POLICE DEPT
DOLF LAMERIGTS
EDDY BLOK
EDDY COPPEE
EDDY SPEER
EDDY VAN BESAUW
ERIC CLIPPE
ERIC DEBOCK
FABIEN OSAER
FILIP VAN LINT
FRANCOIS De BUEGER
FRANK E. JACOPS
FRANKY DE DEURWAERDER
GUIDO BYNENS
GUIDO WOUTERS, ANTWERP POLICE DEPT.
HENRI LACASSE, INSURANCE SMAP-OMOB
HENRI LERMINIAUX
HENRI MANDLER
JACQUES MOLLET, BELGIAN PROFESSIONAL ASS
CAR RENTAL CO
JAN SCHIETECAT
JEAN LEON ROLLIER
JEAN PIERRE DE CUYPER
JEAN PIERRE LAUTERS, INSURANCE P & V
JEAN VIDAL
JEAN-LUC PATARS, GENDARMERIE
JEAN-MARIE DUFRASNE
JOHAN de CONINCK
JOSEPH SIBORGS
KARINE MEUL, ANTWERP (BE) POLICE DEPARTMENT
KOEN MACHTELINCKX
KURT BORREMANS, ANPI/NUBB - INSPECTOR
LEONA DETIEGE, MAYOR OF ANTWERP
LUC LAMINE, ANTWERP (BE) POLICE DEPARTMENT
LUC PIRON, GOCA INSPECTION
LUC VAN BEYLEN, ANTWERP (BE) POLICE DEPART-
MENT

LUC van den BROECK
MANOLI FIDIS
MARC COLYN, GOCA INSPECTION
MARCEL BAUGNIET
MARIO GENTILE
MICHEL BRIERS
MICHEL LECRENIER
P. W. VAN VLASSELAER
PATRICK SCHUMACHER
PETER GORIS, FEDERAL POLICE ANTWERP
PETER VAN ROY
PHILIPPE CHUFFART
PHILIPPE DE WINDT, LOCAL POLICE CHARLEROI
PHILIPPE FROIDMONT
PIERRE SOUGNEZ
PIM ROBYN
RAOUL CASNEUF, KBC INSURANCES, FRAUD UNIT
ROBERT JACOUET
RONALD VAN DEN HOECK, ANTWERP
RONNY ASSELMAN
RUDI GEBRUERS, FEDERAL POLICE
LEOPOLDSBURG
RUDI ROSSEEL, ANTWERP POLICE DEPT.
RUDOLF LENOIR
S. LOMMAERT, ANTWERP (BE) POLICE DEPARTMENT
SERGE DRESENS
SIMON PRZYBYLSKI
STEFAAN BILLIAU, FEDERAL POLICE GDA LEPER
STEFAAN CLAEYS
STEFAAN GROENE
STEFAN VAN GEERT
THIERRY VAN CALOEN
TOUSSAINT TABURY, BRIGADE JUDICIAIRE DE LIEGE
VITO BIVACCO
WILLY STROOBANTS
WIM DE KEYSER, KERSENBOMENLAAN 1
WOUTER ALLEGAERT, FEDERAL POLICE
YVES De MOFFARTS
YVES FIERENS

BERMUDA

PAUL HENRY
TERENCE M. MAXWELL, BERMUDA POLICE SERVICE

BULGARIA

ELENKO MIKOV, DZI-GENERAL INSURANCE PLC.
MARCO MONTECCHI, , BULGARIA
ZDRAVKO DANKOV, DZI-GENERAL INSURANCE PLC.
JIVKO JELEV

CANADA

A. C. PIERETTI, ON
ADRIAN PAUL BALDWIN, ON
ALAN H. PAYNE, ASSOCIATED LOCKSMITHS, ON
ALAN SCOTT, PEEL REGIONAL POLICE, ON
ALISTAIR WATT, HALTON REGIONAL POLICE SER-
VICES, ON
ALLAN FULTON, STATE FARM INS, ON
ANDRE BEAUCHAMP, ICPB, PO
ANDRE DROLET, SHERLOCK ANTI THEFT MARKING
INC, PO
ANDREA AMYOTTE, IBC-ISD/ICPB, ON
ANDREW BABENSEE, PEEL (ON) REGIONAL POLICE,
ON
ANDREW COSE, PEEL (ON) REGIONAL POLICE, ON
ANDREW PACKER, ON
ANNIE JOYAL, RCMP, BC
ARLENE LANGE, ON
BARBARA HUNTER, INSURANCE CORP BRITISH CO-
LUMBIA, BC
BARRY E. DIXON, ROYAL & SUN ALLIANCE, ON
BARRY G. WARD, MANITOBA (CAN) PUBLIC INS, MB
BEN JILLETT, IBC-ISD/ICPB
BILL LYONS, METRO TORONTO (ON) P S, ON
BILL SIRIUNAS, IBC-ISD/ICPB, ON
BLAIR SMITH, PEEL (ON) REGIONAL POLICE, ON
BLAIR YORKE, RCMP, BC
BOB McCLELLAND, VANCOUVER (BC) P D, BC
BOB SEMPLE, CALGARY (AB) POLICE SERVICE, AB
BRIAN AUGUSTYNIAK, 20/20 INFORMATION, ON
BRIAN BELL, OTTAWA-CARLETON REG P S, ON
BRIAN J. CALVIN, ON
BRIAN J. MANNING, ALBERTA MOTOR ASSOC, AB
BRIAN JONES, ON
BRIAN KEGLER, ICBC-SIU, BC
BRIAN T. W. HENRY, STATE FARM INS, ON
BROOKE RYE, SIGNUM CORPORATE SERVICES, ON
BRUCE CROCKER, ICPB - CATB, ON
BRUCE GRATTO, ROYAL & SUN ALLIANCE, ON
BRUCE THOMSON, PEEL (ON) REGIONAL POLICE, ON
CAL P. BODNAR, INSURANCE CORP BRITISH COLUM-
BIA, BC
CAMERON MILLER, ICBC-SIU, BC
CARL A. SWANSON, ON
CARLA WEBB, VANCOUVER (BC) P D, BC
CAROLYN C. DRAMBALAS, ALLSTATE INS, ON
CAROLYN ERICSON, STRATEGIC BUSINESS RISKS
INT'L, ON
CHARLY FLESHER, RCMP, BC

CHRIS ROBERTS, METRO TORONTO (ON) P S, ON
CHRISTINE BRIAND, RCMP, BC
CHRISTINE PARKER, STATE FARM INS, ON
CHRISTOPHER BURKE, TORONTO (ON) POLICE SER-
VICE, ON
CHRISTOPHER DENNISON, BURL-OAK INVESTIGA-
TIVE SERVICES, ON
CHRISTOPHER WILLIAMS, ON
CHUCK GLOVER, RCMP, BC
CLAYTON M. BALLMAN, LETHBRIDGE CITY POLICE
SERVICE, AB
CONSTABLE KALIA, RCMP, BC
COR deGRAAFF, ROYAL & SUN ALLIANCE INS, AB
CRAIG HEATLEY, YORK REGIONAL POLICE, ON
CURTIS C. MELNYCHUK, BC-ATTF, BC
D. GWYNN EDWARDS, ICPB, AB
DAN BEACOCK, ON
DAN BUCH, ON
DAN MURPHY, METRO TORONTO (ON) P S, ON
DAN NADEAU, PEEL (ON) REGIONAL POLICE, ON
DANIEL JOHNSTONE, PEEL (ON) REGIONAL POLICE,
ON
DANIEL RILEY, CHIPPEWA OF THE THAMES FIRST
NATION P D, ON
DARRELL WARE, ON
DARYL K. DUNN, BC
DAVE BROUGHTON, ON
DAVE HERMAN, RCMP, BC
DAVE J. WENGER, DAVE WENGER INVESTIGATIONS,
BC
DAVE ROBINSON, ON
DAVID A. BENDER, FORENSIC ENGINEERING, INC, ON
DAVID BRATT, AXA INS, ON
DAVID JEAR, ICBC-SIU, BC
DAVID MCAREE, OCA BC, BC
DAVID McFARLANE, DURHAM REGIONAL POLICE
SERVICE, ON
DAVID SCHNEIDER, STATE FARM INS, AB
DAVID VAN ALLEN, PEEL (ON) REGIONAL POLICE, ON
DENNIS BLACKBURN, THE CO-OPERATORS INS, AB
DENNIS K. PEARCE, ON
DENNIS ST AUBIN, INSURANCE CORP BRITISH CO-
LUMBIA, BC
DERRICK ALCOCK, STATE FARM INS, ON
DOMINIC MAURINI, HALIFAX INS, ON
DON B. EVERTS, ON
DON DEELEN, PEEL (ON) REGIONAL POLICE, ON
DON FORGERON, INS BUREAU of , NS
DON LICKERS, ONTARIO PROVINCIAL POLICE, ON
DON MONETTE, ON
DON PANCOE, BRANTFORD (ON) POLICE SER, ON
DONALD O'CONNOR, ON
DONALD PELLERIN, OTTAWA (ON) POLICE SERVICE,
ON
DONALD W. IRELAND, AB
DOUG COUSENS, ONTARIO PROVINCIAL POLICE, ON
DOUG DIPLOCK, ON
DOUG FISHER, VANCOUVER (BC) P D, BC
DOUG LOWTHER, ON
DOUGLAS J. WEARMOUTH, AB
DOUGLAS MOIR, ON
DOUGLAS R.E. LINLEY, ALLPRO LOCK & SAFE, BC
EDWARD H. RULTON, ON
EDWIN H. TRETWOLD, COAST IMPORT AUTO SUP-
PLY, BC
ERIC SKINNER, PEEL REGIONAL POLICE, ON
EVELYNN RICHARDS, MANITOBA PUBLIC INS, MB
F. E. ERIC MATTINSON, ON
FORREST KELLERMAN, ICBC-SIU, BC
FREDRIC RICK D. LARSON, INSURANCE CORP BRIT-
ISH COLUMBIA, BC
GARNET C. THOMPSON, GARNET INVESTIGATIONS,
ON
GARRET HOOGESTRAAT, RCMP, AB
GARRY S. POTTS, AB
GARY W. KERNAGHAN, ON
GARY W. ROBERTSON, BURL-OAK INVESTIGATIVE
SERVICES, INC., ON
GAYE POKOL, ON
GEOFF A. BEAN, ON
GEORGE A. KLONOWSKI, ONTARIO PROVINCIAL
POLICE, ON
GEORGE KLEINSTEIBER, ON
GEORGE R. BEARSE, ON
GEORGE R. GREEN, RCMP, AB
GERALD R. GARAND, ON
GERRY DE SAUTNIERS, RCMP, BC
GLENN T. STODDARD, AB
GORDON OLIVER, OLIVER-YASKIW & ASSOC, MB
GREG BISHOP, RCMP, BC
GREG MacPHEE, WHITEHALL BUREAU OF , NS
GREG SULLIVAN, HALTON REGIONAL POLICE SER-
VICES, ON
GUY OUELLETTE, ICPB, NB
HARRY S FOX, ON
HEATHER RAMORE, PEEL REGIONAL POLICE, ON
HENRI MAHER, PQ
IRWIN AXNESS, RCMP, SK
J. D.DALE WALKER, ON

J. RON BALDWIN, CFE, ROYAL INS, ON
J.E. CALVIN WHITE, J.E.C. WHITE CONSULTING, ON
JAMES (JIM) JONES, CALGARY (AB) POLICE SERVICE, AB
JAMES A. DOUGLAS, IBC-ISD/ICPB, ON
JAMES F. HAMILTON, UCDA - ONTARIO, ON
JAMES GOERTZ, ROYAL INS, ON
JAMES McINTOSH, ON
JAMES W. COWAN, ON
JAMIE PORTER, PEEL (ON) REGIONAL POLICE, ON
JANE ROGERS, IBC-ISD/ICPB, ON
JAY HODGSON, PEEL (ON) REGIONAL POLICE, ON
JEAN DAGENAIS, INS BUREAU OF , PO
JEAN TURCOTTE, JEAN TURCOTTE EVALUATIONS, INC, PO
JEAN-CLAUDE CLOUTIER, ON
JEAN-LUC LANGLOIS, MORIN, BOURGET & DENIS, PO
JEFF DAVIS, PEEL (ON) REGIONAL POLICE, ON
JEFF HENRY, NAVLYNX TECHNOLOGIES INC, ON
JERRY SOULLIERE, ALLSTATE INS, ON
JIM ADAMS, ON
JIM CARKENER, ICPB, BC
JIM McKINLEY, PEEL (ON) REGIONAL POLICE, ON
JIM STEINBACK, VANCOUVER (BC) P D, BC
JIM TAIT, FBIG INVESTIGATIONS, BC
JOE FIUME, ON
JOE NEWBOLD, O.M.V.I.C, ON
JOHN AUCOIN, NB
JOHN BANKS, THE CO-OPERATORS, ON
JOHN CARSON, LONDON (ON) POLICE, ON
JOHN FAROUHARSON, PEEL REGIONAL POLICE, ON
JOHN G. FLEMING, NORTH WATERLOO INS CO, ON
JOHN LeGUERRIER, PO
JOHN R. SHEA, RCMP, MB
JOHN RENNIE, VANCOUVER (BC) P D, BC
JOHN SKANES, ON
JOHN TALBOT, ON
JOHN WARD, VANCOUVER (BC) P D, BC
JOSEPH E. CARIGNAN, RCMP, BC
JUDY HEAD, BC
KARL LAYNE, PEEL REGIONAL POLICE SERVICE, ON
KATHY GAGNON, PEEL REGIONAL POLICE, ON
KATHY METZGER, CERTAS DIRECT INS, ON
KELLY COUSINS, PEEL (ON) REGIONAL POLICE, ON
KEN CARLIN, INDEPENDENT APPRAISAL SERVICE, ON
KEN G. HAYWOOD, AUTOTHEFT.COM, AB
KEN J. SMITH, AB
KEN MARCHANT, CAGARY (AB) POLICE SERVICE, AB
KENNETH BASS, CATB, ON
KENNETH D. BYERS, ORIGIN & CAUSE, INC, ON
KERRY MAH, RCMP, BC
KEVIN J. BELFORD, ONTARIO PROVINCIAL POLICE, ON
KEVIN R. GLOVER, RCMP, AB
KEVIN W. CALHOUN, ON
KEVIN WILLSON, ON
KIRK QUINN, STATE FARM INS, ON
KIRK SAYLES, ONTARIO PROVINCIAL POLICE, ON
KRISTINE E. LEES, STATE FARM INS, ON
LANCE M. COLBY, AB
LISA EASTERBROOK, STATE FARM INS, ON
LLOYD WANT, AB
LOUIS W SPRY, ON
LUCY BERNHARDT, YORK REGIONAL POLICE, ON
LYLE PARKER, ON
LYNN L. COUSINS, INSURANCE CORP BRITISH COLUMBIA, BC
MACE ARMSTRONG, ON
MALCOM R. BARBER, ON
MARGARET QUINN, EOUITABLE APPRAISAL SER, ON
MARGERY McLEOD, ALBERTA MOTOR ASSOC. INS CO., AB
MARIE-CLAUDE COTE, RCMP, BC
MARK BARKLEY, ON
MARK DICOSMO, STATE FARM INS, ON
MARK NOBLE, PEEL REGIONAL POLICE SERVICE, ON
MARK STEVENS, ON
MARK W. STONEHILL, PILOT INS CO, Ltd, ON
MARLENE VIAU, ON
MARTIN JAEKEL, WHITEHALL BUREAU of Ltd, ON
MARY LOU O'REILLY, INS COUNCIL of , ON
MICHAEL B. DAMM, INS SEARCH BUREAU , ON
MICHAEL D. LAKE, STATE FARM INS, ON
MICHAEL FOLK, MONEX INSURANCE MGNT, ON
MICHAEL G. NORTON, IBC-ISD/ICPB, ON
MICHAEL PLANTE, PEEL (ON) REGIONAL POLICE, ON
MICHAEL PROSKA, BURL-OAK INVESTIGATIVE SERVICES, INC., ON
MICHAEL T. HAYES, ON
MIKE HAZLETT, ICBC-SIU, BC
MIKE KEAN, PEEL (ON) REGIONAL POLICE, ON
MIKE LIDSTONE, RCMP, BC
MIKE McCARTHY, VANCOUVER (BC) P D, BC
MIKE PURDY, BC-ATTF, BC
MYLES KIDDER, OTTAWA-CARLETON REG P S, ON
NEIL D.B. FERGUSON, STATE FARM INS, ON
NOLA CREWE, CREWE & MARKS, ON
OLIVER BODEMANN, CIBC INS, ON

PATRICE PILON, RCMP, BC
PATRICK WARREN, LOMBARD , ON
PAUL F. HAYNER, ALBERTA MTR ASSOCIATION INS CO., AB
PAUL FEENEY, METRO TORONTO (ON) P S, ON
PAUL S. GRACE, STATE FARM INS, ON
PAUL TAYLOR, VANCOUVER (BC) P D, BC
PAUL W. REID, SIGNUM CORPORATE SERVICES, ON
PAUL WHATTAM, RCMP, AB
PETER GROENLAND, VANCOUVER (BC) P D, BC
PETER MACKINNON, ESTEVAN (SK) P D, SK
PHIL ENS, VANCOUVER (BC) P D, BC
PHIL G. EDGAR, DURHAM (ON) REGIONAL POLICE, ON
PIERRE P. JODOIN, SHERLOCK ANTITHEFT MARKING INC, PO
R. EDWARD LAWRENCE, LAWRENCE & ASSOCIATES, NB
RAE BANWARIE, BC
RANDALL WILES, ON
RANDY INOUYE, VANCOUVER (BC) P D, BC
RAY GINGRAS, STATE FARM INS, ON
RICHARD CHALKE, VANCOUVER (BC) P D, BC
RICHARD HEINE, ALLSTATE INS, AB
RICHARD LOWEN, WINNIPEG (MB) POLICE SERVICE, MB
RICHARD WATTS, TORONTO (ON) POLICE SERVICE, ON
RICK MUIR, ON
RICK MULDER, VANCOUVER (BC) P D, BC
RICK PENGELLY, METRO TORONTO (ON) P S, ON
RICK RUSTICUS, ON
ROBERT DE GROOT, STATE FARM INS, ON
ROBERT G. BEATTIE, USED CAR DLRS ASSOC, ON
ROBERT HUNTER, CORPORATE CONSULTANTS INTL, ON
ROBERT MORRIS, ON
ROBERT S. KELMAN, BELAIR DIRECT INS, ON
ROBERTO SAVIO, ON
RODGER SHEPARD, VANCOUVER (BC) P D, BC
ROGER L. LICHTY, ON
ROLAND SIMPSON, ON
RON CASEY, IBC-ISD/ICPB, ON
RON KANUIT, THE CO-OPERATORS INS, AB
RON McCRACKEN, IBC-ISD/ICPB, ON
RONALD ROLOSON, ON
ROSS PATTEE, INSURANCE CORP BRITISH COLUMBIA, BC
ROSS PENNY, IBC-ISD/ICPB, ON
RUTH HART-STEPHENS, TORONTO AUTO AUCTION, ON
RYAN TEDESCO, RVT SYSTEMS, BC
SANDRA LAVALLEE, RCMP, BC
SCOTT COOKE, VANCOUVER (BC) P D, BC
SERGE BEAUDIN, PO
STEPHEN BLOM, PEEL (ON) REGIONAL POLICE, ON
STEPHEN BOYD, ONTARIO PROVINCIAL POLICE, ON
STEPHEN E. GOBBY, AB
STEPHEN JACKEL, VANCOUVER (BC) P D, BC
STEVE ASTIN, YORK (ON) REGIONAL POLICE, ON
STEVE DAWSON, DNS LOCK SERVICE, MB
STEVE GARDNER, OTTAWA-CARLETON REG P S, ON
STEVE J. KEARNEY, STATE FARM INS, ON
STEVE PATTERSON, PEEL REGIONAL POLICE, ON
STEVE VROLYK, BC-ATTF, BC
STEVEN D. BARCHAM, ONTARIO PROVINCIAL POLICE, ON
SUE CARSON, STATE FARM INS, ON
SUE COLLINGS, ZURICH , ON
SYLVIA LIM, VANCOUVER (BC) P D, BC
SYLVIE NAULT, RCMP, BC
TERRY WHIN-YATES, BC
TERRY WHIN-YATES, CPAL INC., BC
THOMAS WARFIELD, PEEL REGIONAL POLICE, ON
TIM E. THOMAS, METRO TORONTO (ON) POLICE, ON
TIM FLYNN, ON
TOM POKORNIK, ON
TONY ROMANIC, ON
VICTOR LOUIE, RCMP, BC
WARREN N. BARNARD, ON
WAYNE COOKE, DILIGENT BAILIFF SERVICE LTD., ON
WAYNE CUMMINGS, IBC-ISD/ICPB, ON
WAYNE E. CUMMINGS, INSURANCE BUREAU OF , ON
WAYNE HUMMEL, ON
WES WATERS, RCMP, BC
WILL MURRAY, RCMP, BC
WILLIAM BILL ROBINSON, RCMP, MB
WILLIAM A. SMITH, THE CO-OPERATORS INS, AB
WILLIAM BOOGAARD, YORK (ON) REGIONAL POLICE, ON
WILLIAM F. LAROCOUE, AB
WILLIAM GOETZ, YORK (ON) REGIONAL POLICE, ON
WILLIAM H. CAMERON, ICPB - CATB, ON
WILLIAM HAND, PEEL (ON) REGIONAL POLICE, ON
WILLIAM J. FUHRMAN, ON
WILLIAM R. KENNEDY, ON

COLUMBIA
JESUS E. BLANDON, SEIPRI, ANTIOQUIA

CZECH REPUBLIC
PETR SKORNOK
VLASTIMIL FRIC, CEBIA, SPOL.s.r.o.

DENMARK
ARNE E.M. KNIPPEL
ARNE KNIPPEL
BERNHARD LINDHOLM, TRYG-BALICA INS
HANS MEJLSHEDE, MEJLSHEDE LASE/NOGLER A/S
PAUL E. JOHANSEN, TRYG-BALTICA INS
SVEN HANSEN, ALM BRAND INS CO

ENGLAND
ANN SIBLEY
CAS SMITH, SUFFOLK
CLIVE RAW, AVON & SOMERSET CONSTABULARY, BRISTOL
DAVID JAMES GODDEN, KENT COUNTY CONSTABULARY
DAVID JONATHAN GODDARD
DAVID NEIL
DAVID RICHARDS, SURREY
DUNCAN BRETT, BRITISH CREDIT TRUST
IAN PLATT, VEHICLE SECURITY INSTALLATIONS LTD, LIVERPOOL
IAN ROLLASON
JASON STOPPS, BRITISH CREDIT TRUST
JOHN BAILEY, DEVON
JOHN MICHAEL BARRON, PRESTON
JULIAN NICHOLAS MATTHEWS, BEDFORDSHIRE POLICE, BEDFORD
KEITH SADLER, W MIDLANDS
KEVIN SMITH
KEVIN STREET, KRS INTERNATIONAL
LESLEY K. EMMETT, GLOS
MARTIN PARR, BMW FINANCIAL SERVICES LTD, HAMPSHIRE
MICHAEL ADDIS, GLOS
NEIL CHARLES LOY
NIGEL M.J. HUNT, HERTFORDSHIRE CONSTABULARY
PAUL DEVERE, KENT
PAUL J. WATTS
PAUL JONATHAN VINCENT, DEVON
PAUL THOMAS BAKER, STAFFORDSH
RHIAN BANHAM
ROBERT BUDD, GLOUCESTER
ROBERT HILLIER, APAK GROUP LTD
ROBERT READ
SCOTT BOWERS
STEPHEN WILLIS, METROPOLITAN POLICE, HEATH
STEVE MORT, BRITISH TRANSPORT POLICE
STUART K. FAIRCLOUGH
TERRY HILL, BRITISH TRANSPORT POLICE
TONY MULLANE, BRITISH CREDIT TRUST LTD

FINLAND
ARI HUHTINEN
HARRI TAVIKANGAS, HELSINKI POLICE DEPT
JARI KANTONEN, A-VAKUUTUS MUT INS CO
JARI TIAINEN
JUKKA POHJALAINEN
KAJ-ERIK BJORKVIST, POHJOLA GROUP INS
KARI AALTIO
KARI PUISTO, POHJOLA GROUP INS
KARI WIHLMAN, VEHICLE ADMINISTRATION SERVICE
KIMMO SIMOINEN
MAARIT KAAKKOMAKI
MARKO MELENDER
MARTTI JAAKO, A-VAKUUTUS MUTUAL INS
MARTTI OJALA, POHJOLA GROUP INS
MATTI JYSKE
MATTI MOISIO, A-VAKUUTUS MUTUAL INS
MIKKO MASALIN, HELSINKI POLICE DEPT
NIKO MARONEN, BORDER GUARD
PERTTI KALEVA
VEIJO MOILANEN, SAMPO INS

FRANCE
ALAIN BARBIER, OIPC GENERAL SECRETARIAT INTERPOL
ALAN R. TAYLOR
CHRISTIAN ALSINET, AGENCE D'INVESTIGATIONS
DAVID DOUCH, RENAULT ADVANCED ENGINEERING
FRANCOISE MOIREZ, ARGOS
GILLES DESBOS, ARGOS
JEAN MARC DALIDO, POLICE SURETE DEPARTMENTALE 94
JEAN-FRANCOIS SUIRE, ARGOS
JEAN-PIERRE CASSAN, ARGOS
JOEL RAYMOND - AURIBAULT, AGENCE d'INVESTIGATIONS
PASCAL CHEVALIER, ZURICH INS
STEVEN POLIFKO, IPSG INTERPOL

GERMANY
ANDREAS PROBST, EUROPCAR CONTROL SECURITY
GEORG ILLE
GUNTHER SEIDEMANN, SACHVERSTANDIGENBURO

HEINER-JURGEN SCHIERMANN
JAROSLAW DOMANSKI, EUROPCAR CONTROL SECURITY
KEES SCHULTINGE, HERTZ RENTAL CAR
MANFRED KRAEMER, LOCK EXAMINING & REPORTING
THOMAS HEISTER

HERZEGOVINA
DINO OSMANKADIC, SARAJEVO CANTON POLICE, BOSNIA

HUNGARY
GABRIELLA VERBOVSZKY, MGA KFT
HEDVIG KORNIDESZ, MGA KFT

IRELAND
PAUL A BURKE, CO CAVAN

ISRAEL
DAVID RABAN, LOCK-VISION LLC
BULLER MOSHE

ITALY
ALLESSANDRO CIUCHI
ANTONELLA RIVA, COBRA AT
ANTONIO MONTANARO, N.C.B. INTERPOL ROME
EMANUELE NICOSIA, ARGOS ITALY
RENATO SCHIPANI, N.C.B. INTERPOL ROME
SEBASTIANO BONINA, EUROTRUSTEE INVESTIGATIONS S.a.s

JAMAICA
VINCENT A. ROYAL, VINEL CTRL INV & SEC CONS LTD

JAPAN
DAVE EBIHARA, J TRADE CORPORATION

KENYA
CHRISTOPHER M. MacDONALD, CARTRACK KENYA, Ltd

MALAYSIA
YUSOF MOHD.RAZALLI, MALAYSIAN POLICE FORCE-GOVT DEPT

MEXICO
ALFONSO NOVOA NOVOA, SONORA
BENJAMIN T. VADA-GONZALEZ
CARLOS RAMON VEGA COTA, SONORA
DANIEL ARMANDO GOVEA, CORPRATIVO PLUS PARA LA PRESTACION, JALISCO
JORGE PICAZO-SOSA
JUAN MIGUEL ARIAS SOTO, SONORA
MANUEL EMILIO HOYOS DIAZ, SONORA
MANUEL EMILIO HOYOS SOTELO, SONORA
MARIO GONZALEZ-GAMEZ, CTY
PERLA GARCIA-ALCOCER, NICB, DF

NETHERLANDS
A. H. VERHOEVEN
A. HAEN, INTERPOLIS
A. J. van der LEE
ANDRE' J. de PAAUW
BOB SPRINGVLOED
CORNELIS FEENSTRA, NATIONAL POLICE AGENCY - CRI
DAAN VAN WIJCK, NATIONALE NEDERLANDEN ING GROUP
DICK SNATERSE, POLITIE REGIO ROTTERDAM
DIRK PELLIKAAN, REGIO POLITIE ROTTERDAM - RIJNMOND
EVELINE KLAASSEN, POLICE ROTTERDAM
GERARD W.M. VAN WARMERDAM
GERRIT WALGEMOET, ISB 4 EUROP
GOOS H. KROEZE, NATIONALE NEDERLANDEN ING GROUP
H.J.S.M. VAN OOSTERBOSCH, SCHADEBUREAU O & O NEDERLAND BV
HARRY van BREE, STICHTING VAR
HEROLD BRINKMAN, ZURICH INS
J. A. van PELT, AEGON VERZEKERINGEN
J. W. KOUDIJS, DETECTIVE RECHERCHEBUREAU ALKRIS
J.C.B. HANS KOOIJMAN
JOHANNES KOK, REGIO POLITIE ROTTERDAM - RIJNMOND
JOHN P.B. VAN WATERSCHOOT, RIVER POLICE ROTTERDAM RIJNMOND
JOOP ROOS
KEES PETTER, KONINKLIJKE MARECHAUSSEE, SCHIPHOL
LAMMECHIENA VAN WIJK, REGIO POLITIE ROTTERDAM - RIJNMOND
M. M.J. WETTER
MATTHEUS J. KALJOUW
PIET J. VROLIJK
RENE' B.G. ENGELEN

RENE VAN DUIN, POLICE ROTTERDAM
ROBERT J. GERRITSEN
RUUD van der VEKEN
TINO KEMPF, DUTCH REGISTRATION AUTHORITIES
TJIP A. KOOPMANS

NEW ZEALAND
MARK A. GIBSON, NEW ZEALAND POLICE, NZ
PETER RUDOLF HENTSCHEL

NORTHERN IRELAND
ROBERT V. GRIBBEN

NORWAY
ERIK HAGELSTEEN VIK, FNH NORWEGIAN FINANCIAL
   SERVICES ASSN
NILS K. BREKKE, GJENSIDIGE NOR INS
OLAV PAUL FJAELBERG, GJENSIDIGE NOR INS
RONALD ERIKSEN, IF SKADEFORSIKRING NUF
SVEIN JAKOBSEN, VESTA FORSIKRING AS
THOR BORGE, IF SKADEFORSIKRING NUF

PHILIPPINES
JOSE ERWIN T. VILLACORTE

POLAND
A. MICHAEL MIODUSZEWSKI, CAR INVESTIGATION
   OFFICE
ADAM MIODUSZEWSKI, CAR INVESTIGATION OFFICE
DOROTHY PIETKA, CAR INVESTIGATION OFFICE
KAROL A. BELKA, KBI - WARSAW
MARIUSZ PERENC

PORTUGAL
PAULO G.A.V. CRAVEIRO, ARGOS PORTUGAL

PUERTO RICO
CHARLES S. DeFRANCE

SCOTLAND
ANDREW BOAG HACKETT
ANDREW DOUGLAS KAYE, FIFE
DAVID CRAWFORD
DOUGLAS REID
GARY GALLACHER, STRATHCLYDE POLICE
GRAHAM LINDSAY MURRAY, DUMFRIES &
   GALCOWAY CONSTABULARY
IAIN DAVIS MCKINLAY
IAIN DAVIS MCKINLAY
IAIN DAVIS MCKINLAY, GLASGOW
IAN C. KERR
JOHN B. BLACK, J. B. INVESTIGATIONS
JOHN H. LEITCH, ENQUIRY SERVICES SCOTLAND
KEITH MALCOLMSON, STRATHCLYDE POLICE

SLOVAK REPUBLIC
RADKO VODA, OLYMPO CONTROLS Ltd
ROBERT ZRUBAK, IRIS SLOVAKIA

SOUTH AFRICA
ALBERT E. PIATER, CP CLAIMS ADJUSTERS, FREE
   STATE
ANDRE' SMIT, ESTRN CAPE
CARL S. VAN ZYL, TRACKER NETWORK, GAUTENG
CLEMENT OLIVIER, TRACKER NETWORK,
   JOHANNESBU
D J SWART, TRACKER NETWORK, GAUTENG
D S BOOYSEN, KWAZUL
DANIEL T. NEL, GAUTENG
ERIC HAYNES, THE KEMPSON GROUP, EAST CAPE
FRANCOIS KRUGER, KRUGER & ASSOCIATES,
   GAUTENG
I. J. SCHEEPERS, TRACKER NETWORK, NO PROVINC
J. G. SCHEEPERS, TRACKER NETWORK, NO
   PROVINC
JACQUES MULLER, TRACKER NETWORK
JOSE' RIBEIRO, EASTERN PR
KOBUS DU PREEZ, THE KEMPSTON GROUP, EAST
   CAPE
LEON BRAND, TRACKER NETWORK, RSA MPUMAL
M. H. ODENDAL, GAUTENG
N. A. POTGIETER, TRACKER NETWORK, CAPE TOWN
PAUL MEYER, GAUTENG
PIERRE B. de CLERK, TRACKER NETWORK,
   JOHANNESBU
R J BEZUIDENHOUT, TRACKER NETWORK
R. COETZEE, TRACKER NETWORK, JOHANNESBU
RON BARRIE, NISSAN , GAUTENG

SPAIN
JOSE MANUEL CARCANO, INSTITUTO DE
   INVESTIGACION VEHICULOS
JOSE' ANTONIO MORENO MOYA, GUARDIA CIVIL-
   POLICIA AMBITO ESTATAL
JUAN C. SOBRINO, ARGOS SPAIN
MICHAEL L. LINARES
MIGUEL ALVAREZ EXPOSITO, GUARDIA CIVIL-
   POLICIA AMBITO ESTATAL

SWEDEN
ANDERS GUSTAFSON, LANSFORSAKRINGAR WASA
BENGT GUSTAFSSON
CARL-GOREN CARLSSON, LARMTJANST AB
CHRISTER BERGLUND
CHRISTER HALLESTRAND, FOLKSAM INS INV
CLAES CAROLI, TRYGG-HANSA
DAN OHLSSON
DAVID ANDERSSON, SAAB AUTOMOBILE AB
GERT-OVE ANDERSSON
GORAN JURLAND, SPECIAI INVESTIGATION IF INSUR-
   ANCE
GORAN KELLNER, LARMTJANST AB
JERKER SKOLDEFALK
JOEL LUND, FOLKSAM INS INV
LEIF BJORKLUND, LARMTJANST AB
MATS CARLSSON
PER NORSTROM
ROLF LEWIJN
STEFAN SKOGLUND
THOMAS ULFSTEDT, FOLKSAM INS INV
TORBJORN SERRANDER, STOCKHOLM COUNTY
   POLICE
TORE BJORKMAN, LARMTJANST AB

SWITZERLAND
ADRIANO Di LALLO
DANIEL SENN, DETEKTIVBUREAU
DANIEL ZOLLINGER
DIETER SIEGRIST, HELVETIA PATRIA ASSURANCES
FRANCOIS DI FRISCO, ELVIA
MARC STAUFFER, PHENIX ASSURANCES-FRAUD IN-
   VESTIGATIONS
PASCAL FOURNIER
ROGER MAZENAUER, HELVETIA PATRIA ASSUR-
   ANCES

UNITED KINGDOM
ALAN ALDRIDGE, HERTS
ALAN CHRISTIAN HILTON, W YORKSHIR
ALISON BURGESS, FRAUD INVESTIGATION
ANDREW JAMES LONGSDEN, LANCS
ANTHONY B. ARNOLD, KENT
ANTHONY GREEN, KENT
ANTHONY J. WELLING, DERBYSHIRE
ANTHONY P. WAPPNER, OXON
BARRY CAWDELL, SALOP
BARRY HANCOCK, B R INTERNATIONAL, LTD, E/SUS-
   SEX
BOB RADFORD
BOYD JEREMY HOWELLS, WEST MIDLANDS POLICE,
   WEST MIDS
BRIAN J. GLEDHILL
BRIAN WARD, HERTS
BRIAN WHITTAKER, KENT
BRUCE BICKERDIKE
BRYAN KING-WILLIAMS
BRYAN SHEPPARD, AVON & SOMERSET CONST,
   AVON
CHRISTOPHER A. LORDAN
CHRISTOPHER BUNDOCK
CHRISTOPHER CHARLES DALTON, APAK GROUP
   PLC, HERTFORDSH
CLIVE CROSS, E YORKS
COLIN STUART WILSON, ESSEX
DAVID A. BELL, SECURED BY DESIGN
DAVID E. DOUCH, WILTSHIRE
DAVID F. RYAN, LONDON
DAVID G. BENSON, KENT
DAVID J. de la COUR
DAVID MOORE
DAVID S. OUICK, BRITISH CREDIT TRUST LTD
DENNIS W. LAVERS
DONALD J. CARSLEY
DOUGLAS CHARLES LYND, KENT COUNTY CON-
   STABULARY, KENT
EDWARD SPITZER, ENTERPRISE RENT-A-CAR, SUR-
   REY
EDWARD YOUNG, NORTHUMBER
FRANK KEDDLE
FRANK WILSON, DEVON
GARY DIXON, HERTS
GARY J. RUSSELL
GAVIN ROBERTSON, ESSEX
GEORGE SCAMMELL, HMS INVESTIGATIQNS
GERALD P. CAIN, MILLER FTM, LTD
GERALD T. POPE, BEDS
GLEN ROBERT HILL, HERTS
GRAHAM GEORGE BANKS, ESSEX
GRAHAM HATFIELD, KENT COUNTY CONSTABULARY,
   KENT
GRAHAM J. BIRD
GRANT A. BIRD, ESSEX () PQLICE- STOLEN VEH,
   ESSEX
HENRY COWDRY, JAGUAR CARS LTD, COVENTRY
IAN FAIRLEY
IAN LAURANCE PLAYLE, SUFFOLK
JAMES G. BROWN
JAMES G. FRY, DATATAG ID LIMITED

JEFFREY D. MARSHALL
JEREMY WORTHINGTON, SECURED BY DESIGN LTD
JERRY OAKES, WILTSHIRE POLICE, WILTSHIRE
JERRY O'BRIEN
JIM McNULTY
JOHN BALDOCK, BERKSHIRE
JOHN C. HOPE, NATIONWIDE INV GROUP
JOHN FOULKES, J. FOULKES & SONS
JOHN FRANCIS RUDDEN, KENT
JOHN HANCHETT, J.A. HANCHETT & ASSOC.
JOHN NEAVERSON, NOTTINGHAM
JOHN P. BATTEN
JOHN R. PENN, SURREY
JOHN R. SMALLBONE, HAMPS
JOHN S. RUSSELL
JOSEPH F. LENIHAN
KARL HAMILTON, METROPOLITAN POLICE SERVICE
KEITH J. HOPE, KENT
KENNETH HOWARD, OXON
KEVIN A HOWELLS
KEVIN BARRETT, KENT
LEE RADLEY, HIGHWAY INSURANCE, SUFFOLK
LINDA MAYNE, ALPHA RESPONSE
LYALL P.N. CORY, BMW (GB) Ltd, BERKS
MALCOLM FINCH
MALCOLM KYLE, TYNE&WEAR
MARK ALFREDO BRAHAM, KENT
MARK J.C. JONES, W SUSSEX
MARK JOHNSON, APAK GROUP, BRISTOL
MARK KEWLEY, CLEVELAND POLICE - OCU
MARTIN BRASSELL, HPI, WILTS
MARTIN GILL
MARTIN J. KEY, CAMBS
MARTYN C. RANDLE, MTR INS REPAIR RESEARCH
   CTRE
MASOOD ALI RAI, BIRMINGHAM
MICHAEL A. OUAYLE
MICHAEL ENGEL, WEST SUSSE
MICHAEL HINCHLIFFE
MICHAEL J. CARTER, ESSEX
MICHAEL J. HARVEY
MIKE COWAN, THAMES VALLEY POLICE
NEIL FOX, CLEVELAND POLICE - OCU
NEIL LESLIE LONGSDEN, RTA INVESTIGATIONS,
   LANCS
NICHOLAS A. MAYELL
NICK SUMMERS
NICOLA OWEN, METROPOLITAN POLICE SERVICE
NIGEL R. BARTER, WORCS
PAUL DUNWELL, BRISTOL
PAUL J. COOKE, KENT
PAUL KENYON, KENYON INVESTIGATIVE SERVICE,
   LANCS
PAUL W. HEDGES, STH WALES
PAUL WILLIAM DYER, E SUSSEX
PETER C. GATFIELD
PETER D. SCOTT, HERTFORDSHIRE CONSTABULARY
PETER FREDERICK WEBSTER, CLEVELAND
PETER G. HYDE, SURREY
PETER GEORGE BOLTON
PETER J. RUSSELL
PETER JOHN WELLING
PETER RANDHAWA
PETER STANLEY, SECURI-GUARD LTD, DEVON
PETER TAYLOR, MILLER FTM, LTD
PHILIP ANTHONY WALSH, STH GLOS
PHILIP EDGERLEY
PHILIP J. ROBINSON, HAMPSHIRE
PHILIP LOWE
PHILLIP SLIGHT
RICHARD BROOMFIELD, CAMBSHIRE
ROBERT BARRY CALKIN, IPSWICH
ROBERT BUNNEY, DEVON & CORNWALL CONSTABU-
   LARY, DEVON
ROBERT G. WELCH, WST SUSSEX
ROBERT W. HARDING
ROBIN J. NELSON, ALPHA RESPONSE LTD, KENT
ROGER J. ELLIOTT
ROGER K. MOSS
RONALD E. HARRIS
S. LENNEY, POLICE STATION, KENT
SHAUN CREED, KENT COUNTY CONSTABULARY,
   KENT
SIMON BILBIE, WARWICKSHIRE POLICE TRAFFIC INV
   UNIT
SIMON BROWN, KENT
SIMON ERIC GORDON, C.D.A. LEGAL SERVICES LTD,
   BUCKS
SIMON F. WHITTAKER
SIMON JOHN MASTERSON, KENT
STEFAN STANISLAW JOCHAN, SUFFOLK CONSTABU-
   LARY, SUFFOLK
STEPHEN ALLAN LEE, ALTERNATIVE VEHICLE IN-
   SPECTIONS LTD, ESSEX
STEPHEN FOSTER, AUTOTRAC PLC, WEST SSX
STEPHEN JQWITT, STRANGE, STRANGE &
   GARDNER, BIRMINGHAM
STEVE GAYWOOD, DIRECT LINE INSURANCE, SUR-
   REY

STEVE L. MILLER, WALES
TERRY WINSTON-ROY JONES, SPIRE VEHICLE RE-
   COVERY, BUCKINGHAM
TINA KNOWLES
TOM NAYLOR, BLACK HORSE LTD
TONY PRYOR, NISSAN MOTORS (GB) LTD,
   HERTFORDSH
TONY SIMMS
WILLIAM HOLT
WILLIAM L.N. TRUEMAN, DIRECT LINE GROUP SER-
   VICES, SURREY

UKRAINE
YURIY KAVUN

UNITED ARAB EMIRATES
GEORGE P.K., MILLER INTERNATIONAL, DUBAI
   BRANCH

UNITED STATES OF AMERICA
A. J. MEDINA, TX
A. J. WALSH, TX
A.J ROCKY YANNONE, CERTIFIED SIU SERVICES, NY
ADALBERTO ZAPATA, NY
ADAM C. HAYES, CO
ADAM S. MARAKOVITS, NATIONWIDE INSURANCE, PA
ADRIA GALLAGHER, MA
ADRIAN L. CALLAHAN, TX
AL NORRIS, NICB, MI
AL PATON, MARYLAND STATE POLICE, MD
ALAN D. ORRINGER, ALAN ORRINGER AUTO ENTER-
   PRISES, PA
ALAN E. WYCHE, STATE FARM INS, SC
ALAN FISHER, NY
ALAN HAMMAKER, STATE FARM INS, PA
ALAN J. PFEIFER, CO
ALAN STEWART, STATE FARM INS, MS
ALAN TATE, METRO INVEST/RECOVERY SYSTEMS,
   MA
ALAN WILSON, NY
ALBERT ANDRADA, NEW DPS-MTD, NM
ALBERT B. MASON JR, RICHMOND (VA) P D, VA
ALBERT MARTINEZ, TX
ALBERT MELINO, STATE FARM INS, NY
ALBERT R. FRANCH, NEW STATE POLICE, NM
ALBERTO R. RAVELO, NY
ALDA MARZAN, STATE FARM INS, NJ
ALEX PEREZ, HOLLYWOOD (FL) P D, FL
ALEX PERRY, NY
ALEXANDER A. SOUTOS, PA
ALICE E. MILES, PHILADELPHIA (PA) P D, PA
ALICE TOBIASSEN, SAFETY INS, MA
ALICIA HOLMES, STATE FARM INS, NY
ALLEN CARPENTER, LA
ALLEN R. ROBERTS, MD
ALLISON SKINNER, CA
ALQUIMIDES ARROYO, NY
ALTON R. TYNDALL Jr., DURHAM (NC) P D, NC
ALVIN ICE, STATE FARM INS, OK
ANASTACIO TOROC, Jr, VIRGINIA BEACH (VA) P D, VA
ANDERSON GENE HASS, CHATANOOGA (TN) P D, TN
ANDRE THIBODEAU, GOVERNOR'S A/T STRIKE
   FORCE, MA
ANDRE' BELOTTO, CA
ANDRE' FRANCIS, NY
ANDREA DWYER, STATE FARM INS, OH
ANDREA LINDFORD, SAFECO INS, PA
ANDREW BLETHEN, NY
ANDREW C. HEATH, NC
ANDREW ELMORE, NY
ANDREW M. VIGLUCCI, NIAGARA FALLS (NY) P D, NY
ANDREW McFEELEY, FL
ANDREW PIEZGA, PA
ANDREW S. COHEN, METRO DADE (FL) P D, FL
ANDREW SREBROSKI, MD
ANDREW TERSKI, HERNDON & ASSOC, MI
ANGELA WILLINGHAM, U-HAUL INTERNATIONAL, AZ
ANGELO P. CHIOTA, FL
ANGELO P. POLITO, NY
ANITA PRICE, ROBERT PLAN CORP, NY
ANITA R. HILDERBRAND, MD
ANN WYATT, TX
ANNETTE NAZZARO, GEICO, NY
ANTHONY A. BLACKMAN, FL
ANTHONY ANTONACCI, NY
ANTHONY BOGACZ, HERTZ, CO
ANTHONY E. BULVER, AZ
ANTHONY E. DENNIS, NORTH CAROLINA DMV EN-
   FORCEMENT, NC
ANTHONY FARNETI, NY
ANTHONY J. GONZALO, TAMPA MACHINERY AUC-
   TION, INC., FL
ANTHONY J. HENRY, NY
ANTHONY J. MARTIN, Jr, NEW JERSEY STATE POLICE,
   NJ
ANTHONY K. DAVIS, NC
ANTHONY L. SIERRA, PIMA CO (AZ) S O, AZ
ANTHONY PEREZ, NY
ANTHONY R. CENTRONE, ROBERT PLAN CORP, NY

ANTHONY SANTARE, EBS CONSULTANTS LTD, NY
ANTHONY T. SAPIT, IL
ANTONIA RODRIGUEZ, TX ATPA, TX
ANTONIO MONTEIRO, NORTH ASTERN TECHNICAL SERVICE, MA
ANTONIO SANCHEZ, TX
ARLEEN CLAYTON, STATE FARM INS, MI
ARMAND CHOATE, MAINE - DMV, ME
ARMANDO FUENTES, TX
ART HACKETT, NJ
ART M. HOHMAN, OH
ARTHUR F. CAIN, PA
ARTHUR J. ETRINGER, NY
ARTHUR MARCHISELLI, NY
ARTHUR MARTIN, CA
ARTHUR R. BARRERA, TEXAS DPS, TX
ARTHUR T. THIBODEAUX, GEICO, LA
ARTURO SALAS, BUFFALO (NY) P D, NY
ARVIN D. TURNER, ALLIED INS, CA
AUDIE H. MURPHY, BRETHREN MUTUAL INS, MD
AUGUSTUS D. STANSBURY, GEICO, LA
AUSTIN GARRETT, TN
BARBARA D. STOTT, US CUSTOMS, VA
BARBARA KENT, STATE FARM INS, WV
BARBRA FERSTER, PA
BARNET FAGEL, INTERTRACK TRACKING, IL
BARRY B. MILAM, NC
BARRY BARBER, BALTIMORE CO (MD) P D, MD
BARRY I. BECK, DELAWARE DMV, DE
BARRY K. WHITE, MANHEIM AUTO AUCTION, PA
BARRY L. SHERMAN, MIDDLESEX TWNSP (PA) P D, PA
BARRY T. RILEY, NJ
BARRY V. BROWN, GREENVILLE CO (SC) S O, SC
BECKY L. WHITMAN, SC
BELINDA TAYLOR, ILLINOIS STATE POLICE, IL
BEN SPOLARICH, CA
BENITA L. SHARPE, STATE FARM INS, IL
BENJAMIN DY, PROGRESSIVE INS, WA
BENJAMIN FRITTS, AUTO RECOVERY SYSTEMS, NY
BENJAMIN P. REMAK, STATE FARM INS, WA
BERNARD E. SPANGLER JR., ZURICH NA, MD
BERNARD I. WENTZ, STATE FARM INS, PA
BERNARD J. RILEY, MI
BERNARD L. TURNER, UT
BERRIE BOREN, STATE FARM INS, CA
BERT F. SO, NV
BETH ROHR, CNH, WI
BETTY ANN MOJADDIDI, NICB, VA
BETTY RANES, VIRGINIA DMV, VA
BIENENIDO MARTINEZ, NY
BILL A. BEALL, TX
BILL BRADWAY, AZ
BILL COOPER, TARRANT CO (TX) ATTF, TX
BILL HANSEN, MARICOPA CO (AZ) S O, AZ
BILL HESSE, SC
BILL PETERS, SAN MATEO CO (CA) VEH THEFT TF, CA
BILL REHM, NM
BILL SOMERS, ALLSTATE INS, CT
BILL THOMPSON, FARMERS INS, CA
BILLIE M. CRAWFORD, AL
BILLY C. HOOD, SMYRNA (GA) P D, GA
BLAINE ALLMON, MARICOPA CO (AZ) S O, AZ
BLAINE TELLIS, DES MOINES (IA) P D, IA
BOB BURKE, CALIFORNIA HWY PATROL, CA
BOB COOPER, NJ
BOB HAGAN, FARMERS INSURANCE GROUP, TX
BOB HARSHAW, OSBI, OK
BOB HOLMES, NC
BOBBY G. OWENS, NICB, AZ
BOBBY K. RAKES, VIRGINIA STATE POLICE, VA
BOBBY L. STATON, NICB, OK
BOBBY OWENS, NICB, AZ
BOBBY R. SMITH, TN
BONNIE M PIKE, GA
BRAD ANDERSON, LANCASTER (PA) P D, PA
BRAD GREINER, NICB, VT
BRAD HARDIN, TX
BRAD JEFFERIS, STATE FARM INS, CA
BRADEN BAZILUS, UNELKO SECURITY SYSTEMS, AZ
BRADLEY M. MINGER, FAYETTE CO (IA) S O, IA
BRADLEY S. KEEFER, FT WORTH (TX) P D, TX
BRANDON PARKER, NORTHERN ILLINOIS ATTF, IL
BRANDY L. TORQUATO, BREVARD CO (FL) S O, FL
BRANT BECK, STATE FARM INS, VA
BRENDA CULLY, VA
BRENDAN BYRON, NY
BRENDAN R. MAGUFFIN, NY
BRENDHAN B. HARRIS, PROGRESSIVE INS, ME
BRENT DuPONT, EDEN PRAIRIE (MN) P D, MN
BRENT J. BATES, PORTLAND (OR) P B, OR
BRENT K. FIGUEIRA, EUCLID (OH) P D, OH
BRENT L. NELSON, SD
BRENT R. RICHTER, MN
BRENT R. SELLS, MONTANA MVD-INV & ENF UNIT, MT

BRET CHARLES TEMPLIN, BAJA RECOVERY, CA
BRETT E. KELLEY, PROGRESSIVE INS, FL
BRIAN A. BLOME', AMERICAN HONDA MTR CO, CA
BRIAN A. KRUSZKA, PA
BRIAN BRENNAN, MD
BRIAN C. MICHELIN, MI
BRIAN C. WINANT, NY
BRIAN CARPENTER, LEXINGTON FAYETTE CO (KY) P D, KY
BRIAN D. EVANS, TX
BRIAN E. McALLISTER, NY
BRIAN FITZPATRICK, GA
BRIAN G. OSTERHOLT, CA
BRIAN GUNDERSON, EAGAN (WI) P D, WI
BRIAN J. BOLCHOZ, MT PLEASANT (SC) P D, SC
BRIAN K. DIMETROSKY, NJ
BRIAN KELLY, PA
BRIAN KITTRELL, MS
BRIAN P. CAPUTO, NY
BRIAN SALATA, PINAL CO (AZ) ATTORNEY, AZ
BRIAN TROUT, ARIZONA DPS, AZ
BRIAN YORI, LOS ANGELES (CA) P D, CA
BRIGIT HARTZ, NEW DPS-MTD, NM
BRODIE M. MACK, Jr, NY
BRUCE A LESLIE, ZURICH, U S, NY
BRUCE A. MADISON, NE
BRUCE BODENSTEIN, MARK-N-GARD, INC, NC
BRUCE C. SUMNER, NJ
BRUCE D. McCLURG, MANHEIM AUTO AUCTION, PA
BRUCE E. HULL, MA
BRUCE E. HURLEY, MAINE - DMV, ME
BRUCE ELLISON, WAYNE CO (MI) AIRPORT P D, MI
BRUCE J. FLAUGHER, MD
BRUCE McDONALD, MI
BRUCE McKINLEY, DEALER SECURITY SOLUTIONS, CA
BRUCE R. BONNER, CONNECTICUT STATE POLICE, CT
BRUCE ROGERS, ORANGE CO (CA) DA'S OFF, CA
BRUCE SAVILLE, PA
BRUCE SPENCE, TX
BRUCE TISCHOFER, CT
BRYAN E. REED, INDIANAPOLIS (IN) P D, IN
BRYAN JACKSON, PHILADELPHIA (PA) PD, PA
BRYAN R. GALKE, STATE FARM INS, NY
BRYAN S. SITTON, NC
BRYAN TYITYE, MI
BUCKY BARLOW, FAIRFAX COUNTY (VA) POLICE, VA
BUD HOOD, ORANGE CO (CA) S O, CA
BURLEIGH LOCKLAR, TEXAS DPS, TX
BURLEY COPELAND, ARIZONA DPS, AZ
BURLEY M. COPELAND, ARIZONA DPS, AZ
BYRON C. DYER, AMERICAN INTL GROUP, NY
C. C. BENSON, TX
C. W. McADAMS, NC
CAL RIX, MI
CALIXTO BULNES, NY
CALVIN A. DEYERMOND, LAWRENCE (MA) P D, MA
CALVIN McKINNEY, VA
CARL C. CARRICO III, CHRYSLER FINANCIAL, MO
CARL E. ARNETT, MICHIGAN STATE POLICE, MI
CARL J. DELROSARIO, NY
CARL J. DuFOUR, AVAYELLES PARISH (LA) S O, LA
CARL L. BOOMHOWER, SANDY (OR) P D, OR
CARL LANGE, LANGE TECHNICAL SERVICES, NY
CARL N. CLIFFORD, DAYTONA AUTO AUCTION, FL
CARL S. STOWELL, NY
CARL WADDELL, ORANGE CO (CA) ATTF, CA
CARLA CHAMBERS, STATE FARM INS, CA
CARLA K. SCOUTEN, STATE FARM INS, VA
CARLECTON PETERSON, ST LOUIS CO (MO) P D, MO
CARLITA BALLARD, NHTSA - DEPT OF TRANSPORTATION, DC
CARLO D. MARZOCCA, CA
CARLO W. PETR, NY
CARLOS I. FEBO, NY
CARLOS LEE, PROGRESSIVE INS, NV
CARMEN SWANSON, AZ
CAROL FORSYTH, AVIS, IL
CAROL J. RIPOLI, NJ
CAROL KOSTELNIK, VT
CAROL S. FARRIS, STATE FARM INS, VA
CAROL VANNATTER, CA
CAROLE ACUNTO, CHASE COMMUNICATIONS, NY
CAROLYN CHALECKI, STATE FARM INS, CA
CARTHEL W. WILLIAMS, TX
CATHERINE McLELLAN, STATE FARM INS, WA
CECIL SMITH, CALIFORNIA HWY PATROL, CA
CELSO VILLARREAL II, COASTAL BEND ATTF, TX
CHAD BLACK, STATE FARM INS, MD
CHAD STEPHEN KILBY, OK
CHALOUEY NEWT SHOUP, MICHIGAN STATE POLICE, MI
CHARLES A. CHRISLEY, Jr, SC
CHARLES A. MINCH, NY
CHARLES A. NICASTRO, FL
CHARLES C. MOLLA, ST LOUIS CO (MO) P D, MO
CHARLES CALDWELL, TX
CHARLES D. BANKS, FL

CHARLES D. BISHOP, NJ
CHARLES DALEY, GOVERNORS AUTO THEFT STRIKE FORCE, MA
CHARLES DICKERSON, EMC INS, IA
CHARLES E. LEE Jr., WARM SPRINGS (GA) POLICE DEPT, GA
CHARLES E. MALSAN, Jr, WEST HARTFORD (CT) P D, CT
CHARLES E. PADGETT, JR, INDIANA STATE POLICE, IN
CHARLES E. WALTER, TX
CHARLES F. KEE, Jr, NY
CHARLES G. WILLIAMS, KEMPER INS, IL
CHARLES GUYTON, ROCK HILL (SC) P D, SC
CHARLES J. AUGUSTINE, SECURITY SERVICES CTR, OH
CHARLES J. PAKULIS, LEE CO (FL) S O, FL
CHARLES KELLY, CT
CHARLES KNAPP, ARIZONA VEHICLE THEFT TASK FORCE, AZ
CHARLES L. ELINGBURG, NORTH CAROLINA DMV ENFORCEMENT, NC
CHARLES MOSS, CA
CHARLES NELSON CAVEY, VA
CHARLES P. DUNCAN, FL
CHARLES R. DALT, BOSTON (MA) P D, MA
CHARLES R. PENNEY, MONTGOMERY CO (MD) P D, MD
CHARLES R. WARD, MD
CHARLES REAGLE, TX
CHARLES ROSSER, TX
CHARLES T. MEADE, NY
CHARLES W. BURR, SC
CHARLES WENDORFF, FL
CHARLIE COX, FL
CHARMAYA SMITH, AMERICAN NATIONAL INS, MO
CHERYL D. REESE, WI
CHERYL R. ZOFKIE, IL
CHIP BAYLES, TULSA (OK) P D, OK
CHRIS A. BIMONTE, METRO DADE (FL) P D, FL
CHRIS A. McKINNEY, FBI, DC
CHRIS A. RATHBUN, CA
CHRIS B. MOORE, AL
CHRIS BLEVINS, YORK CO (SC) S O, SC
CHRIS BRIGGS, WA
CHRIS DAVIS, STATE FARM INS, MI
CHRIS DENGELES, ARLINGTON CO (VA) P D, VA
CHRIS HEISER, BERGEN CO (NJ) PROSECUTOR'S OFF, NJ
CHRIS KURSCHNER, NJ
CHRIS MAGYAR, GEICO, MI
CHRIS MAUNTZ, STATE FARM INS, CA
CHRIS POOL, STATE FARM INS, KS
CHRIS ROWLAND, TRAVIS CO (TX) S D, TX
CHRIS S. BRIDGES, OK
CHRIS SPRANGER, STATE FARM INS, DC
CHRISTI CHARLTON, STATE FARM INS, OH
CHRISTINE MANGAN, PA
CHRISTOPHER A. FRIEDMAN, NY
CHRISTOPHER A. MILLER, NY
CHRISTOPHER B. CONNOLLY, NY
CHRISTOPHER C. CANASKI, LA
CHRISTOPHER CALI, IL
CHRISTOPHER COLE, MI
CHRISTOPHER D. GREENE, EMC INS, RI
CHRISTOPHER GAHN, NY
CHRISTOPHER J. BARBER, MD
CHRISTOPHER J. BLOCK, IL
CHRISTOPHER J. LEACH, TX
CHRISTOPHER J. MALEK, TX
CHRISTOPHER J. O'CONNOR, NY
CHRISTOPHER L. HUBBARD, HI
CHRISTOPHER L. HUDGENS, OK
CHRISTOPHER M. ERB, LANCASTER (PA) P D, PA
CHRISTOPHER M. ZERMENO, TX
CHRISTOPHER PALAZZO, NY
CHRISTOPHER T. McDONALD, MD
CHUCK PINSKA, MN
CHUCK WRIGHT, ARIZONA DPS, AZ
CINDI A. BURKEWITZ, AZ
CINDY J. COHN, DURHAM (NC) P D, NC
CLARENCE E. ROBERTSON, HAYES LEASING CO, INC, CT
CLARENCE O. BRICKEY, VA
CLARK W. BAKER, SD
CLAUDE JACK JACKSON, CINCINNATI INS, OH
CLAUDIA PELTON, STATE FARM INS, MI
CLAYTON DAVIS, HOWARD CO (MD) P D, MD
CLEO BATTON, GA
CLEVE FRANKLIN, GEICO DIRECT, LA
CLIFF BABBITT, TEXAS D P S, TX
CLIFF BIEDER, NY
CLIFF CHEZUM, WA
CLIFF McCRARY, WINDSOR EOUITY GROUP, TX
CLIFFORD R. GRAY, CA
CLINT VARNELL, NEW STATE POLICE, NM
CLYDE CONKLIN JR., NICB, FL
COLIN V. PATTERSON, NY
COLLEEN CASSIDY, NICB, MA

COLLEEN P. RICHARTS, MD
CONLEY A. RAY, MECHANICAL EVALUATION, MI
CONNIE M. GEARHART, ARIZONA MVD, AZ
CONRAD D. GOLEMBA, MI
CORBY MARSHALL, STATE FARM INS, NE
CRAIG D. FARRA, STATE FARM INS, PA
CRAIG D. MILLER, VILLAGE OF PEWAUKEE (WI) P D, WI
CRAIG DUNCAN, MD
CRAIG M. BEEK, DEERE & CO, IL
CRAIG OLSON, WASAHINGTON CO (MN) S O, MN
CRAIG P LONG, IL
CRAIG R. BENES, VIN VERIFIER PRODUCTS, CA
CRAIG T. HINTZE, NY
CRAIG VAN ATTA, GEICO, GA
CRAIG W. HAMBLIN, NJ
CRAIG WALKUP, WESTFIELD COMPANIES, OH
CURTIS A. GREGORY, IL
CURTIS STODDARD, UTAH MOTOR VEHICLE ENF, UT
D. A. BURDETTE, JR., DIVERSIFIED INVESTMENTS, SC
D. DARLENE GREENY, STATE FARM INS, VA
D. DENISE MAJOR, KILLEEN (TX) P D, TX
D.T. RUSTY RUSSELL, SAINT LUCIE CO (FL) S O, FL
DALE GESNER, NICB, OR
DALE MACE, AZ
DALE R. BINKERT, TX
DALE R. FIELDS, MD
DAN BEALL, BEALL INV, CA
DAN BOHNET, EPHRATA PD, WA
DAN BROWN, PRUDENTIAL P & C, TX
DAN MOSOUERA, CORAL GABLES (FL) P D, FL
DAN R. ROGERS, NY
DAN S. JUSTUS, MO
DAN WINSLOW, AZ
DAN ZIEBER, SAN DIEGO ADJUSTERS, CA
DANA PARKER, GRETNA (LA) P D, LA
DANA SCIAVICCO, ELECTROGUARD, LLC, GA
DANA W. KALLAHAN, VT
DANA WICKLAND, TEXAS DPS, TX
DANE L. WOOD, NICB, UT
DANIEL A. PISCULLI, NY
DANIEL A. YOUNG, SAN MATEO CO (CA) VEH THEFT TF, CA
DANIEL BRACHT, GALVESTON CO (TX) AUTO CRIMES, TX
DANIEL BRODNICK, RIVERSIDE (OH) P D, OH
DANIEL BROWN, NIAGARA CO (NY) S D, NY
DANIEL CANNELL, KEMPER INS, NJ
DANIEL DEERE, EXECUTIVE INV. BUREAU, INC., MD
DANIEL ENGLERT, PHILADELPHIA (PA) P D, PA
DANIEL F. RYAN, CA
DANIEL HALLIDAY, ADESA IMPACT, NH
DANIEL I. METZGER, TORRANCE (CA) P D, CA
DANIEL J. BARRETT, NY
DANIEL J. COTTER, NY
DANIEL J. GLATZ, NY
DANIEL J. HURLEY, Sr, LO/JACK, IL
DANIEL J. STRAUB, WASHINGTON DC METRO P D, DC
DANIEL JACKSON, IL
DANIEL M. BROGDON, AUTO CLUB of S. CALIFORNIA, CA
DANIEL M. MILLER, NY
DANIEL M. WEBBER, HARRISBURG (PA) BUREAU OF POLICE, PA
DANIEL MORAN, NY
DANIEL NATHAN DOWNS, ALLSTATE INS, OK
DANIEL P. GREEN, MI
DANIEL P. JAYKEL, OH
DANIEL P. LEE, STATE FARM INS, WA
DANIEL P. WELLS, GOVERNOR'S A/T STRIKE FORCE, MA
DANIEL PEARSON, TARRANT CO (TX) ATTF, TX
DANIEL R. ANDERSON, LA
DANIEL R. LOCATELLI, CA
DANIEL R. WRIGHT, TN
DANIEL S. BYBEE, STATE FARM INS, OH
DANIEL S. SMITH, JR, FL
DANIEL STEIN, OH
DANIEL W. BESSECK, MD
DANIEL W. LOWRANCE, NC
DANNY C. BLACKBURN, SELECTIVE INS, VA
DANNY McGLOTHLIN, CA
DANNY W. COMPTON, BLACKSBURG (VA) P D, VA
DARREL R. CONN, TX
DARRELL ADAMS, GALVESTON CO (TX) AUTO CRIMES, TX
DARRELL L. EHLERS, WA
DARRELL L. STRIPLING, DOLLAR RENT-A-CAR SYS, TX
DARRELL M. SMITH, STATE FARM INS, OH
DARRELL WILSON, PLANT CITY (FL) P D, FL
DARREYL R. WALKER, SC
DARRIN T. GRONEL, WASHINGTON STATE PATROL, WA
DARRYL C. HARRIS, NEW YORK STATE POLICE, NY
DARRYL NORRIS, TX
DAVE E. HUNT SR., NATIONWIDE INS, CT

DAVE McKEEHEN, STATE FARM INS, WA
DAVE PETRELLI, STATE FARM INS, CA
DAVE RITSON, GREAT AMERICAN INS, OH
DAVE SMITH, PHOENIX (AZ) P D, AZ
DAVE TJEPKEMA, MICHIGAN STATE POLICE, MI
DAVE WATSON, AL
DAVID SCOTT OWEN, AZ
DAVID A. ARGENTI, BROWARD CO (FL) S D, FL
DAVID A. BANO, NY
DAVID A. BENTE, MIAMI SPRINGS (FL) P D, FL
DAVID A. DAVIS, FLORIDA HWY PTL, FL
DAVID A. DREW, FL
DAVID A. HOFFER, PHILADELPHIA (PA) P D, PA
DAVID A. SCHAROUN, NY
DAVID A. WEBER, OLATHE (KS) P D, KS
DAVID AZUR, MD
DAVID B. GORDON, NY
DAVID B. HILL, ALLSTATE INS, CT
DAVID BRONSTEIN, BERNSTEIN AND CHACKMAN, P A, FL
DAVID C. DUNKELBERGER, INDIANA INS, OH
DAVID C. MACE, SR., IL
DAVID C. MacGILLIS, FL DEPT ENVIRONMENTAL PROTECTION, FL
DAVID CANDELARIA, NEW STATE POLICE, NM
DAVID COTTEY, CA
DAVID D. RICE, AZ
DAVID D. SCHWEBE, BADGERLAND AUTO RECOVERY, WI
DAVID DeWALLACE, PROGRESSIVE INS, CT
DAVID E. MARSH, WV
DAVID E. MCCAMLEY, GEICO, VA
DAVID F. ELLER, GA
DAVID FISHER, PENNSYLVANIA STATE POLICE, PA
DAVID G. GRAM, PASADENA (TX) P D, TX
DAVID G. HUMESTON, NY
DAVID G. OBAL, MONTGOMERY CO (MD) P D, MD
DAVID G. SCHWARTZKOPF, NICB, AZ
DAVID GIBSON, TX
DAVID H. DEMPSEY, AUTO CLUB -AAA-SIU, CA
DAVID HENRY, NY
DAVID HIRSCH, LIBERTY MUTUAL INS, FL
DAVID HOLLINGSHEAD, STATE FARM INS, KS
DAVID J. CHRISTIANA, CT REG AUTO THEFT TASK FORCE, CT
DAVID J. FLADTEN, WALWORTH CO (WI) S O, WI
DAVID J. GATZ, MICHIGAN STATE POLICE, MI
DAVID J. SHILLINGFORD, NATIONAL EQUIPMENT REGISTER, NY
DAVID J. WALSH, NY
DAVID KLOS, PROGRESSIVE INS, CO
DAVID L. COHEN, NJ
DAVID L. DICKERSON, EAST TEXAS ATTF, TX
DAVID L. WEISER JR, LANCASTER CITY (PA) P D, PA
DAVID M. BECKNER, VIRGINIA STATE POLICE, VA
DAVID M. DUDA, STATE FARM INS, NY
DAVID M. ECKLUND, FT LAUDERDALE (FL) P D, FL
DAVID M. HART, FORT COLLINS (CO) P D, CO
DAVID M. MEDLIN, NC
DAVID M. ROONEY, UNITED RENTALS, MD
DAVID M. WALKER, Sr, HINCKLEY (IL) P D, IL
DAVID M. ZOLNA, WEST BLOOMFIELD (MI) P D, MI
DAVID MENDENHALL, TX
DAVID P. CAREY, MONROE CO (FL) SO, FL
DAVID P. EMOND, WA
DAVID P. LINKLETTER, NY
DAVID PAGE, TX
DAVID POSTIFF, STATE FARM INS, CA
DAVID POWELL, GEICO, MI
DAVID R. HICKMAN, TX
DAVID R. MAUSER, MESA (AZ) P D, AZ
DAVID R. McCANN, LA
DAVID R. SALZMAN, CINCINNATI (OH) P D, OH
DAVID RAMOS, Jr, SAN ANTONIO (TX) P D, TX
DAVID REHRIG, FL
DAVID ROCCAFORTE, CA
DAVID SPARKS, US DOT - NHTSA, DC
DAVID T. FAIR, SC
DAVID T. PROEFKE, MI
DAVID T. WITT, NORTH TEXAS AUTO THEFT TF, TX
DAVID TEUSCHER, OK
DAVID THISTLEWOOD, GOVERNORS AUTO THEFT STRIKE FORCE, MA
DAVID TURNER, SMITH CO (TX) S D, TX
DAVID TYMRAK, MI
DAVID VAN CLEVE, FARMERS INS, IL
DAVID VERDERESE, LANSING (MI) P D, MI
DAVID W. BUCHANAN, TX
DAVID W. GUILMETTE, MAINE - DMV, ME
DAVID W. LINDH, NATIONWIDE INS, NH
DAVID W. TUCK, ALACHUA CO (FL) S O, FL
DAVID W. WALLACE, TX
DAVID WAYNE MAYBERRY, NC
DAWN KIELY, NY
DAWN PALMIERI, STATE FARM INS, AZ
DEAN CAIN, ALLSTATE INS, OK
DEAN O. HOUSTON, ALAMO INVESTIGATIVE SERVICES, INC., KS
DEB NOONE, STATE FARM INS, PA

DEBORAH A. GEER, NICB, IL
DEBORAH K. PENDERGRASS-LIETO, PROGRESSIVE INS, MD
DEBORAH MAZYCK, DOT - NHTSA, DC
DEBORAH STANFILL, JACKSON (TN) P D, TN
DEBORAH STEVENSON, VA
DEBRA CRAIN, CA
DEDRA N. POWELL, LA
DEE ROSELL, TULSA (OK) P D, OK
DEL SLAVENS, US CUSTOMS, VA
DENISE K. BAUM, MONTANA DEPARTMENT OF JUSTICE, MT
DENNIE HUGGINS, WV
DENNIS A. DELANO Sr., BUFFALO (NY) P D, NY
DENNIS A. MENSCH, FL
DENNIS A. ROSKE, MN
DENNIS BAGOZZI, METROPOLITAN INS, MI
DENNIS J. DAMEK, TX
DENNIS J. FITZPATRICK, NY
DENNIS J. MIGNOGNO, NORTH EASTERN TECHNICAL SERVICES, DE
DENNIS K. KLINE, MI
DENNIS L. MEYER, IL
DENNIS LEGGIO, NY
DENNIS LESSIAK, NICB, CA
DENNIS M. SCHULKINS, STATE FARM INS, IL
DENNIS P. BURGESS, MA
DENNIS R. WEAVER, AR
DENNIS SCHARES, JOHN DEERE GLOBAL VEH COMM, GA
DENNIS TRAMMELL, ALABAMA BUREAU OF INVESTIGATION, AL
DENNIS W. BAKER, GRAND BLANC (MI) P D, MI
DENNIS W. MIDGETTE, JR, VA
DENVER L. BREWSTER, GA
DEREK R. WOODS, BURNS LOCKSMITHS, INC, WA
DEVIN C. JORDAN, HERNDON & ASSOCI, MI
DIANA B. MCGINNES, STATE FARM INS, WA
DIANA M. RUMMEL, CRIME PREVENTION PROGRAM, CA
DIANE A. MANDEVILLE, VIRGINIA STATE POLICE, VA
DIANE JANEDIS, STATE FARM INS, CA
DIANE M. ROBERSON, STATE FARM INS, MI
DIANE SKIRMONT, NICB, IL
DIANNE McGOWAN, FL DEPT HWY SAFETY, FL
DIANNE STUBBS, NY
DIEGO A. URBINA, PR
DILIA CAMACHO, NY
DOMENIC ZAFFINO, PHILADELPHIA (PA) P D, PA
DOMINIC A. D'ONOFRIO, NJ
DOMONIC D. CARO, MI
DON BARTON, MICHIGAN STATE POLICE, MI
DON CAMPOS, SAN ANTONIO (TX0 P D, TX
DON FAIRCLOTH, OSBI, OK
DON G. PERILLO, NY
DON HANRAHAN, STATE FARM INS, NY
DON KESSLER, N A D E - MANHEIM AUCTIONS, NJ
DON L. FRISCH, PROGRESSIVE INS, TX
DON L. GUY, CALIFORNIA HWY PATROL, CA
DON LENHART, FAIRFAX COUNTY (VA) POLICE, VA
DON M. JOHNSON, UT
DON MACINTOSH, PROGRESSIVE INS, OK
DON MARTIN, TEXAS DPS, TX
DON McCASLIN, STATE FARM INS, NY
DON MOLCHAN, ARIZONA VEHICLE THEFT TASK FORCE, AZ
DON R. CAMPBELL, IN
DON STEVENSON, ALEXANDRIA (VA) P D, VA
DON WEEKS, STATE FARM INS, LA
DON WILLSEY, STATE FARM INS, WA
DONA JONES, GA
DONALD A. MINER, CA
DONALD A. SOREL, MA
DONALD A. VAN HOUTTE, MI
DONALD B. LEWIS, CA
DONALD C. CHECKAN, PA
DONALD C. MURTHA, PA
DONALD C. SUMPTER, PA
DONALD CARROLL, KIRKLAND (WA) P D, WA
DONALD COURTHEYN, FL
DONALD DAVID, SAFEWAY INS, LA
DONALD E. DERMA, STATE FARM INS, IL
DONALD G. DOWLESS, NC
DONALD G. TIMKO, CT
DONALD H McCLURE, TEXAS AUTO TITLE, TX
DONALD HOWE, TN
DONALD J. FOSTER, CA
DONALD L. DURBIN, ILLINOIS STATE POLICE, IL
DONALD L. HOWELL, MN
DONALD M McNAIR, SR, BERGEN COUNTY AUTO CRIME, NJ
DONALD M. LUSK, MICHIGAN STATE POLICE, MI
DONALD N. THOMPSON, NATIONWIDE INS, CT
DONALD SINSKI, NY
DONALD T. SCHUG JR., NY
DONALD THOMAS BROWN, LA
DONALD V. HOSEK, STATE FARM INS, IA
DONALD W. ROBERTSON, VA
DONALD W. SWANGER, WAYNESVILLE(NC) P D, NC

DONALD WEBER, FBI, NY
DONNA AUGUSTYNIAK, NJ
DONNA E. PENTON, VIRGINIA STATE POLICE, VA
DONNA J. CONICK, IL
DONNA M. ELAM, INDIANA STATE POLICE, IN
DONNA STEWART, CA
DONNIE G. NICHOLS, TX
DONNIE J. KING, PASADENA (TX) P D, TX
DOUG A. THOMAS, ORANGE CO (CA) ATTF, CA
DOUG L. MAHOE, HERTZ, CA
DOUG MURRAY, NJ
DOUG SHELLEY, NJ
DOUGLAS E. CASH, MD
DOUGLAS F. DUNNAGAN, NC DMV ENFORCEMENT SECTION, NC
DOUGLAS FICK, STATE FARM INS, IL
DOUGLAS G. TATE, KANSAS HWY PATROL, KS
DOUGLAS K. SIMMONS, SIOUX FALLS (SD) P D, SD
DOUGLAS L. CLEMENTS, TX
DOUGLAS M. DEMANGONE, YORK CO (PA) DA OFFICE, PA
DOUGLAS M. McCALLISTER, MI
DOUGLAS McMEEKIN, PA
DOUGLAS MERCEREAU, NY
DOUGLAS O'DELL, UCSD P D, CA
DOUGLAS URBANI, NV
DOUGLAS W. FENDER, VA
DOW D. CHRISWELL, TX
DRENNAN JACKSON, Jr, MICHIGAN STATE POLICE, MI
DUANE A. AVERY, MICHIGAN STATE POLICE, MI
DUANE D. PUDGIL, CA
DUANE RAGAN, NY
DWAYNE BOROWICZ, NEW BALTIMORE (MI) P D, MI
DWAYNE L. PRUETT, TX
DWIGHT A SCHWABROW, NY
DWIGHT J. BELL, CA
DWIGHT J. CLINTON, UNIVERSAL UNDERWRITERS GROUP, KS
DWIGHT L. CLIFFORD, PRUDENTIAL P & C, TX
DYON P. HARPER, RAYTOWN (MO) P D, MO
E. DAVE HOWELL, JR, PLANO (TX) P D. TX
E. STEVE GENTRY, VA
E.C. TIM LAWSON, COLONIAL PENN INS, CT
EARL D. CHEWING, Jr, VA
EARL D. HAYNES, Jr, WESTFIELD COMPANIES, GA
EARL HENRY SNYPES, NORTH CAROLINA DMV, NC
EARL HYSER, STATE FARM INS, IL
EARL MELTON, AL
EARL SMITH, PROGRESSIVE INS, MI
ED BRADLEY, EBS CONSULTANTS LTD, NY
ED WEIL, VIRGINIA DMV, VA
EDDIE EVANS, STATE FARM INS, NM
EDDIE LYNCH, NY
EDMOND J.K. O'BRIEN, OCEAN CITY (MA) P D, MD
EDUARDO TORE, VIRGINIA DMV, VA
EDWARD B. KIELY, PA
EDWARD CASTALDI, HONDA R & D AMERICAS, INC, CA
EDWARD FRISCHKORN, NJ
EDWARD FUZY, NATIONWIDE INS, VA
EDWARD G. GERDS, MICHIGAN STATE POLICE, MI
EDWARD HARSCH, NASSAU CO (NY) P D, NY
EDWARD HART, AVIS, NY
EDWARD J. KURATHOWSKI, STATE FARM INS, NY
EDWARD J. MAIER, NY
EDWARD J. McLAUGHLIN, STATE FARM INS, NY
EDWARD J. MENGANI, NY
EDWARD J. SHEPHARD, BURNSVILLE (MN) P D, MN
EDWARD J. SILVESTRINI, NEW YORK STATE INS FRAUDS BUREAU, NY
EDWARD J. SITLER, REGIONAL AGENCY MARKETS, NH
EDWARD KASCHE, CT
EDWARD KAZIO, PENNSYLVANIA STATE POLICE, PA
EDWARD L. CHARRON, OH
EDWARD L. GESSER, Jr, MD
EDWARD L. HUDE, MASON (MI) P D, MI
EDWARD M. HACKER, FL
EDWARD MAXWELL, FL
EDWARD NOWAK, IL
EDWARD R. DWYER, PA
EDWARD R. POLSTEIN, NY
EDWARD R. WOODS, KEYED RITE, INC, IN
EDWARD T. COX, NY
EDWARD T. PARSONS, NY
EDWARD W. NIGHTINGGALE, HERNDON & ASSOC, MI
EDWARD W. SIXBERRY, Sr, SIXBERRY, INC, FL
EDWIN CZELATKO, NJ
EDWIN J. DRISCOLL, Jr, NY
EDWIN L. JOHNSON, CT
EDWIN P. SPARKMAN, NICB, IL
EDWIN W. DIXSON, GWINNETT CO (GA) DEPT OF FIRE & EMERG SERV, GA
EILEEN A. WOLCK, NY
EILEEN M. TIANO, PA
ELAINE SMITH, FL
ELIAS CAMACHO, NICB, TX

ELISABETH SCHILTZ, WESTFIELD GROUP, ND
ELIZABETH ADAMS, IL
ELIZABETH I. ROWAN, STATE FARM INS, NV
ELIZABETH J. DARGA, MICHIGAN STATE POLICE, MI
ELIZABETH O'CONNOR, STATE FARM INS, IL
ELLEN JOAS, STATE FARM INS, NM
ELLIOT J. HANSEN, FARMERS INS, CA
ELLIOTT A. ROUSSEAU, TX
EMMETT B. BOOZER, SPECIALTY RESEARCH INC, MS
EMMETT MONEYHUN, KANECO (IL) ATTF, IL
EMZLA PITTS, OK
ERIC BUXTON, HYUNDAI MOTOR AMERICA, CA
ERIC C. DONALDSON, MILWAUKEE (WI) P D, WI
ERIC C. ELLE, ID
ERIC HOFFMAN, ENTERPRISE RENT A CAR, WI
ERIC J. MILLER, STATE FARM INS, PA
ERIC J. PUGH, VA
ERIC J. SIEBER, E. J. SIEBER & CO, CA
ERIC J. WILLIAMS, TEXAS DPS, TX
ERIC K. DOWDLE, LEHIGH CO AUTO THEFT TF, PA
ERIC M. WEAVER, NC
ERIC RATLIFF, ALEXANDRIA (VA) P D, VA
ERIC REICHERT, NY
ERIC SIMONTON, STATE FARM INS, MI
ERIC SMITH, TX
ERIC TURK, PENNSYLVANIA STATE POLICE, PA
ERIC WISEMAN, ORANGE CO (CA) DA'S OFF, CA
ERICK OSTROWSKI, DOUGLAS CO (CO) S O, CO
ERILYN ROGERS, ELECTROGUARD, LLC, GA
ERNEST M. FALCONER, ALLSTATE INS, NY
ERNEST R. ZWICKE, WI
ERVIN SIERRA-TORRES, PR
ERWIN H. MOORE, MA
EUGENE GENE R. DROZD, A INS, TX
EUGENE A. TRUE, NEBRASKA STATE PATROL, NE
EUGENE GARRANZA, TX
EUGENE H. MAROUARDT, OR
EUGENE J. ALDRICH, MICHIGAN STATE POLICE, MI
EUGENE J. KUCHARCZYK, NICB, IL
EUGENE L. CAPAUL, MN
EUGENE M. SULLIVAN, IL
EUGENE MARCHESE, JR, MASTERSLEUTH INVESTIGATIONS, FL
EUGENE R. KACZMAREK, FL
EVERETT F. DUNTON, VIRGINIA FARM BUREAU INS, VA
EVERETT KAHERL, ME
FELIX ENCARNACION, NY-NJ PORT AUTHORITY P D, NY
FIDENCIO HINOJOSA, TX
FORREST AUSTIN, LA
FORREST E. FOLCK, CA
FORREST E. REESE, IA
FRANCIS G. FAGAN, NY
FRANCIS LEONARD, NY
FRANCIS M. JOYCE, RI
FRANCIS POITRAST, GOVERNORS AUTO THEFT STRIKE FORCE, MA
FRANCIS R. HANNIGAN, NY
FRANCIS T. SHERIDAN, PA
FRANCIS X SZTUK, ALLMERICA FINANCIAL, NJ
FRANCISCO J. SANTIAGO, PR
FRANK A. GRABER, CA
FRANK A. KOVACS, CT
FRANK A. RUZICKA, NJ
FRANK A. ZANGAR, NICB, WA
FRANK C. SHOR, NEW YORK CITY SHERIFFS OFFICE, NY
FRANK GABRIELLE III, FL
FRANK H WALLACE, IL
FRANK H. SHARE, STATE FARM INS, MI
FRANK HEALEY, GREAT AMERICAN INS, NJ
FRANK J STEFFEN, CA
FRANK J. DeLEO, NY
FRANK J. DeMARTINO, NJ
FRANK J. HUBERT, NY
FRANK J. HUNT, NYS INS FRAUDS BUREAU, New York
FRANK J. KEEGAN, PA
FRANK J. PUGLIESE, STATE FARM INS, IL
FRANK L. MOORE, IL
FRANK L. VANEK, GARLAND (TX) P D, TX
FRANK MALINAK III, TEXAS D P S, TX
FRANK P. HENRY, NY
FRANK P. MURPHY, NY
FRANK P. WALSH, STATE FARM INS, NY
FRANK R. MORRIS, MA
FRANK RAMIREZ, TX
FRANK S. MORRIS, ARIZONA DPS, AZ
FRANKIE G. FLOIED, TN
FRED B. WALSER, WA
FRED BREINER, NY
FRED C. BAMOUTE, MESA (AZ) P D, AZ
FRED J. GRECO, NY
FRED J. KERSTIENS, LAKEWOOD (CO) P D, CO
FRED J. KLECKA, TX
FRED L. SOLOMON, VIRGINIA STATE POLICE, VA
FRED MUTUM, NY
FRED PATTERSON, CO
FREDERICK G. HAAS, WI

FREDERICK HANSEN, NY
FREDERICK L. DAVIS, MI
FREDERICK LOMBARDI, CA
FREDERICK P. LOHMANN, TEXAS FARM BUREAU, TX
FREDERICK S. TRUE, HANOVER INS, MA
FREDERICK WILLIAMS, STATE FARM INS, AL
G. MICHAEL McKEE, CA
GABRIEL A. BIDOT, PROGRESSIVE INS, FL
GABRIEL MORGAN, VIRGINIA DMV, VA
GABRIEL NARVAEZ, NY
GAETANO C. SAVA JR, BRISTOL TWNSHP (PA) P D, PA
GAIL ARMAND, STATE FARM INS, CA
GAIL NOVACK, MET HOME & AUTO INS, MA
GALEN J. PAPE, KS
GARRET LACOUR, I.A.S., INC/THEFT AVERT, TX
GARRY A. FERGUSON, NY
GARTH WILSON, ORANGE CO (CA) ATTF, CA
GARY A. BOARDMAN, NY
GARY A. LaROUCHE, UTICA MUTUAL INS, NJ
GARY B. DEESE, HOME DETECTIVE COMPANY, NC
GARY BARBADILLO, AIG HAWAII INS, HI
GARY BEACH, VIRGINIA DMV, VA
GARY C. KEISER, TX
GARY C. KEISER, NICB, TX
GARY D. KING, TX
GARY D. LOWRIE, STATE FARM INS, IL
GARY D. MUNKENS, CLASSSIC HEAVY EQUIP ADJUSTING CO, NJ
GARY E. ADAMS, FBI, NY
GARY F. KELSHAW, EAST ORANGE(NJ) P D, NJ
GARY H. HOPPER, CA
GARY HOME, TEXAS DPS, TX
GARY HORNE, TX
GARY J. DAYTON, NORFOLK (VA) P D, VA
GARY J. FISCHER, JEFFERSON CO (KY) P D, KY
GARY J. LEONE, NY
GARY L. KUPSAK, ILLINOIS MVTPC, IL
GARY L. NELSON, VA
GARY L. SYVERTSON, MONTANA MVD - FIELD OPS BUREAU, MT
GARY LEE RIVET, MN
GARY M. DeBLASIS, PA
GARY P. WRIGHT, NY
GARY RAMSEY, NORTH CAROLINA DMV, NC
GARY RAY STONE, TX
GARY RENICK, TX
GARY SCHILD, IL
GARY SMITH, NY
GARY STEVEN LABB, CA
GARY STOVALL, PROGRESSIVE INS, MD
GARY W. PINKSON, DFW AIRPORT (TX) DPS, TX
GENE L. CROCE, CHESAPEAKE (VA) P D, VA
GENE SIMPSON, STATE FARM INS, WA
GENNARO J. ASSORGI, PA
GEORGE A. WEBBER, IL
GEORGE C. MANNING, NY
GEORGE C. WORSHAM, GA
GEORGE D. BONILLA, LANCASTER (PA) P D, PA
GEORGE E CRABB, TN
GEORGE F. MERCADO, NY
GEORGE HISATAKE, CALIFORNIA DEPT OF JUSTICE, CA
GEORGE HOKE, ARIZONA VEHICLE THEFT TASK FORCE, AZ
GEORGE J DAVIS, JR, NY
GEORGE K. ADAMS, WV
GEORGE KLIPPEL, CT
GEORGE L. GRAHAM, NY
GEORGE M. GANDY, TX
GEORGE P. VITONE, JR, DARIEN (CT) P D, CT
GEORGE R. THOMAS III, CA
GEORGE R. WILSON, AZ
GEORGE S. ALBOFF, FIRE TECH ASSOC, CA
GEORGE S. HICKLER, REPUBLIC WESTERN INS, NY
GEORGE SCHEMENAUER, MICHIGAN STATE POLICE, MI
GEORGE SYDLAR, NY
GEORGE TAPIA, NY
GEORGE W. YANKOVICH, OH
GEORGE WINISTORFER, WARRIOR INSURANCE GROUP, IL
GEORGE WINNEGAR, FL
GERALD A. BRAVE, QUEENS CO (NY) D A, NY
GERALD A. FAY, COLORADO IND AUTO DLRS ASSOC, CO
GERALD ALSUP, UNIFIED INV. AND SCIENCES, INC., TN
GERALD B. RHODES, STATE FARM INS, OH
GERALD D BOYER, WA
GERALD E COLE, CO
GERALD F. PITSTICK, STATE FARM INS, CA
GERALD G. DERFUSS, FL
GERALD L. PARK, SAN DIEGO (CA) P D, CA
GERALD R. McNAMARA, VT
GERALD R. SCHULTE, CA
GERALDINE GARY, AAA - SOUTHERN CALIFORNIA, CA

GERARD J. MARONEY, NY
GERARD J. ROBERSON, EAST POINT (GA) P D, GA
GERRY ESTRADA, TEXAS DPS, TX
GIL HERNANDEZ, TX
GILBERT E. LARSON, IL
GILBERTO E. FUENTES, Jr, SIERRA VISTA (AZ) P D, AZ
GILBERTO R. LOSOYA JR., TX
GINO RADOVIC, STATE FARM INS, NY
GLEN H. MCLAUGHLIN, TX
GLEN HOLIFIELD, MS
GLEN S. GREENWALT, DELAWARE CO (PA) P D, PA
GLEN SIDER, NATIONAL EQUIP REGISTER, NY
GLENN C. BYRNES, CT
GLENN DAVIS, TN
GLENN H. DEVILEY, GREEN BAY (WI) P D, WI
GLENN M. COLE, ARLINGTON (TX) P D, TX
GLENN R. KIRKPATRICK, SUFFOLK CO (NY) P D, NY
GLENN R. WHEELER, STATE FARM INS, IL
GLENN WELTER, TEXAS DPS, TX
GLORIA J. WOODARD, NC
GLORIA LAURO, STATE FARM INS, NY
GORDON CARROLL, MAINE - DMV, ME
GORDON E. IVORY, GEI PROFESSIONAL INVESTIGATIONS, NY
GRACE M. ISGRO, NYS DMV, NY
GRAHAM F. BUTLER, NC
GRANT A. EATON, GLENDALE (AZ) P D, AZ
GRAYDON L. DUCK, AL
GREG A. HUTCHINSON, NICB, CA
GREG A. RULE, NJ
GREG CORVI, STATE FARM INS, CA
GREG DROTT, STATE FARM INS, TX
GREG EAKENS, TX
GREG EBERT, KILLEEN (TX) P D, TX
GREG GEHMAN, MANHEIM AUTO AUCTION, PA
GREG HALL, CALIFORNIA HWY PATROL, CA
GREG J. GAGNE', NY
GREG J. GAYNOR, NY
GREG JACOBSON, SAN MATEO (CA) P D, CA
GREG L. HUMRICHOUSE, IOWA CITY (IA) P D, IA
GREG LEITZ, STATE FARM INS, MI
GREG LEROY, STATE FARM INS, LA
GREG MacDONALD, BELLEVILLE POLICE DEPT, NJ
GREG McCOMAS, COLORADO STATE POLICE, CO
GREG MINICK, FARMERS INS, CA
GREG S. DOC HOLLIDAY, TX
GREG TERP, METRO DADE (FL) P D, FL
GREG TUCCI, SHAKOPEE (MN) P D, MN
GREG ZIEGLER, CALIFORNIA HWY PATROL, CA
GREGG P. WARGO, NY
GREGORY A. CAMPUS, NY
GREGORY C. GARVER, CALIFORNIA HWY PATROL, CA
GREGORY D. PERRY, FOUNTAIN (CO) P D, CO
GREGORY E. MALSAM, CO
GREGORY H. GORDDARD, PA
GREGORY HUNT, NC
GREGORY J. FOLEY, GOVERNORS AUTO THEFT STRIKE FORCE, MA
GREGORY J. HEIDEL, IL
GREGORY J. MAKAREWICZ, MI
GREGORY J. RILEY, PA
GREGORY KLICHOWSKI, IL
GREGORY M. HARDY, STATE FARM INS, AZ
GREGORY MELANSON, METROPOLITAN INS, MA
GREGORY R. BUCHANAN, MANATEE CO (FL) S O, FL
GREGORY S. KLEES, MD
GREGORY S. MCCORMICK, TX
GREGORY TASICH, MI
GREGORY THOMAS, LOWER ALLEN TWP (PA) P D, PA
GREGORY V. CARR, NATIONWIDE INSURANCE, TX
GREGORY VERN McKINNEY, NC
GREGORY W. NEWHOUSE, ST LOUIS (MO) METRO P D, MO
GREGORY W. SILVERMAN, NEW YORK CITY POLICE DEPT, NY
GUILLERMO E. TRUJILLO, KANECO (IL) ATTF, IL
H PAUL TELLOCK, STATE FARM INS, VA
H. D. BURR, BURR INVESTIGATION, ID
H. D. NEWMAN JR, WASHINGTON DC METRO P D, DC
H. GEORG SPINNATO, ATLAS INVESTIGATIONS, MD
H. HARDY GILLAM, NC
H. L. RATCLIFF, TX
H. LEE BALLARD, FL
H. R. BOB BUCK, AUSTIN (TX) PD, TX
HAL PARRISH, GA
HANS SEGBOER, NJ
HAROLD GENSLER, NY
HAROLD MUNROW, GREENWICH (CT) P D, CT
HAROLD STECH, SAN ANTONIO (TX) P D, TX
HAROLD V. MAEDER, QUICK INVESTIGATIONS, INC., MI
HARRY F BILLINGS, FORENSIC EVENTS, MA
HARRY I. MAYER, MIAMI SPRINGS (FL) P D, FL
HARRY J BRADY, SR, MD
HARRY J. BRADY, JR, NY

HARRY MARKLE, MA
HARVEY ALONI, STATE FARM INS, NY
HARVEY C. ALTES, FL
HARVEY S. MESHEL, FL
HEATHER CHRISTIAN, GA
HECTOR BLANCO, TX
HEIDI ENGEL, STATE FARM INS, FL
HEIDI HELLBAUM, STATE FARM INS, WA
HEIDI J. MACOMBER, RI
HEIDI M. JORDAN, NICB, NH
HENRY F. CAMBRON, SMYRNA (GA) PD, GA
HENRY H. BRUNE, JR, TX
HENRY J. BENAVIDES, NJ
HENRY LIPE, TX
HENRY W. FEARNOW Jr., VA
HENRY W. HEISEY, SPECTRUM INS AGENCY NC, NC
HERBERT ATWOOD, FL
HERBERT F. BAILEY II, FL
HERBERT L. BURR, MASSACHUSETTS REG MTR VEH, MA
HERBERT T. MILLER, SR, V I N INC, IN
HERMAN SALZ, SALZ LOCK & SAFE, HI
HERVEY SKIP .O. DAVIDSON, DAVIDSON INVENTIGATIONS, CA
HILARIO RUIZ, TX
HOLT WALKER III, NJ
HOWARD B. JOHNSON, WA
HOWARD DUNN, VENICE (FL) P D, FL
HOWARD E. KOENIG, CT
HOWARD G. TITUS, OH
HOWARD H. FRONK, NY
HOWARD R. SMITH, JR, AL
HOWARD R. TOLIVER, IL
HOWARD SMITH, A INS, VA
HOWARD W. CRAIG, LOUDOUN CO (VA) S O, VA
HOWARD W. REMSON, NY
HUGH J. BRADSHAW, NY
HUGHIE L. LAWTER, NORTH CAROLINA DMV - ENFORCEMENT, NC
IDA KLAYNMAN, GEICO, NY
IGNACIO PULIDO, STATE FARM INS, CA
IRA G. BEATY, CA
IRA GALBREATH, CHESAPEAKE (VA) P D, VA
IRA K. TROW, NY
IRENE M. McREYNOLDS, CA
J. A. TEAGUE, NC
J. BYRON ROACH, ALLSTATE INS, TX
J. CRAIG LEMOINE, LOUISIANA FARM BUREAU INS, LA
J. D. HOUGH, ARIZONA DPS, AZ
J. D. PLAYER, SC
J. HESS, LEXINGTON FAYETTE CO (KY) P D, KY
J. KEITH HENLEY, STATE FARM INS, OK
J. LAURENCE COSTIN, CCC INFORMATION SERVICES, INC, IL
J. PEAKS, NEWPORT NEWS (VA) P D, VA
JACK D. COLTRANE JR, NC
JACK E. EANES, DELAWARE DMV, DE
JACK G. CHARLESWORTH, CHARLESWORTH ENTERPRISES, GA
JACK HOSFORD, CA
JACK L. GENTRY, IRVING (TX) P D, TX
JACK MACAULEY, PROGRESSIVE INS, MD
JACK R. BAUM, NEW YORK STATE POLICE, NY
JACK SULLIVAN, FL
JACKIE DEANE, TX
JACKSON K. CHAMBERS, MD
JACQUELINE VIQUE-PAZMINO, STATE FARM INS, NY
JACQUES I. DEREMER, FL
JAMES C. HARDING, PA
JAMES A. BRYANT, STATE FARM INS, WA
JAMES A. DeLASHMUTT, LAKEWOOD (CO) P D, CO
JAMES A. McKINNEY, DES MOINES (IA) P D, IA
JAMES A. STEWART, SAN DIEGO (CA) P D, CA
JAMES A. TEDESCO, AVIS, CA
JAMES A. VITALE, STATE FARM INS, IL
JAMES A. WOLLENBERG, MO
JAMES A.JIM BERRIGAN, CRUM & FORSTER INS, NJ
JAMES B. CAMP, TX
JAMES B. CARLTON, STATE FARM INS, AL
JAMES B. JACKSON, NJ
JAMES B. LYNCH, MO
JAMES BITTICK, ALLSTATE INS, OK
JAMES BLICHARZ, NY
JAMES BURSON, TEXAS DPS, TX
JAMES C. BOND, Sr, ROUND ROCK (TX) PD, TX
JAMES C. GILBERTSON, VIRGINIA DMV, VA
JAMES C. HASKELL, PROGRESSIVE INS, NH
JAMES CARROLL, MO
JAMES CHERRY, FARMERS INS, VA
JAMES COUCH, OH
JAMES D. DeCARLO, DE
JAMES D. FOLEY, MI
JAMES D. HOLMES, METRO TRANSIT POLICE, DC
JAMES D. HUNTE, HENRICO (VA) P D, VA
JAMES D. McMANUS, OH
JAMES D. PALLADINO, LIBERTY MUTUAL INS, NY
JAMES DENARDO, PHILADELPHIA (PA) P D, PA

JAMES DePIETRO, CA
JAMES E. BRUNER, JR, SC FARM BUREAU CAS INS, SC
JAMES E. CACKETT, NY
JAMES E. COLE, NY
JAMES E. DENNIS, FORT WORTH (TX) P D, TX
JAMES E. DROTAR, MD TRANSPORTATION AUTHORITY P D, MD
JAMES E. EANE, CHESAPEAKE (VA) P D, VA
JAMES E. GARVIN, PEERLESS INS, NH
JAMES E. IVERSON, CA
JAMES E. POTTS, NEW YORK CENTRAL MUT FIRE INS, NY
JAMES E. STONER Jr., SHIREMANSTOWN BOROUGH (PA) P D, PA
JAMES E. WHITAKER, WESTFIELD COMPANIES, OH
JAMES F. DORSEY, BUDGET RENT A CAR, MD
JAMES F. KEELEY III, GREAT AMERICAN INS, PA
JAMES F. LALLY, NY
JAMES F. WOODS, TX
JAMES FISHER, PENNSYLVANIA STATE POLICE, PA
JAMES FRAUENHOFFER, MD
JAMES H KAUTZ, JR, WESTMINSTER (CO) P D, CO
JAMES H WHEATLEY, HARRISONBURG AUTO AUCTION, VA
JAMES H. COPELAND, NICB, AL
JAMES H. CROWNING, PALM BEACH CO (FL) S O, FL
JAMES H. GLAZIER, MD
JAMES H. KUHN, STATE FARM INS, IL
JAMES H. STANCER, JR, KS
JAMES HARRIS, CT
JAMES HOWARD SESSOMS JR, NC
JAMES J CADIGAN, FBI, DC
JAMES J SPANEL, LINCOLN (NE) P D, NE
JAMES J. BORDINO, BERGEN CO (NJ) PROSECUTOR'S OFF, NJ
JAMES J. MASTERSON, NYS INS FRAUD BUREAU, NY
JAMES K. BROWN, LAKE PARK (FL) P D, FL
JAMES K. DIESTEL, STATE FARM INS, GA
JAMES K. SEIBERT, DONEGAL INS GROUP, PA
JAMES KOTERAS, TX
JAMES L. EDWARDS, MI
JAMES L. JEFFREY, BRANCH CO (MI) S D, MI
JAMES L. REICHLIN, STATE FARM INS, MD
JAMES L. RIEHMAN, INFINITY INS, PA
JAMES L. STEWART, FL
JAMES LAWLOR, STATE FARM INS, NJ
JAMES M. CLONTZ, NY
JAMES M. GAVIGAN, LO/JACK, MI
JAMES M. GRAMMER, TX
JAMES M. PARKER, GREENBELT (MD) P D, MD
JAMES MARINUCCI, NY
JAMES MARK BURGER, BALTIMORE CO (MD) P D, MD
JAMES MARRON, NY
JAMES McDONOUGH, CT
JAMES MURTAGH, NY
JAMES N. CASTONGUAY, CT
JAMES N. RAGLAND, HENDERSON (NC) P D, NC
JAMES N. TURNER Jr., TENNESSEE HWY PATROL, TN
JAMES O'DONOVAN, GOVERNORS AUTO THEFT STRIKE FORCE, MA
JAMES P RUHLIG, MI
JAMES P. McNELLIS, NATIONWIDE INS, IL
JAMES P. MEEHAM, CT
JAMES R. BARTEE, Jr, SC
JAMES R. COUGHLIN, PA
JAMES R. CROTTS, HAMPTON (VA) P D, VA
JAMES R. EDDY, NEFCO, NH
JAMES R. ELLERBY, PT WASHINGTON (NY) P D, NY
JAMES R. GRAY, ST PAUL (MN) P D, MN
JAMES R. JENKINS, MI
JAMES R. PENNIMAN, GOVERNOR'S A/T STRIKE FORCE, MA
JAMES ROCKER, OCATT, CA
JAMES S. SHUTT, IL
JAMES S. SPILLER, NICB, IL
JAMES STANDIFORD, ANNE ARUNDEL CO (MD) P D, MD
JAMES T. BECK JR, NORTH CAROLINA DMV, NC
JAMES T. MALONE, CORAL SPRINGS (FL) P D, FL
JAMES TANNER, SAN MATEO CO (CA) VEH THEFT TF, CA
JAMES W. DAVIS, CHARLESTON (SC) CITY P D, SC
JAMES W. HOFFMAN, ADELANTO (CA) P D, CA
JAMES W. LYNCH, CT
JAMES W. MARTIN Jr., NYS-DMV-AUTO THEFT, NY
JAMES W. MOLLOY, WI
JAMES W. PAROLSKI, NJ
JAMES ZACCARI, NY
JAN BODON, TX
JAN G. ROESCH, PINAL CO (AZ) ATTORNEY, AZ
JAN STUKEL, PALM BEACH CO (FL) S O, FL
JANE A. KURN, EYEWITNESS INVESTIGATIONS, FL
JANE E. BAGLIER, WINNER INTL., LLC, PA
JANET H. FISHER, STATE FARM INS, SC
JANET RODGERS, TARRANT CO (TX) ATTF, TX
JANET RODGERS, TARRANT CO (TX) ATTF, TX
JANICE M. DiLEMMO, NY
JANINE TRUJILLO, NEW DPS-MTD, NM

JAOMES A. TOLLES, GEICO, NY
JARRAD P. BERKIHISER, LANCASTER (PA) P D, PA
JASON A. LENTZ, IL
JASON D. BRINKER, HARRISBURG (PA) BUREAU OF POLICE, PA
JASON GAGLIANO, LA
JASON L. BUTLER, NEW YORK CITY POLICE DEPT, NY
JASON M. POLZ, KANECO (IL) ATTF, IL
JASON S. ICE, CARY (NC) P D, NC
JASON VIORAL, PA
JAY A. SCHRAMM, OH
JAY A. YOUNG, BUFFALO (NY) P D, NY
JAY E. NORRIS, NICB, TX
JAY GROOB, AMERICAN INVESTIGATIVE SERVICES, iNC., MA
JAY J. ZAGURSKY, RENSSELAER CO (NY) DA'S OFF, NY
JAY M. EINHORN, OK
JAY P. TODRAS, FL
JAY TRUELOCK, TEXAS DPS, TX
JEAN-HENRI A. LAPRIME, MA
JEANETTE NORRIS, STATE FARM INS, CA
JEANINE PAULY, DULUTH (MN) P D, MN
JEANNE BOOMHOWER, MAINE - DMV, ME
JED A. BURGER, FL
JED APPELBAUM, NY
JED LETCHFORD, UNITREN DIRECT INS, PA
JEFF . BROWN, IL
JEFF BLAIR, ILLINOIS STATE POLICE, IL
JEFF CARTER, UTAH MOTOR VEHICLES, UT
JEFF CROW, STATE FARM INS, GA
JEFF DELINSKI, METRO TRANSIT POLICE, DC
JEFF HESTER, GA
JEFF KEARNEY, GMAC INS, NY
JEFF MAEKER, TEXAS D P S, TX
JEFF MARSHALL, STATE FARM INS, NH
JEFF PODWIKA, CORAL SPRINGS (FL) P D, FL
JEFF POHLAR, TIS INC., FL
JEFF SAVAGE, TX
JEFF SEAHOLM, AUSTIN (TX) P D, TX
JEFF STROBL, STATE FARM INS, WA
JEFF TURNER, GEICO, MI
JEFF VAN BUSKIRK, GEICO, MI
JEFFERY R.K. BRUCHAL, HONOLULU (HI) PD, HI
JEFFORY J. SCHIEBEL, HENNEPIN CO (MN) S O, MN
JEFFREY A. ARTIKES, MIDDLETOWN (CT) P D, CT
JEFFREY A. GEORG, P.A.D.E., PA
JEFFREY C. MOULD, CT
JEFFREY D. ANDERSON, PA
JEFFREY D. REARDEN, CHATTANOOGA (TN) P D, TN
JEFFREY D. TERSKI, HERNDON & ASSOC, MI
JEFFREY ESHING, LIBERTY MUTUAL INS, MO
JEFFREY FINDLAY, NY
JEFFREY FISHER, CT
JEFFREY GILLEN, PENNSYLVANIA STATE POLICE, PA
JEFFREY HOSKOWITZ, PENNSYLVANIA STATE POLICE, PA
JEFFREY JAGOE, INNOVATIVE AFTERMARKET SYSTEMS, TX
JEFFREY LANGE, LANGE TECHNICAL SERVICES, NY
JEFFREY M. ADAMS, ABBEY, ADAMS, BYELICK, KIERNAN, MELLER & LANCASTER, FL
JEFFREY M. LaFRANCE, CT
JEFFREY MERMON, PENNSYLVANIA STATE POLICE, PA
JEFFREY N. SYTAR, NAPERVILLE (IL) P D, IL
JEFFREY PFOTENHAUER, ILLINOIS STATE POLICE, IL
JEFFREY R. ABRAMS, THE PRONET GROUP, INC., TX
JEFFREY R. KRAUSE, LANCASTER CITY (PA) P D, PA
JEFFREY R. LARA, NEW DPS-MTD, NM
JEFFREY T. MAIN, PALM BEACH GARDENS (FL) P D, FL
JEFFREY TRACEY, MD
JENNIFER HAMILTON, STATE FARM INS, MI
JENNIFER R. PIERCE, OR
JENNINGS E. HARRISON, EYEWITNESS INVESTIGATIONS, FL
JEREMIAH B. WALSH, NJ
JEREMIAH SMITH, VA
JEROME HONEYCUTT, NC
JERREL W. JERRY SMITH, HERTZ, GA
JERROLD LEE JOHNSON, TN
JERRY BECK, SAN ANTONIO (TX) P D, TX
JERRY F. PAWELSKI, QUICK INVESTIGATIONS, INC, MI
JERRY G. WQOD II, TX
JERRY J. JANECEK, IL
JERRY L. AUCH, NORTH DAKOTA DEPT OF TRANSPORTATION, ND
JERRY L. HARRIS, PEMCO INS, WA
JERRY L. HOLDEN, LIBERTY MUTUAL INS, TX
JERRY L. McCURRY, TARRANT CO (TX) ATTF, TX
JERRY MALON, GEICO, MI
JERRY R. CARTER, TECHNIFIRE SERVICES CO, TN
JERRY R. LOVEJOY, DES MOINES (IA) P D, IA
JERRY S. WEIDNER, PA
JERRY SZYMANSKI, LOS ANGELES (CA) P D, CA

JERRY TAUSEND, STATE FARM INS, OR
JERRY VESELY, TX
JERRY W. ALTIERI, NATIONWIDE INS, VA
JERRY W. DAUGHERTY, SC
JERRY WESTLUND, CT
JESSICA C. TURNER, FL
JESUS BECERRA, TX
JILL K. MIMBS, STATE FARM INS, FL
JILL REUTELER, COLORADO STATE PATROL, CO
JILL SPEIGHTS, US CUSTOMS, VA
JIM ABELE, CA
JIM BENITEZ, ARIZONA VEHICLE THEFT TASK FORCE, AZ
JIM CARTER, CALIFORNIA HWY PATROL, CA
JIM CARTWRIGHT, CA
JIM COOKSEY, MARBLE FALLS (TX) PD, TX
JIM DEVASHER, KY
JIM G. LANIGAN, NATIONWIDE INS, PA
JIM L. VANDERVEEN, STATE FARM INS, OK
JIM NORWOOD, ARIZONA DEPT OF INSURANCE, AZ
JIM RICE, ORANGE CO (CA) ATTF, CA
JIM RUDISELL, NICB, CO
JIM STANLEY, DOTHAN (AL) P D, AL
JIM T. SPAULDING, FL
JIM TOWE, TEXAS DPS, TX
JIMMIE E. JETER, LA
JIMMY C. BALL, NICB, IL
JIMMY J. COMBS, IL
JIMMY L. HESTER, TN
JO-ANNE RIDDLE, MD
JOAN M KLOPF, MA
JOAN PITTS, CA
JOANNE F. ROBERTS, NJ
JOANNE PICKERING, GILBERT (AZ) P D, AZ
JOCELYN REILLY, STATE FARM INS, NY
JODI B. INSANA, NICB, PA
JODY R, PARKER, Jr, SC FARM BUREAU CAS INS, SC
JODY W FORE, TEXAS D P S, TX
JOE C. MARETT III, GREENVILLE CO (SC) S O, SC
JOE ESCARENO, STOVACT INC., CA
JOE F. BROSIUS, TEMPE (AZ) PD, AZ
JOE F. RABAGO SR., TX
JOE GOSSET, JR, KY
JOE L. HUNT, COON RAPIDS (MN) P D, MN
JOE MARK PORTMAN, TX
JOE TINGLE, LEXINGTON FAYETTE CO (KY) P D, KY
JOE TUBOLINO, STATE FARM INS, AZ
JOE WALLACE HOOD JR, TX
JOE WATTERS, TX
JOEL ANTHONY POPE, NY
JOEL D. BELSKY, PHILADELPHIA (PA) HSG P D, PA
JOEL OFFORD, STATE FARM INS, AK
JOEY CANADY, TX
JOEY GARDNER, NC DMV ENFORCEMENT, NC
JOHN A. BREHM, CINCINNATI (OH) PD, OH
JOHN A. BRUNETTI, PARKWAY CAR STEREO, NY
JOHN A. GARWOOD, PROGRESSIVE INS, OH
JOHN A. GUZMAN, PHOENIX (AZ) P D (CSB), AZ
JOHN A. HODA, INDEPENDENT SPECIAL INVESTIGATIONS, CT
JOHN A. KOSLOSKY SR, PA
JOHN A. MARTINEZ, NV
JOHN A. REUTTER, SUPERIOR INVESTIGATORS OF FLORIDA, INC, FL
JOHN B. McHUGH Jr., NY
JOHN BABER, IOWA STATE POLICE, IA
JOHN BARLOW, HONDA R & D AMERICAS, INC, OH
JOHN BROLLY, SAFECO INS, MN
JOHN C. HOWARD III, INTERSCIENCE, FL
JOHN C. OLIVEIRA, NJ
JOHN C. THOMPSON, FARMERS INS, NV
JOHN CAMPBELL, PENNSYLVANIA STATE POLICE, PA
JOHN CANNON, NY
JOHN CARGAN, PENNSYLVANIA STATE POLICE, PA
JOHN CARROUTHERS, GEICO, GA
JOHN D. DIMINNO, LIBERTY MUTUAL INS, NY
JOHN D. HARRIS, NORTH TEXAS AUTO THEFT TF, TX
JOHN D. KLOC, CNA INS/INV. OPTIONS, IL
JOHN D. SIDES, NM
JOHN DAVID IVEY, NORMAN (OK) P D, OK
JOHN DIVITTORIO, GREENVILLE CO (SC) S O, SC
JOHN DONVITO, NY
JOHN E GALLIVAN, WARRIOR INSURANCE GROUP, IL
JOHN E. JASPER, IL
JOHN E. MONTALBANO, GEICO, LA
JOHN E. NICHOLES, OK
JOHN E. SIMMONS, SUPERIOR BANK - FSB, IL
JOHN E. TURNER Jr, NY
JOHN E.M. HOBAN, STATE FARM INS, CA
JOHN ESPINOSA, NY
JOHN F. ALVES, NY
JOHN F. LOGAN, PA
JOHN F. MATULA, EXECUTIVE CLAIM SERVICE, NY
JOHN G. KESSLER, STATE FARM INS, IL
JOHN G. SCHROEDER, NY
JOHN GASPICH, PITTSBURGH (PA) P D, PA
JOHN H. EDMONSON, MI
JOHN H. JONES, UT

JOHN HAYES, NY
JOHN HUBER, SR, NY
JOHN HUNTLEY, DISTRICT ATTY OFFICE (NM), NM
JOHN J. ALBANESE, CT
JOHN J. BOYD, MD
JOHN J. BURKE, IL
JOHN J. CLARK, KEMPER INS, NY
JOHN J. GELOSO III, VA
JOHN J. KENNEDY, NY
JOHN J. PIKOLCZ, WARRENVILLE (IL) P D, IL
JOHN J. POWERS, FIREMANS FUND INS, MA
JOHN J. QUINN, Jr, PA
JOHN J. VAN HOUTEN, NY
JOHN J. VENZA, NY
JOHN K. MOORE, LAKEWOOD (CO) P D, CO
JOHN K. POTRATZ, KEMPER INS, FL
JOHN L. CALICO, GEICO, LA
JOHN L. LAGIOIA, IL
JOHN L. STEFFEL, GA
JOHN LANZETTA, MD
JOHN LINDBOE, CA
JOHN M. BEDINGFIELD, TX
JOHN M. BOLOGNA, NY
JOHN M. CASSIDY, AL
JOHN M. CULLEN, JMC INVESTIGATIONS, RI
JOHN M. EHRMANN, NY
JOHN M. HANNON, NY
JOHN M. HICKEY, CLARENDON INS, NY
JOHN M. McDONALD, NEW YORK INS FRAUD BUREAU, NY
JOHN M. SHAW, MONTGOMERY CO (MD) P D, MD
JOHN M. ZARANIS, NY
JOHN MALANDRINO, METROPOLITAN INS, NY
JOHN MARSHALL, HALL CO (GA) S O, GA
JOHN McCOLLUM, STATE FARM INS, OH
JOHN MOORE, CA
JOHN MROSZCZYK, NORTHEAST CONSULTING ENG, MA
JOHN NOVOSEL, IN
JOHN NUTTER, GOVERNOR'S A/T STRIKE FORCE, MA
JOHN P. CARRELL, TN
JOHN P. DAEMERS, STATE FARM INS, PA
JOHN P. HILDERBRAND SR., POTOMAC PRIVATE INVESTIGATIONS, MD
JOHN P. NEVLUD, FAIRFAX CO (VA) P D, VA
JOHN P. NICHOL, IL
JOHN P. NOVAK, NY
JOHN P. SEPANIK, STATE FARM INS, IL
JOHN P. SLATER, WHITE CO (AR) S O, AR
JOHN PAVLINEC, AURORA (IL) P D, IL
JOHN PERKINS, NATIONAL GRANGE MUTUAL INS, NY
JOHN POLKINGHORN, AMERICAN FAMILY INS, SD
JOHN PREXTA, OH
JOHN R. BAINBRIDGE, Jr, CASUALTY CONSULTANTS, Inc, PA
JOHN R. DEAR, NICB, MN
JOHN R. GAMBERZKY, CIVIL & FRAUD INVESTIGATIONS, CA
JOHN R. HENDRICKSON, NJ
JOHN R. MARSHALL, OH
JOHN R. MURSU, HARCO NATIONAL INS, IL
JOHN R. NARDOLILLA, W.I.R.E.D., FL
JOHN R. WHITACRE, JRW ENTERPRISES, MO
JOHN R. WINKLER, NE
JOHN RONAYNE, NY
JOHN ROOD, MACOMB CO (MI) S O, MI
JOHN RUBERTI, KANE CO (IL) ATTF, IL
JOHN RUFO, EBS CONSULTANTS LTD, NY
JOHN S. RIENZO, Jr, NY
JOHN SANDERS, NORTHERN ILLINOIS ATTF, IL
JOHN SAULLO, GREATER TAMPA BAY AUTO AUCTION, FL
JOHN SCHLINGER, TX
JOHN SOLTYS, NIAGARA FALLS (NY) P D, NY
JOHN T. BURKE, JACK BURKE & ASSOC, Ltd, IL
JOHN T. SHAW, SHAW INVESTIGATIONS, FL
JOHN T. TAYLOR, NIAGARA CO (NY) S D, NY
JOHN T. WHELAN III, STATE FARM INS, PA
JOHN V. ABOUNADER, NEW YORK DMV AUTO THEFT, NY
JOHN VALENTINE, SMITHTOWN (NY) P D, NY
JOHN VIGIL, TEXAS DPS, TX
JOHN W. ALEXANDER, AUSTIN (TX) P D, TX
JOHN W. BAILEY, Jr, COMAL CO (TX) S O, TX
JOHN W. CARR, DALLAS (TX) P D, TX
JOHN W. GANTT, AZ
JOHN W. HANNAH, NJ
JOHN W. MURPHY, HALL CO (GA) S O, GA
JOHN W. STUBBLEFIELD JR., MYRTLE BEACH (SC) P D, SC
JOHN W. THOMAS, TX
JOHN W. VALENTINE, TX
JOHN WRIGHT, NM
JOHN ZEVETCHIN, BIG EAST APPRAISAL SER & EQUIP CO, CT
JOHNNIE JONES, JR, VIRGINIA STATE POLICE, VA
JOHNNY BURKS, HEART OF TEXAS ATTF, TX
JOHNNY D. HICKS, GRAND PRAIRIE (TX) P D, TX
JOHNNY L. HOLUB, NORTH TEXAS AUTO THEFT TF, TX

JOHNNY M. SHOEMAKER, STATE FARM INS, MS
JOHNNY T. NEAL, STATE FARM INS, TX
JON BACHELDER, STATE FARM INS, AK
JON J. RAPPARD, ALLSTATE INS, NE
JON KING, TEMPE (AZ) P D, AZ
JONATHAN L. SITEK, JONATHAN SITEK INV., CT
JONATHAN R. DELA VEGA, HI
JORGE A. DeJESUS JR., HARTFORD (CT) P D, CT
JORGE BENITEZ, FT LAUDERDALE (FL) P D, FL
JORGE F. N. MARTIN, PR
JORGE RINCONES, TX
JOSE L. CLEMENTE COTTO, PR
JOSE MORA, TX
JOSE SAUCEDA, TX
JOSEPH A. GALLO III, STATE FARM INS, LA
JOSEPH A. LONGMORE, PHILADELPHIA (PA) P D, PA
JOSEPH A. MURPHY, BOSTON (MA) P D, MA
JOSEPH A. SCANDARIATO, STATE FARM INS, NY
JOSEPH A. SENICA, Jr, NJ
JOSEPH A. STASIO, HOLLYWOOD (FL) P D, FL
JOSEPH A. YANNONE, CERTIFIED SIU SERVICES, NY
JOSEPH B. GALIAZZI, CAMDEN (NJ) P D, NJ
JOSEPH C. ADAMS, HARLEYSVILLE INS, MD
JOSEPH C. MCHALE, PROGRESSIVE INS, FL
JOSEPH CHAMIE, WAYNE CO (MI) AIRPORT P D, MI
JOSEPH DI BENEDETTO, NY
JOSEPH E. TAVARES, JET FORENSIC INVESTIGATIONS, RI
JOSEPH F. GROSSO, PA
JOSEPH F. KING JR., HOWARD CO (MD) P D, MD
JOSEPH F. WALSH, PHILADELPHIA (PA) P D, PA
JOSEPH FASONE, STATE FARM INS, IL
JOSEPH GRANT, GOVERNOR'S A/T STRIKE FORCE, MA
JOSEPH I. deVILLE, RICHMOND (CA) P D, CA
JOSEPH J. KALTZ, MICHIGAN STATE POLICE, MI
JOSEPH J. ROGERS, STATE FARM INS, OR
JOSEPH J. SEPANIK, CA
JOSEPH KNOPP, JPK INVESTIGATION SERVICE, NE
JOSEPH L. DATESMAN, PENNSYLVANIA STATE POLICE, PA
JOSEPH L. O'HARA, FBI, MD
JOSEPH M. SHAYTER, SHIREMANSTOWN BOROUGH (PA) P D, PA
JOSEPH M. SMITH, MA
JOSEPH M. ZUROMSKY, PEERLESS INS, MA
JOSEPH MARINO, NY
JOSEPH MASON, GOVERNORS AUTO THEFT STRIKE FORCE, MA
JOSEPH MURPHY, GOVERNOR'S A/T STRIKE FORCE, MA
JOSEPH N. GIAMMONA, IL
JOSEPH NELSON, CORAL GABLES (FL) P D, FL
JOSEPH OSBORNE, PA
JOSEPH P. BANAHAN, NY
JOSEPH P. DOUGHERTY, NEW YORK STATE POLICE, NY
JOSEPH P. NANNERY, SAN FRANCISCO (CA) P D, CA
JOSEPH P. SCHAEDLER, AMICA MUTUAL INS, CT
JOSEPH PRINZO, NORTH ARLINGTON (NJ) P D, NJ
JOSEPH RAINONE, LO/JACK, NJ
JOSEPH RAUCH, WESTFIELD COMPANIES, OH
JOSEPH S. BORING, KS
JOSEPH SANCHEZ, PA
JOSEPH SCAMARDELLA, HERTZ, NJ
JOSEPH T. KOCHAN, LEHIGH CO (PA) AUTO THEFT, PA
JOSEPH T. McMAHON, NY
JOSEPH T. NADOLSKI, PA
JOSEPH TOBIN, STATE FARM INS, PA
JOSEPH V. WASLH JR, FBI, MD
JOSEPH VERILLE, CITY OF RYE (NY) P D, NY
JOSEPH W BOISSO, IL
JOSEPH W. BROWN, MD
JOSEPH W. WALTERS, VIRGINIA STATE POLICE, VA
JOSHUA A. CANULLI, VA
JOY A. PAGENKOPP, CA
JOY MALONEY, STATE FARM INS, NY
JUAN G. PAGAN, PR
JUAN G. PAGAN JR., TX
JUAN JOSE LOPEZ RAMIREZ, S.G. SECRETARIA DE GOBERNACION, CA
JUDD BROWN, PALM BEACH CO (FL) S O, FL
JUDD LEVENSON, SPRINGFIELD (NJ) P D, NJ
JUDI DeMARTIN, STATE FARM INS, MI
JUDITH B. BURK, STATE FARM INS, CO
JULIAN SAENZ, VA
JULIAN UPSHAW, NEW DPS-MTD, NM
JULIE A. SMITH, NICB, IL
JULIUS O. BELTON, TX
JUNE L. CHADWICK, LA
JUSTIN OWEN, TX
JUSTIN P. SPAULDING, LOWER ALLEN TWP (PA) P D, PA
KANDY M. WALKER, PROGRESSIVE INS, OH
KAREN K. HUTTON, STATE FARM INS, OR
KAREN KALLAS, STATE FARM INS, IL
KAREN L. METZ, FL
KAREN M. DEAN JOHNSON, STATE FARM INS, WA

KAREN S. RADCLIFFE, STATE FARM INS, PA
KARL C. DEITER, GA
KARL H. NESLER, STATE FARM INS, ND
KARL W. INTEMANN, PROGRESSIVE INS, MI
KATHLEEN A. BROOKS, THE HARTFORD, NJ
KATHLEEN A. REYES, CALIFORNIA HWY PATROL, CA
KATHLEEN HOCKLER, ALLSTATE INS, NY
KATHRYN A. JEFFERIES, IL
KATHY A. MIROUX, IL
KATHY J. ANDERSON, TX
KAY MARTIN, STATE FARM INS, OK
KEITH CHANCE, NC
KEITH E. WOODRUFF, MO
KEITH F. WILKINS, NJ
KEITH FRANSON, CT DMV, CT
KEITH GOSS, NY
KEITH J. LUMINAIS, ALLSTATE INS, LA
KEITH KUCIFER, TEXAS D P S, TX
KEITH R. CARLOUGH, CT
KEITH R. HAIRELL, ALLSTATE INS, TN
KEITH R. LEVIN, CA
KEITH W. COX, AL
KEITH W. PEARCE, STATE FARM INS, FL
KELLI ANDERSON, MO
KELLY D. ROBERTS, STATE FARM INS, NM
KELLY S. GLEASON, TX
KELLY S. MOLANDES, TX
KELLY S. WEISSINGER, MO
KEN BERGER, MONTGOMERY CO (MD) P D, MD
KEN M. SCHIMNOSKI, MICHIGAN STATE POLICE, MI
KEN MILLIS, FL
KEN PHILLIPS, FREDERICKSBURG AUTO AUCTION, VA
KEN PROPES, NM
KEN VITTY, STERLING INVESTIGATION SER, NJ
KENN ROSENBERG, ORANGE CO (CA) ATTF, CA
KENNETH A. LAMB, BOSTON (MA) P D, MA
KENNETH B. MacKENZIE, TX
KENNETH C. HOUCK, INDIANA STATE POLICE, IN
KENNETH CARNER, IL
KENNETH E. NORRIS, MD
KENNETH F. DePRETTO, WA
KENNETH G. LANINGA, MI
KENNETH J. FANTOZZI, NJ
KENNETH J. GRANICZMY, TEXAS DPS, TX
KENNETH J. SCHAEFFER, NY
KENNETH KELLY, NY
KENNETH KINCADE, NORTH LITTLE ROCK (AR) P D, AR
KENNETH L. SIMPSON, STATE FARM INS, TX
KENNETH LAMB, GOVERNOR'S A/T STRIKE FORCE, MA
KENNETH LEE HYDEN SR., VA
KENNETH M. DEISCHER, FL
KENNETH M. ROBERTS, AUSTIN (TX) P D, TX
KENNETH MASH, TN
KENNETH P. HAWCOTT, IA
KENNETH R. TASSIE, MICHIGAN STATE POLICE, MI
KENNETH R. BENSON, STATE FARM INS, CA
KENNETH R. DODGE, FAIRFAX CO (VA) POLICE, VA
KENNETH R. OVERTON, PROGRESSIVE INS, FL
KENNETH R. STEELMAN, MI
KENNETH R. YOUMANS, NJ
KENNETH S. HAYNIE, PASADENA (TX) P D, TX
KENNETH SANTARE, EBS CONSULTANTS LTD, NY
KENNETH W. BEIJEN, NY
KENNETH W. GRAHAM, BUSINESS CONS. INVESTIGATIONS, PA
KENNETH W. HAMMOND, MO
KENNETH W. REAMS, NC
KENNETH ZION, AUTOMOTIVE COLLISION CONSULTANTS, CA
KENNY McCAFFERY, LA
KENNY SCHULL, TX
KENT D. EMERICK, TX
KENT E. MILLER, WHITTIER (CA) P D, CA
KENT W. MAWYER, TEXAS D P S, TX
KENT ZABEL, TRI-STATE AUCTION, ND
KENT ZWICKER, OREGON STATE POLICE, OR
KERRI CHADWICK, FL
KERRY COLE, UTAH MOTOR VEHICLE ENF, UT
KERRY L. VINCENT, MECHANICSBURG BOROUGH (PA) P D, PA
KERRY P. GALLEGOS, UTAH MOTOR VEHICLES, UT
KEVIN A. STRANGE, MD
KEVIN B. KELLEY, OH
KEVIN COOK, MA
KEVIN DUCHARME, NORTH EASTERN TECHNICAL SERVICE, MA
KEVIN GREBIN, SD
KEVIN H. BOGNER, VIRGINIA DMV, VA
KEVIN HASSETT, NY
KEVIN J. CURRY, 3-M, MN
KEVIN J. O'REILLY, LIBERTY MUTUAL INS, MI
KEVIN J. SULLIVAN, NJ
KEVIN J. TAYLOR, ASHEVILLE (NC) P D, NC
KEVIN K. CHEVRIER, PROGRESSIVE INS, NY
KEVIN L. BALANCIER, LA
KEVIN L. THOMAS, BALTIMORE CO (MD) P D, MD

KEVIN LYNCH, HANOVER INS, MA
KEVIN M. DONOVAN, STATE FARM INS, FL
KEVIN M. HANNA, PA
KEVIN M. JOHNSON, OKLAHOMA CITY (OK) P D, OK
KEVIN M. LEE, NY
KEVIN McCONNELL, WASHINGTON DC METRO P D, DC
KEVIN McCONVILLE, NJ
KEVIN McHUGH, MA
KEVIN O'CONNOR, LIBERTY MUTUAL INS, NY
KEVIN O'NEILL, WEST ST PAUL (MN) P D, MN
KEVIN P. RICHARD, FIREMANS FUND INS, MA
KEVIN R. LEARY, CONSTABLES OFFICE, MA
KEVIN S. McCANN, MI
KEVIN SAY, ARIZONA VEHICLE THEFT TASK FORCE, AZ
KEVIN T. GOODNIGHT, STATE FARM INS, OH
KEVIN VIDAL, HUNTINGTON BEACH (CA) P D, CA
KIM EVERITT, PLYMOUTH ROCK ASSURANCE, MA
KIM G. GREENWOOD, NC
KIM M. KAZARNOWICZ, PA
KIM TRIPLETT, WASHINGTON STATE PATROL, WA
KIMBERLY A. PACE, TX
KIMBERLY M. WOOD, MN
KIRK LANE, PULASKI CO (AR) S D, AR
KLAUS E. HIRNSCHAL, CT
KOLLEEN OLSEN, STATE FARM INS, CA
KORINNE PAOLO, GENERAL ACCIDENT INS, NY
KRISTIE L. DWYER, NICB, IL
KRISTIE SAMPSON, OR
KRISTY HASKINS, UTAH MOTOR VEHICLE ENF, UT
KURT A. PEPPER, WA
KYLE COOK, WICHITA FALLS (TX) P D, TX
KYLE EDWARDS, TEXAS DPS, TX
KYLE G. WILLIAMS, NY
KYLE W. MCPHEE, MI
L. EDWARD EGLY, ANOKA CO (MN) S O, MN
LANCE A. FRY, WA
LANDIS CRAVENS, TEXAS CITY (TX) P D, TX
LARRY A. WARCH, OHIO CASUALTY GROUP, MD
LARRY B. WILLIAMSON, NC
LARRY C. CHOLEWIN, IL
LARRY D. HARRIS, DES MOINES (IA) P D, IA
LARRY D. LEE, WESTFIELD COMPANIES, OH
LARRY E. BARKSDALE, LINCOLN (NE) P D, NE
LARRY E. WILLIAMS, NC
LARRY FORTIER, MICHIGAN STATE POLICE, MI
LARRY G. JOHNSON, ANOKA CO (MN) S O, MN
LARRY G. PARKER, NH
LARRY J. LEE, BELLAIRE P D, TX
LARRY KOCUREK, TX
LARRY L. CAPP, TX
LARRY L. LUNSFORD, TX
LARRY MELLINA, VA
LARRY OLIVER, AUSTIN (TX) P D, TX
LARRY PATRICK, 166 AUTO AUCTION, MO
LARRY PEREZ, NJ
LARRY SWINFORD, EAST TEXAS AUTO THEFT TASK FORCE, TX
LARRY TRIBBLE, SOUTHERN AUTO AUCTION, CT
LARRY W.W. WILSON, IN
LAURA A. SUAREZ, IL
LAURA CAMPBELL-BISHOP, STATE FARM INS, CA
LAURA L. KIRN, GEICO INS, LA
LAURANCE R. BURZYNSKI, WI
LAWRENCE E. RUNYAN, NATIONWIDE TRUCK ADJUSTERS, MN
LAWRENCE GOMEZ Jr, NY
LAWRENCE HINRICHS, NY
LAWRENCE J. RAWLE, PHILADELPHIA (PA) P D, PA
LAWRENCE J. WYMAN, NY
LAWRENCE M. SENESKI, STATE FARM INS, MI
LAWRENCE MASSONE, MA
LAWRENCE R. DUGUAY, FL
LAWRENCE SMITH, MD
LEE A. JOHNSON, WI
LEE ANN FINK, STATE FARM INS, NY
LEE ANN ROADS, PIMA CO (AZ) ATTORNEYS OFF, AZ
LEE DeVANEY, NORTH TEXAS ATTF, TX
LEE ESWORTHY, BALTIMORE (MD) P D, MD
LEE ROTHGEB, SENTRY INS, VA
LEN SILVA, CA
LEN WHITNEY, WA
LENARTH R. SANDBERG, ALLSTATE INS, NJ
LEO H. GROTHAUS, MISSOURI DEPT of REVENUE CIB, MO
LEO J. FITZHENRY, COMMERCE INS CO, MA
LEON DAVID BRIDGERS, NC
LEON R. PUTYRSKI, IL
LEONARD ADIS, NJ
LEONARD J. BUNACH, NE
LEONARD J. MACIEJEWSKI, SEMINOLE CO (FL) S O, FL
LEONARD McFADDEN, TEXAS DPS, TX
LEROY C. TYLER, HENRICO (VA) P D, VA
LEROY F. FUJISHIGE, HONOLULU (HI) P D, HI
LEROY G. STARR, FL
LES BROWN, SACRAMENTO CO (CA) D A, CA
LESLIE A. JOHNSON, FARMERS INS, AZ

LESLIE E. CRAVENS, FL
LESTER E. JOHNSON, JR., DE
LESTER KNIFFIN, CT
LESTER R. ALEXANDER, VAN ZANDT CO (TX) S O, TX
LINCOLN GEE, NY
LINDA A. GUNDERSON, STATE FARM INS, LA
LINDA AKESSON, STATE FARM INS, CA
LINDA LAMBERT, STATE FARM INS, NV
LINDA MENDOZA, TX
LINDA PERKINS, PHILADELPHIA (PA) D A OFFICE, PA
LINDA RILEY-WARREN, NM
LINDA S. BAUMANN, NE
LINWOOD E. SMITH, TN
LISA A. WEINER, PROGRESSIVE INS, VA
LISA De ROJAS, METRO DADE (FL) P D, FL
LISA HAMPTON, NEW YORK DEPT HEALTH - PRO MEDICAL, NY
LISA THORNE, SCHENECTADY CO (NY) DA, NY
LIZ ANDERSON, NORTH TEXAS AUTO THEFT TF, TX
LIZ DOWLING, NICB, IL
LLOYD E. LaLONDE, VOLUSIA CO (FL) FIRE SERVICE, FL
LOIS F. KEENAN, VIRGINIA IND AUTO DLRS ASSOC, VA
LONZALE RAMSEY, NE
LORAN GRASSL, TX
LORRAINE GARZIANO, GEICO DIRECT, NY
LOU KOVEN, LOS ANGELES POLICE DEPT, CA
LOUIE BROOKS, MS
LOUIS J. CHRIST, IN
LOUIS M. BADALAMENTI, LA
LOUIS R. CARDINAL, TEXAS D P S, TX
LOUIS SMALLBERGER, PA
LOUIS W. BROWN, IN
LOWELL W. DOUBLIN, TX
LUCY GUIDO, NY
LUIS A. COLLAZO Jr, NY
LUIS E. CARREON, TX
LUKE DELAGARZA, NEW DPS-MTD, NM
LYLE WATANABE, STATE FARM INS, HI
LYNN A. COX, STATE FARM INS, GA
LYNNDON P. ANG, NASSAU CO (NY) P D, NY
LYNNICE TULLOS, STATE FARM INS, MS
M. ELISA ANDERSON, VIRGINIA DMV INVESTIGATIONS, VA
M. O. TILLMAN, Jr, GA
MADELYN M. RUPERTO, NY
MALCOLM A. BALLARD, LA
MAMIE BRODEUR, PALM BEACH CO (FL) S O, FL
MANDY THOMAS, GEICO, GA
MANUEL GONZALEZ MENENDEZ, JARDINES de ARECIBO, PR
MANUEL RAMOS, OCATT, CA
MANUEL RENE CARDONA, TX
MARC J. YOUNGQUIST, MIDDLESEX MUT ASSURANCE CO, CT
MARC MICCICHE, COLORADO STATE PATROL, CO
MARCIA HANCOCK, PIMA CO (AZ) S O, AZ
MARCIA McALLISTER, INSURANCE AUTO AUCTIONS, INC, IL
MARGARET H. FLEMING, SC
MARGARET SCOTT, OAKLAND CO (MI) PROS ATTY, MI
MARIA D. MORELAND, STATE FARM INS, NV
MARIA E. ADAMS, FLORIDA DMV, FL
MARIA LARSON, NY
MARIANNE E. FINNEY, CA
MARIANNE MITCHELL, STATE FARM INS, LA
MARIE R. HARDEN, CHAMPAIGN (IL) P D, IL
MARION L. MILES, VA
MARK A. DAVID, OSCODA TWNSP (MI) P D, MI
MARK A. EASTMAN, VIRGINIA BEACH (VA) P D, VA
MARK A. LANE, VA
MARK A. McGUFFIN, FARMERS INS, AZ
MARK A. McKAIN, WESTFIELD COMPANIES, OH
MARK A. STOWELL, NICB, CA
MARK A. ZADNIK, ILLINOIS STATE POLICE, IL
MARK ALLEN, TEMPE (AZ) P D, AZ
MARK AMOS, MI
MARK B. STIKE, STATE FARM INS, DE
MARK BUCSKO, MD
MARK BUTLETT, AURORA (IL) P D, IL
MARK C. HOERRMANN, AZ
MARK CASSISTA, CT
MARK D. CULVER, KEY FIRE INV INC, IN
MARK D. SANDERS, INDIANA STATE POLICE, IN
MARK EATON, KANE CO (IL) ATTF, IL
MARK ENGLISH, IL
MARK F. HOUSTON, ST. LOUIS CO P D, MO
MARK FRANEY, MO
MARK G. HUKEL, FORT WORTH (TX) P D, TX
MARK GUSTAD, EDAN PRAIRIE (MN) P D, MN
MARK HARRINGTON, EDAN PRAIRIE (MN) P D, MN
MARK HECKMAN, VA
MARK J. DEARING, NICB, NY
MARK J. YANITELLI, NEW YORK STATE POLICE, NY
MARK K. GIBBLE Jr., PA
MARK KELLY, PENNSYLVANIA STATE POLICE, PA
MARK LEWIS, PORTSMOUTH (VA) P D, VA

MARK MENDEZ, TX
MARK P. MEAGHER, VA
MARK R. FRENZO, GOVERNORS AUTO THEFT STRIKE FORCE, MA
MARK R. HODGES, TULSA (OK) P D, OK
MARK RUTLEDGE, TX
MARK RYCHEN, NORFOLK (VA) P D, VA
MARK S. AUGUSTUS, STATE FARM INS, NY
MARK S. WAGNER, SCOTTSDALE (AZ) P D, AZ
MARK SILK, ME
MARK STEVEN HANLON, SAN MATEO CO (CA) VEH THEFT TF, CA
MARK TRAUB, LEHIGH CO (PA) DA OFFICE, PA
MARK W. LOVERN, VA
MARK W. STANFORD, TN
MARK WALLDORF, STATE FARM INS, MI
MARK ZIMMERHANZEL, TX
MARLON HARRIS, PROGRESSIVE INS, FL
MARRIANN M. SCANLAN, STATE FARM INS, CA
MARTHA JONES-JOSEPH, AAA - SOUTHERN CALIFORNIA, CA
MARTHA L. GURNEY, PA
MARTHA SIMONS, STATE FARM INS, NY
MARTIN A. WHITE, THE HARTFORD, NJ
MARTIN E. DAHLSTROM, WEXFORD CO (MI) S O, MI
MARTIN E. MEDEIROS Jr, AIG HAWAII INS, HI
MARTIN J. CUNNINGHAM, A INS, TX
MARTIN J. SMITH, TAMPA (FL) P D, FL
MARTIN JASSO, TX
MARTIN KEVIN TUOHY, GA
MARTIN L. KRAKOWER, NY
MARTIN OUATTLEBAUM, SC
MARTY PARKER, GREENBELT (MD) P D, MD
MARY ANN MYERS, STATE FARM INS, NC
MARY DODSON, STATE FARM INS, KS
MARY E. LeROY, AZ
MARY J. AFTANAS, NICB, IL
MARY K. McINTYRE, VT
MARY LOUISE DAVIS, NY
MARY McBRIDE, STATE FARM INS, WA
MATT BERRY, ANPAC, MO
MATT DIXON, GEICO, GA
MATT FRANCIS, ENTERPRISE RENT A CAR, CA
MATT LYNCH, PRUDENTIAL FINANCIAL, AZ
MATT McMILLEN, WASHINGTON STATE PATROL, WA
MATTHEW C. MILLER, MD
MATTHEW I. SOLON, SOLON INVESTIGATIVE SERVICES, IA
MATTHEW J. SLEAR, NY
MATTHEW J. WALSH, LEE CO (FL) S O, FL
MATTHEW LOMIS, PHILADELPHIA (PA) P D, PA
MATTHEW M. DENNY, MD
MATTHEW R. FURSTENFELD, NY
MAUREEN THOLEN, 3 M SECURITY MARKET CENTER, MN
MAX BELLARD, LIBERTY MUTUAL INS, PA
MAYRA LICIAGA, NY
MEDGAR GIBBS, MS
MEGAN R. SAVAGE, IL
MEL COHEN, NY
MELANIE COLE, FARMERS INS, CA
MELISSA VAN DREW, IL
MELODIE BALDWIN, TARRANT REGIONAL ATTF, TX
MELVIN C. MOOERS, MT
MELVIN R. DELANEY, NY
MELVYN MILNER, NEW YORK DMV AUTO THEFT, NY
MICHAEL A. CAULFIELD, NY
MICHAEL A. DIMINO, NY
MICHAEL A. FEDISH, BROOME CO (NY) S O, NY
MICHAEL A. GATES, TX
MICHAEL A. GILBERT, MONGOMERY CO (PA) D A OFFICE, PA
MICHAEL A. GRASS, NY
MICHAEL A. JONES, STATE FARM INS, IL
MICHAEL A. MAURO, PALM BEACH CO (FL) S O, FL
MICHAEL A. NARDOLILLO, NY
MICHAEL A. SABO, DEARBORN (MI) P D, MI
MICHAEL A. SCARBROUGH, WAYNE CO (MI) AIRPORT P D, MI
MICHAEL ARBIT, FT LAUDERDALE (FL) P D, FL
MICHAEL B. HOLLY, NORTH LAS VEGAS (NV) P D, NV
MICHAEL B. KAUFOLD, GA
MICHAEL B. McMAHON, NY
MICHAEL B. PURPURA, MET LIFE - HOME AND AUTO, NY
MICHAEL BEDARD, OCATT, CA
MICHAEL BENDER, NICB, AZ
MICHAEL C. ANFUSO, NY
MICHAEL C. HOEPPNER, JEFFERSON CO (CO) S D, CO
MICHAEL CANNY, HAMPTON (VA) P D, VA
MICHAEL CARPENTER, RI
MICHAEL CARROLL, TUCSON (AZ) P D, AZ
MICHAEL CHACONGS Jr, MONTGOMERY CO (MD) P D, MD
MICHAEL CIOFFI, ENGLEWOOD CLIFFS (NJ) P D, NJ
MICHAEL CLUNE, NY
MICHAEL D. BORUFF, CALIFORNIA DEPT OF JUSTICE, CA

MICHAEL D. DONSKY, FL
MICHAEL D. INGELS, TX
MICHAEL D. KELSO, NICB, IL
MICHAEL D. LENNON, STATE FARM INS, CO
MICHAEL D. WAGNER, IA
MICHAEL DEAN, STATE FARM INS, KS
MICHAEL DORTO, NY
MICHAEL DRZONSC, NY
MICHAEL E. ARMENTROUT, MANHEIM AUTO AUCTION, PA
MICHAEL E. LEWIS, MICHIGAN STATE POLICE, MI
MICHAEL E. PETROSKI, NY
MICHAEL F. MULCAHY, NY
MICHAEL F. SECKENDORF, NY
MICHAEL F. SUGRUE, MD
MICHAEL F. TEN EYCK, NY
MICHAEL F. TOWER, PROGRESSIVE INS, WA
MICHAEL FERRARI, MA
MICHAEL GRAZIOSE, NY
MICHAEL GRIFFIN, WV
MICHAEL H. SYMMONDS, NH
MICHAEL HARRIS, PROGRESSIVE INS, MD
MICHAEL HIGGINS, STATE FARM INS, NY
MICHAEL HILDEBRAND, SC
MICHAEL I. JOHNSON, WASAHINGTON CO (MN) S O, MN
MICHAEL J McMULLEN, VERNON (CT) P D, CT
MICHAEL J. CARNAKIS, CA
MICHAEL J. FLAHERTY, NY
MICHAEL J. GALLANTE, FBI, AZ
MICHAEL J. KENARY, NY
MICHAEL J. LULLO, ELMHURST (IL) P D, IL
MICHAEL J. MARTINKO, LEHIGH CO AUTO THEFT TF, PA
MICHAEL J. MULQUEEN, MD
MICHAEL J. NAVIN, NICB, NY
MICHAEL J. RAMOS, STATE FARM INS, FL
MICHAEL J. RODRIGUEZ, NJ
MICHAEL J. VALDEZ, GLENDALE (CO) P D, CO
MICHAEL J. VOLPE, ALLSTATE, NY
MICHAEL JOHN MULLEN, PHILADELPHIA (PA) PD, PA
MICHAEL K. HIGGINS, SR., K-CHEM LABORATORIES, MA
MICHAEL K. SHEETS, IOWA DOT - MTR VEHICLE ENFORCEMENT, IA
MICHAEL K. SMITH, NC
MICHAEL KANE, NEW JERSEY STATE POLICE, NJ
MICHAEL KENESTON, ONE BEACON INS, NY
MICHAEL L. DALTON, NY
MICHAEL L. FISHER, HENRICO (VA) P D, VA
MICHAEL L. HARRELL, NC
MICHAEL L. MAGGARD, WV
MICHAEL L. SOELBERG, MESA (AZ) P D, AZ
MICHAEL LAPASNICK, TX
MICHAEL LARNER, TX
MICHAEL M. SANOVAL, NM
MICHAEL MECHOW, NY
MICHAEL NAGLIERI, STATE FARM INS, NY
MICHAEL O. ADAMS, SC
MICHAEL O. MULCONERY, ID
MICHAEL P. BUCHANAN, IL
MICHAEL P. CANNY, HAMPTON (VA) P D, VA
MICHAEL P. KARCEWSKI, PA
MICHAEL P. MANGAN, IL
MICHAEL P. MILKE, PA
MICHAEL PURDIE, STATE FARM INS, PA
MICHAEL R. BURKE, NY
MICHAEL R. FERGUSON, LAKEWOOD (CO) P D, CO
MICHAEL R. GRENON, WESTFIELD COMPANIES, MI
MICHAEL R. LINN, NAT'L IND AUTO DEALERS ASSOC, TX
MICHAEL R. PARIS, TN
MICHAEL R. RUTH, IL
MICHAEL R. WILLIAMS, KING CO (WA) S O, WA
MICHAEL REA, NJ
MICHAEL REDMON, WHITTIER (CA) P D, CA
MICHAEL REYNOLDS, UIS, IN
MICHAEL RINALDI, INVESTIGATIVE SERVICES, NY
MICHAEL ROGOZIK, COLORADO STATE POLICE, CO
MICHAEL RUSSELL, GEICO, NY
MICHAEL S. MURPHY, NY
MICHAEL SAVALLO, NY
MICHAEL SCHINASI, NY
MICHAEL SCHLOMAS, IL
MICHAEL SHEAHAN, AVIS, NY
MICHAEL SIKA, NJ
MICHAEL SIMEONE, NY
MICHAEL STARACE, NEW YORK CITY FIRE DEPT, NY
MICHAEL STOPLER, NY
MICHAEL T. MARKS, FL
MICHAEL TAM, STATE FARM INS, CA
MICHAEL TINSLEY, COVINGTON (GA) P D, GA
MICHAEL TOWERS, TX
MICHAEL TRUSDELL, STATE FARM INS, PA
MICHAEL W. COKER, DALLAS (TX) P D, TX
MICHAEL W. PIRTLE, NV
MICHAEL WALLACE, FL
MICHAEL WHEATON, GOVERNOR'S A/T STRIKE FORCE, MA

MICHELLE DUBOIS, FAIRFAX COUNTY (VA) POLICE, VA
MICHELLE KLEISS-GARCIA, SAN ANTONIO (TX) P D, TX
MICHELLE R. LANHAM, TEXAS ATPA, TX
MICHELLE SCRIBNER, PROGRESSIVE INS, OK
MIGUEL E. FLEITAS, FL
MIGUEL E. ZAYAS, PR
MIKE BUTLER, IL
MIKE COSKER, CT
MIKE CREECH, GALVESTON CO (TX) ACTF, TX
MIKE GERIK, TEXAS FARM BUREAU, TX
MIKE H. CARMODY, NY
MIKE JARRETT, TULSA (OK) P D, OK
MIKE LOEWE, ILLINOIS STATE POLICE, IL
MIKE M. COOK, STATE FARM INS, SD
MIKE MANNING, UTAH MOTOR VEHICLE ENF, UT
MIKE MASKARICH, CALIFORNIA HWY PATROL, CA
MIKE McCLARY, MD
MIKE McCREARY, SPARKS (NV) P D, NV
MIKE MILLER, NEWPORT NEWS (VA) P D, VA
MIKE MILLER, CA
MIKE MILLIGAN, TX
MIKE MITCHELL, DAYTONA AUTO AUCTION, FL
MIKE MODRA, NV
MIKE NICOLS, PROGRESSIVE INS, VA
MIKE PETERSON, NATIONWIDE INS, CT
MIKE ROSS, SAN ANTONIO (TX) P D, TX
MIKE WIEDEMANN, MO
MIKE WOHLHETER, STATE FARM INS, OH
MIKEL ALLEN, ARIZONA DPS, AZ
MIKEL LONGMAN, ARIZONA AUTO THEFT AUTHORITY, AZ
MILES H. WATTERS, JR., STATE FARM INS, OH
MILLARD WOLFGANG, PA AUTO DEALERS EXCHANGE, PA
MILTON RODRIGUEZ, V.I.C.E. SCRIPT INC, CT
MIQUEL J. RAMIREZ, TEXAS D P S, TX
MITCH HERMANN, STEIN INVESTIGATION AGENCY, CA
MITCH SAUCIER, FARMERS INS, CA
MITCH SZEMPRUCH, NY
MITCH VIPOND, TUCSON (AZ) P D, AZ
MITCHELL J. PRICE, EMC INS, IA
MONTE L. McGOWEN, OH
MONTE R. CZAPLEWSKI, VA
MONTY C. KING, OREGON IND AOTO DLRS ASSOC, OR
MORRIS R. BROWN, ASPU, CA
MOSES McCOWN, NORFOLK (VA) P D, VA
MYRON J. SMITH, CA
NANCY A. HORTON, STATE FARM INS, MI
NANCY J. LILLEY, AMERICAN NATIONAL P & C, MO
NANCY P. BARR, VA
NANCY STEVENS, STATE FARM INS, MS
NATALIE MURDOCK, OK
NATHAN TAARUD, WI
NATHAN WHYBREW, AVIS RENT-A-CAR, GA
NATHAN WOLFE, PA
NEAL R. WISNER, MI
NEIL LOVORN, TEXAS DPS, TX
NEIL M. HALPERN, NY-NJ PORT AUTHORITY P D, NY
NEIL R. DEWEY, WA
NEIL SPECTOR, ORANGE CO (CA) ATTF, CA
NELSON IVAN MARTINEZ, PEMBROKE PINES (FL) P D, FL
NELSON S. RHODES, NC
NELSON TATE, MS
NELSON THAU, A INS, NY
NICHOLAS A. WALTZ, STATE FARM INS, OH
NICHOLAS BAGGETTA, GOVERNOR'S A/T STRIKE FORCE, MA
NICHOLAS C. STAGLIANO, JR, ORANGE CO (NY) D A OFFICE, NY
NICHOLAS DELLA VALLE, NJ
NICOLE COX, NY
NICOLE L. FREDRICKS, DAKOTA CO (MN) ATTORNEY, MN
NICOLE REVELEN, STATE FARM INS, NY
NILES DAVIES III, CLARKSTOWN (NY) P D, NY
NOLAN A. BURNS, TX
NORBERT HEUSER, NY
NORM BERTH, IL
NORMAN CROHN, IL
NORMAN D. ADAMS, OH
NORMAN F. HODGSON, NICB, IL
NORMAN J. MAXWELL, JR, MI
NORMAN O. BUREAU, ME
NORMAN R. COCHRAN, MD
NORMAN W. ANDERSON JR, MD
ODELL MORGAN, OK IND AUTO DLRS ASSOC, OK
OLIVER G. GARRISON, OH
OLIVIA MENDEZ, TX
OSCAR MARTINEZ, NICB VENDOR, TX
OSCAR MARTINEZ, NICB, TX
OWEN McSHANE, NY
PAM RODGERS, STATE FARM INS, AZ
PAM THIERRY, STATE FARM INS, MI
PAMELA HAST, STATE FARM INS, CA

PAMELA L. COCHRAN, STATE FARM INS, VA
PAT A. SHEETS, CA
PAT BREEDLOVE, TX
PAT WEIDEL, NIAGARA CO (NY) S D, NY
PAT WILKERSON, OSBI, OK
PAT ZNAJDA, MN
PATRICIA A. HESTER, TENNESSEE HWY PATROL-PLANNING& RESEARCH, TN
PATRICIA HERNDON, STATE FARM INS, MI
PATRICIA O'SULLIVAN, NY
PATRICIA R. GIUMARRA, FLORIDA DMV, FL
PATRICK A. GOUGH, VIRGINIA BEACH (VA) P D, VA
PATRICK A. TUCKER, VIRGINIA BEACH (VA) P D, VA
PATRICK B. McGRAIL, TX
PATRICK BYRNE, MICHIGAN STATE POLICE, MI
PATRICK CAMPONARO, STATE FARM INS, NC
PATRICK DOYLE, WEST PALM BEACH (FL) P D, FL
PATRICK G. CAMPBELL, NY
PATRICK GREEN, MD
PATRICK J. BAILEY, TX
PATRICK J. ODONNELL, CA
PATRICK J. YATES, STATE FARM INS, IA
PATRICK MARTIN, OCATT, CA
PATRICK R. ERNST, TX
PATRICK T. CRONIN, GA
PATRICK W. CLANCY, LO/JACK, MA
PATTI S. HAMBLIN, CT
PATTY BERLIN, GLOBAL PRODUCT SALES, CA
PATTY CUSCADEN, MO
PAUL A PELLETIER, CT
PAUL B. BIANCO, KALAMAZOO (MI) DPS, MI
PAUL B. CHRISTENSEN, MESA (AZ) P D, AZ
PAUL C. JENSEN, NY
PAUL CLAPPER, C N A INS, NY
PAUL D. ANGLIN, STATE FARM INS, KY
PAUL D. FRIDAY, NY
PAUL D. GALLO, NJ
PAUL DOTEN, ME
PAUL E. EARLS, NC
PAUL EVERSON, BARNSTABLE (MA) P D, MA
PAUL F. TAMBURELLI, XTRA CORPORATION, AZ
PAUL G. AMADO, STATE FARM INS, AZ
PAUL G. JOHNSON, MD
PAUL G. MORGAN, CHARLES CO (MD) S O, MD
PAUL G. RUDY, NY
PAUL HICKEY, OH
PAUL HOLLAND, NORTH TEXAS AUTO THEFT TF, TX
PAUL J. D'ALESSANDRO, NY
PAUL J. PUTKOWSKI, NY
PAUL J. SEFCIK, NATIONWIDE INS, AL
PAUL J. SEILER, IL
PAUL L. REITCHEL, ME
PAUL L. WOOD, GA
PAUL M. BLAIR Jr., MD
PAUL M. BRACCI, STATE FARM INS, NY
PAUL MITCHELL, FL
PAUL R. STUEWER, NY
PAUL RITZENTHALER, OH
PAUL S. ORCUTT, STATE FARM INS, CA
PAUL SERPIS, PLYMOUTH ROCK ASSURANCE, MA
PAUL SKITSKI, PIMA CO (AZ) ATTY, AZ
PAUL SOMERS, US CUSTOMS, VA
PAULA CARDUCCI KELLERMAN, BUFFALO (NY) P D, NY
PEDRO DELPIN, NY
PEDRO J. TORRES ORTIZ, PR
PEDRO VASQUEZ, NJ
PEGGY BEZY, NATIONWIDE INS, MI
PEGGY SHAY, OURISMAN AUTOMOTIVE GROUP, VA
PETE BIGNOTTI, NATIONWIDE INS, VA
PETE FITZSIMMONS, PA
PETE PINELLI, CONNECTICUT STATE POLICE, CT
PETER A. SAMB, AMERICAN FAMILY INS, WI
PETER C. DeTOY, NY
PETER CILENTO, SUFFOLK CO (NY) P D, NY
PETER CIMILUCCA, UTICA INSURANCE, NY
PETER D. SAUBER, N A D E - MANHEIM AUCTIONS, NJ
PETER E. HEPPNER, LYNCH & LYNCH, MA
PETER GANLEY, PROGRESSIVE INS, DE
PETER J SIMET, WI
PETER J. COLLETTE, WI
PETER J. MICHEL, VA
PETER M HADUCH JR., MD
PETER R. CHIMENTI, NY
PETER R. PERRIEN, LA
PETER R. REIHING, NASSAU CO (NY) P D, NY
PETER S. SMITH, NY
PETER VALLAS, PETER VALLAS ASSOC, NJ
PETER W. HOLTZ, LIBERTY MUTUAL INS, NY
PHIL A. SUITT, TX
PHIL P. DONOVAN, TX
PHILIP A. BRAUN, JR, JEFFERSON PARISH (LA) SO, LA
PHILIP C. CULCASI, PCC INVESTIGATIONS, CA
PHILIP C. GOOGIN, CA
PHILIP G. FREDERICK, BLUE RIDGE INS, NY
PHILIP J. CREPEAU, NY

PHILIP J. VAN HOUTEN, CINCINNATI INS, OH
PHILIP KOENIG, NY
PHILIP PASSARO, NY
PHILIP W. CERVASIO, NY
PHILLIP C. RANDAZZO, MICHIGAN STATE POLICE, MI
PHILLIP CHASSEY, GOVERNOR'S A/T STRIKE FORCE, MA
PHILLIP K. HOFFMAN, STATE FARM INS, KS
PIERRE J. KHOURY, PA
PRESTON PINKLETON, CHESTERFIELD CO (VA) P D, VA
PRICE A. SHOEMAKER, IV, STATE FARM INS, IL
QUINN WILHELM, LAKEWOOD (CO) P D, CO
QUINTIN S. WATERS, FT LAUDERDALE (FL) P D, FL
R. D. EDWARDS, NC
R. DAN REMMERS, A INS, TX
R. EDWARD WILLIS, STATE FARM INS, OH
R. M. HAMBY, NORFOLK (VA) P D, VA
R. ODIE WATERS, PROGRESSIVE INS, TX
RACHELLE J. McATEE, KILLEEN (TX) P D, TX
RAFAEL MARTINEZ, NJ
RALPH D. GAULT, PROGRESSIVE INS, NH
RALPH J. PANETTA, AMERICAN INTERNATIONAL ADJ CO, MA
RALPH P. LINEBAUGH, STATE FARM INS, MS
RALPH POLLOCK, NY
RALPH S. KISOR, COLUMBUS (OH) P D, OH
RALPH S. SMITH JR, NC
RALPH SALCIDO, ARIZONA DPS, AZ
RALPH W. NELSON, FT LAUDERDALE (FL) P D, FL
RAMON IRIZARRY, NEWARK ARSON SQUAD, NJ
RANDALL L. HOAGLAND, GA
RANDALL WILSON, NY
RANDY C. GINN, MS
RANDY CALLISON, THE PRONET GROUP, INC, TX
RANDY D. BEESON, VIRGINIA STATE POLICE, VA
RANDY KENNEDY, COLORADO DPS, CO
RANDY L. ANDREWS, DALLAS (TX) P D, TX
RANDY L. CRONE, LEE CO (FL) S O, FL
RANDY L. SMITH, MI
RANDY R. SMITH, STATE FARM INS, MI
RANDY SWICK, TX
RANDY VERA, CALIFORNIA DMV, CA
RAY A. COLLINS, MICHIGAN STATE POLICE, MI
RAY DUSTIN, TX
RAY H. NIBLETT, TX
RAY MAGNO, PALM BEACH CO (FL) STATE ATTORNEYS OFF, FL
RAY SAMPLE, SHERIDAN (CO) P D, CO
RAYMON A. GROSSMAN, GROSSMAN & GRANDI P.C., IL
RAYMOND A. McTAMANY, MD
RAYMOND CLOONEY, KEENE (NH) P D, NH
RAYMOND D. GOMES, VA
RAYMOND DAMIANO, LIBERTY MUTUAL INS, NY
RAYMOND F. ROBERTSON, NY
RAYMOND GARGUILLO, NY
RAYMOND J. BRODEUR, PROGRESSIVE INS, CT
RAYMOND L. PHILO, NEW HARTFORD (NY) P D, NY
RAYMOND MEANY, PT AUTHORITY TRANS CORP PA/NJ, NJ
RAYMOND W. SEILING, LEHIGH CO (PA) ATTF, PA
RAYMUND ROGERS, WEST BRIDGEWATER (MA) P D, MA
REBECCA ATKINSON, WV
REGGIE SMITH, GEICO, NC
REGINA LEWAND, GEICO, NY
REID E. BRAFFORD, GASTONIA (NC) P D, NC
REINHARDT ANDERSEN, NY
RENE' LISOJO, NJ
REYNALDO G. GOMEZ, WASHINGTON STATE PATROL, WA
RICARDO PENTON, HOLLYWOOD (FL) P D, FL
RICH BETHEL, ARIZONA DPS, AZ
RICH HOUGARDY, STATE FARM INS, CA
RICHARAD J. HAGEY, LOUISIANA FARM BUREAU INS, LA
RICHARD A. BENTLEY, CA
RICHARD A. HOWARD, NY
RICHARD A. LOIS, NY
RICHARD A. RIISBERG, MICHIGAN DEPT OF STATE, MI
RICHARD A. RYLLUN, RICHARD RYLLUN ASSOC, NJ
RICHARD B. PITTENGER, NY
RICHARD BRANHAM, STATE FARM INS, CA
RICHARD BREUER, ATLANTIC MUTUAL INS, NJ
RICHARD C. CIRASUOLO, NY
RICHARD C. KNICK III, VIRGINIA DMV - ISO, VA
RICHARD C. STREJLAU, NY
RICHARD CANDEROZZI, NY
RICHARD D McQUOWN, KY
RICHARD D. KIRKLAND, TX
RICHARD D. LAWSON, DELAWARE DMV, DE
RICHARD E. PEDERSON, PETER VALLAS ASSOC, NJ
RICHARD F. LESNIEWSKI, WI
RICHARD FENLON, HOLLYWOOD (FL) P D, FL
RICHARD FULTON, TEXAS DPS, TX
RICHARD FULTON, TX
RICHARD G. HAYWARD, MICHIGAN STATE POLICE, MI

RICHARD GOLDSMITH, STATE FARM INS, FL
RICHARD H. CABRI, ZURICH NA, NJ
RICHARD H. LANE, NJ
RICHARD H. PHILLIPS JR, TN
RICHARD H. POTT, IL
RICHARD HEROLD III, FL
RICHARD I. TALACH, OHIO CASUALTY GROUP, NC
RICHARD IPPOLITO, MANTRACK, INC., FL
RICHARD J. EHLINGER, NYS DMV AUTO THEFT, NY
RICHARD J. HEIM, LANCASTER (PA) P D, PA
RICHARD J. NIEDERMEYER, NY
RICHARD J. OLIVA, ILLINOIS STATE POLICE, IL
RICHARD J. ROZZI, NY
RICHARD J. TAMANOSKY II, LOWER ALLEN TWP (PA) P D, PA
RICHARD KADIEN, NC
RICHARD KLEYNENBERG, STATE FARM INS, MI
RICHARD KOEL, BALTIMORE (MD) P D, MD
RICHARD L. FELTON, MA
RICHARD L. LASHBROOK, STATE FARM INS, AK
RICHARD L. McBRIEN, KS
RICHARD L. MURPHY, Jr, NICB, MA
RICHARD L. WAHTERA, ROSEVILLE (MN) P D, MN
RICHARD L. WALKER, MI
RICHARD LOMBARDI, NY
RICHARD LYONS, STATE FARM INS, VA
RICHARD M. GORDON, PA
RICHARD M. HARRIS, MONTGOMERY CO (MD) P D, MD
RICHARD M. SCHWARTZ, RICHARD SCHWARTZ INVESTIGATIONS, FL
RICHARD MOLONY, CA
RICHARD ORTIZ, FL
RICHARD P. BELYSKI, SC
RICHARD P. WILLIAMS, SC
RICHARD R. BOSCARELLO, OH
RICHARD REYNOLDS, MA
RICHARD S. KING, MURRYSVILLE (PA) P D, PA
RICHARD S. STELZER, OH
RICHARD S. STINGER, LIBERTY MUTUAL INS, PA
RICHARD SALAS, COLORADO STATE POLICE, CO
RICHARD SMITH, NY
RICHARD SPOSATO, NY
RICHARD T. CALDERWOOD, FL
RICHARD T. GUERIN, NY
RICHARD V. MANIS, NJ
RICHARD V. NOVAK, ILLINOIS MVTPC, IL
RICHARD W. LECK, IL
RICHARD W. SLOGGETT, FL
RICK BERNOT, MARIN CO (CA) T F, CA
RICK D. DARBY, TX
RICK PORRAS, BURNSVILLE (MN) P D, MN
RICK VALENTINE, TN
RICK W. REDD, MARIETTA (GA) P D, GA
RICK ZIMMER, OSBI, OK
RICKEY J. STAGGS, CA
RICKEY M. BRUCE, GEICO, LA
RICKY H. GOWDY, STATE FARM INS, NV
ROBBY WEST, STATE FARM INS, NJ
ROBERT A. BACA, NEW DPS-MTD, NM
ROBERT A. BEYRER, OH
ROBERT A. BOROWSKI, MI
ROBERT A. DYER JR., STATE FARM INS, NC
ROBERT A. POPE, OH
ROBERT A. VITO, LAWMAN ARMOR CORP, PA
ROBERT B. BACA, NEW DPS-MTD, NM
ROBERT B. BUTLER, AZ
ROBERT BALIONI, NY
ROBERT BELLANTE, CONNECTICUTT DMV, CT
ROBERT BOWLING, NC
ROBERT C. COLBY, FOUNDERS INS CO, IL
ROBERT C. HASBROUCK, NY
ROBERT C. STRATTON, REDMOND (OR) P D, OR
ROBERT CARLSON, WALWORTH CO (WI) S O, WI
ROBERT COSTA, SAFETY INSURANCE, MA
ROBERT CREPEAU, NY
ROBERT CROOK, TAMPA (FL) P D, FL
ROBERT CZECH, MI
ROBERT D. PERRY, JR, AZ
ROBERT D. SCHURE, MO
ROBERT DETHLEFS, PASADENA (TX) P D, TX
ROBERT DIETRICH, FT LAUDERDALE (FL) P D, FL
ROBERT DIVAGNO, NY
ROBERT E. CAMAIORE, AMERICAN INTL GROUP, NJ
ROBERT E. COOK, FBI, VA
ROBERT E. DOYLE, AVIS, NY
ROBERT E. ENNIS, DETROIT (MI) P D, MI
ROBERT E. JONES, NC
ROBERT E. O'DONNELL, Jr, RI
ROBERT E. SOUTHARD, NASSAU CO (NY) P D, NY
ROBERT E. SUPINGER, VIRGINIA DMV, VA
ROBERT E. SWACKHAMER, MO
ROBERT EUBANKS, FORSYTH CO (GA) S O, GA
ROBERT F. BOROWSKI, IL
ROBERT F. MANGINE, NATS, MD
ROBERT F. MEDLEY, COLUMBUS (OH) A/P AUTH POLICE, OH
ROBERT F. SHEEHAN, KEMPER INS, PA
ROBERT FAILLA, NY

ROBERT G. LIVAICH, NJ
ROBERT G. RITTER, STRATEGIC AUTOMOTIVE SERVICES, PA
ROBERT G. STODDARD, Jr, STATE FARM INS, NY
ROBERT G. SUELTER, TX
ROBERT G. THOMPSON, MS
ROBERT GILBOY, NY
ROBERT H. ANSCHICK, NY
ROBERT H. GARDNER, KEMPER INS, NY
ROBERT J. CHAPMON, TX
ROBERT J. DOHERTY, LIBERTY MUTUAL INS, NJ
ROBERT J. GETSCHMAN, MI
ROBERT J. HESSER, PA
ROBERT J. JAGOE, MD
ROBERT J. JAGOE, BALTIMORE CO (MD) P D, MD
ROBERT J. KENNEY, CT
ROBERT J. LOJEWSKI, STATE FARM INS, IL
ROBERT J. RADOSEVICH, NM
ROBERT J. RING, MA
ROBERT J. RUNGE, STATE FARM INS, KS
ROBERT J. SKOVE, FL
ROBERT J. YANUZZI, NATIONWIDE INS, PA
ROBERT KING, MA
ROBERT KING, PENNSYLVANIA STATE POLICE, PA
ROBERT KNAPP, HOLLYWOOD (FL) P D, FL
ROBERT L. ASHFORD, NY
ROBERT L. BEENER, IA
ROBERT L. BURGESS, NJ
ROBERT L. BURGESS, METROPOLITAN INS, NY
ROBERT L. DEETER, LANCASTER (PA) P D, PA
ROBERT L. EPPES, KS
ROBERT L. FARMER, NICB, WA
ROBERT L. HENDERSON, NY
ROBERT L. LEHAN, CNH, WI
ROBERT L. McFALL, NICB, VA
ROBERT L. STEPHENSON, SC
ROBERT L. VAN DER WISSEL, OH
ROBERT M. CUMMINGS, CUMMINGS ENGINE, WV
ROBERT M. FINLEY, STATE FARM INS, LA
ROBERT M. HILL, MN
ROBERT M. KUROWSKI, OK
ROBERT M. PIKE, MD
ROBERT M. RYAN, IL
ROBERT M. SECKEL, OH
ROBERT M. SMITH, HAMPTON (VA) P D, VA
ROBERT MATTHEW WELCH, FORT WORTH (TX) P D, TX
ROBERT MONIS, MS
ROBERT N. RUTHERFORD, FL
ROBERT P. GLASS, WHITTIER (CA) P D, CA
ROBERT P. RAKER, JR, STATE FARM INS, OH
ROBERT PAINTER, WI
ROBERT PETRO, NY
ROBERT PILCICKI, PENNSYLVANIA STATE POLICE, PA
ROBERT PINTO, NY
ROBERT R. GRIMM, FT LAUDERDALE (FL) P D, FL
ROBERT R. PAUL, STATE FARM INS, FL
ROBERT RAMOS, PA
ROBERT RODRIGUES, MASSACHUSETTS STATE POLICE, MA
ROBERT RUSSELL, STATE FARM INS, NJ
ROBERT S. ROSS, STATE FARM INS, IL
ROBERT SALVIA, NY
ROBERT SPADACCINI, COLONIAL PENN INS, NY
ROBERT SPRINGER, GOVERNOR'S A/T STRIKE FORCE, MA
ROBERT STONE, VIRGINIA DMV, VA
ROBERT SUEHRING, SENTRY INS, WI
ROBERT T. CARR, TX
ROBERT T. KAVICH, NY
ROBERT T. REPIK, GREENWICH (CT) P D, CT
ROBERT T. SMITH, ME
ROBERT VOGT, MI
ROBERT W. AREY, NICB, FL
ROBERT W. GARDNER, NY
ROBERT W. MICHALOWSKY, HARLEYSVILLE INSURANCE, PA
ROBERT W. SUND, R.W.CONSULTING, WA
ROBERT WEIGAND, PA
ROBERT WELTZ, SOUTHERN UNITED FIRE INS, AL
ROBERTA L. TYLER, COLUMBIA (SC) PD, SC
ROBIN A. EMMONS, TX
ROBIN DURANIK, NJ
ROBIN J. MATHWEG, SAFECO INS, MN
ROBIN J. MAXWELL, STATE FARM INS, MI
ROBIN LEACH, WACO (TX) P D, TX
ROBIN P. RUSSELL, MONTGOMERY CO (MD) P D, MD
ROBIN WHEELER, STATE FARM INS, OR
RODGER W. WHITE, PA
RODNEY B. ALLEN, PRUDENTIAL P & C, RI
RODNEY D. JONES, GA
RODNEY L. WATSON, HANOVER INS, NY
RODNEY P. FISHER, STATE FARM INS, IL
ROGELIO TORRES, TX
ROGER A. CLARK Jr., VA
ROGER A. LONG, CALIFORNIA HWY PATROL, CA
ROGER A. TETREAULT, GOVERNOR'S A/T STRIKE FORCE, MA
ROGER BOCK, WESTCHESTER CO (NY) DA'S OFFICE, NY

ROGER COURTNEY, LA
ROGER D. CROSS, MO
ROGER E. ADAMS, MO
ROGER F. MEHL, MI
ROGER H. HILL, MI
ROGER L. VAN DREW, IL
ROGER NAGY, MAINE - DMV, ME
ROLAND D. DUMOND, NICB, TX
RON BRIDGEFARMER, GWINNETT CO (GA) P D, GA
RON C VAN RAALTE, IL
RON CLARK, TULSA (OK) P D, OK
RON F STOUT, LOJACK, VA
RON HENDRICKSON, NEWPORT NEWS (VA) P D, VA
RON HUEY, LA
RON MORIN, ME
RON W. DOHRENDORF, STATE FARM INS, NV
RONALD A. JOHNSON, RAYTOWN (MO) P D, MO
RONALD A. McLEAN, GARLAND (TX) P D, TX
RONALD A. MITCHELL, NY
RONALD B. KOKESH, MI
RONALD C. MUELLER, NASSAU CO (NY) P D, NY
RONALD D. POWELL, MI
RONALD E. WEDEKIND, FLORIDA HWY PTRL, FL
RONALD F. BALZAN, NY
RONALD F. HARSHMAN, MD
RONALD G. MINOR, CALIFORNIA HWY PATROL, CA
RONALD GEORG, NY
RONALD GUTIERREZ, NY
RONALD J BOARDMAN, NE
RONALD J. ANDERSON, NY
RONALD J. GOTTARDI, STATE FARM INS, IL
RONALD J. KIHNEL, LA
RONALD J. SPEDOSKE, FARM BUREAU INS, MI
RONALD LAPOINTE, NCA APPRAISAL CO, INC, NY
RONALD LEWANDOWSKI, CHESTER (PA) P D, PA
RONALD OLSEN, HEMPSTEAD (NY) P D, NY
RONALD ROSATI, PHILADELPHIA (PA) P D, PA
RONALD S. VERWERS, NATIONWIDE INS, VA
RONALD SNYDER, NY
RONALD TEARE, NC
RONALD W. COOK SR., SC
RONALD W. VEA, STATE FARM INS, AK
RONALD Z. KADAR, CT
RONNIE J. DEAN, NC
RONNIE W. TILLER, VIRGINIA STATE POLICE, VA
RORY ROCKY BAILEY, IRVING (TX) PD, TX
ROSEMARY FORKIN, NY
ROSEMARY M. HORTA, NATIONWIDE INS, CT
ROSS AMEND, STATE FARM INS, MI
ROSS P ROGAN, CA
ROSS STUTH, DES MOINES (WA) P D, WA
ROY BOCINA, NY
ROY C. McINTURFF, GASTONIA (NC) P D, NC
ROY D. PARRACK, TEXAS D P S, TX
ROY S. PIERCE, TX
ROYAL DAVENPORT, VIRGINIA DMV, VA
ROYCE E. JORDAN, Jr, TYLER (TX) P D, TX
RUBEN C. SAAVEDRA, COCHISE CO (AZ) S O, AZ
RUBEN LOPEZ, TX
RUDOLF E. HOOGENBOOM, NY
RUDOLPH A. SNYDER, PA
RUDY L. WOODS, TX
RUSS BROMAN, ALLEGHENY CO (PA) DA'S OFFICE, PA
RUSS WELKER, AZ
RUSSELL ATKIN, TX
RUSSELL C. HARVEY, BRIDGEVIEW (IL) P D, IL
RUSSELL CRAETER, BURNET CO (TX) S O, TX
RUSSELL ENGLISH, PEMBROKE PINES (FL) P D, FL
RUSSELL HEYMAN, ZURICH NA, NJ
RUSSELL J. SUESS, FT LAUDERDALE (FL) P D, FL
RUSSELL MCBRIDE, STATE FARME INS, WA
RYAN C. HOLMES, NICB, IL
SALVATORE G. RIGNOLA, NY
SALVATORE LOMBARDO, NJ
SAM H. POPLIN, NC
SAM LANTZ, STATE FARM INS, NY
SAM SMITH, STATE FARM INS, CA
SAMMY M. PRIETO, TEXAS D P S, TX
SAMUEL G. ANGELL, NC
SAMUEL P. DUNLAP, GEICO, PA
SAMUEL W. MORGAN, LOWER ALLEN TWP (PA) P D, PA
SANDRA CABRERA, STATE FARM INS, CA
SANDRA D. CONLON, PRINCE WILLIAM CO (VA) P D, VA
SANDRA K. DRENDEL, STATE FARM INS, MN
SANDY T. GAVIN, LA
SANTO PORTO, ORANGE CO (CA) ATTF, CA
SARAH A. POLING, KANE CO (IL) ATTF, IL
SARAH E. VOGELSBERG, LENEXA (KS) P D, KS
SASCHA O. HERTSLET, HI
SCHUYLER DENHAM, MD
SCOTT A. HENRY, NATIONAL GRANGE INS, NY
SCOTT ADAMS, STATE FARM INS, SC
SCOTT BYERLY, TX
SCOTT COLLINS, GOVERNOR'S A/T STRIKE FORCE, MA
SCOTT D. FREARSON, NATIONWIDE INS, NY

SCOTT FEDER, HOLLYWOOD (FL) P D, FL
SCOTT GREEN, SCOTTSDALE (AZ) P D, AZ
SCOTT GREER, TX
SCOTT H. DAYVAULT, NC
SCOTT HERRING, CA
SCOTT J. GOSSEN, LAWTON (OK) P D, OK
SCOTT J. SCHEER, STATE FARM INS, CO
SCOTT J. WAHL, STATE FARM INS, WA
SCOTT M. REUTTER, AZ
SCOTT MAYFIELD, NY
SCOTT ROBIDEAU, MAINE - DMV, ME
SCOTT V.B. ENGLISH, MD
SCOTTIE TAYLOR, TEXAS FARM BUREAU, TX
SEAN K. GRAY, MARYLAND STATE POLICE, MD
SEAN McNABOLA, FARMERS INS, CA
SEAN P. BURKE, MD
SEBASTIAN J. BONGIORNO, MA
SHAN HAIDER, FARMERS INS, CA
SHANE ROGERS, LA
SHANNON RADECKI, GEICO DIRECT, IL
SHANNON WILDER, GEICO, GA
SHARON WALL, NORTH CAROLINA DMV ENFORCEMENT, NC
SHAUN A. PUGH, HARRISBURG (PA) BUREAU OF POLICE, PA
SHAWN L. ELLIOTT, TX
SHAWN MAHONEY, BURNSVILLE (MN) P D, MN
SHAWN O'GORMAN, TX
SHAWN P. MAROUIS, ME
SHAWN T. RUSSELL, NY
SHEAN L. TEMPLETON, LAKEWOOD (CO) P D, CO
SHEILA L. PICKETT, STATE FARM INS, NY
SHEILA LAWSON, FBI, MI
SHELBY G. BAILEY, VIRGINIA DMV, VA
SHERI L. TAYNOR, FLORIDA DMV, FL
SHERRY ANDERSON, WACO (TX) P D, TX
SHERRY K. IACCARINO, DEERE & CO, IL
SHIGEKO OTANI, CA
SIM CASIMIRO-NG, STATE FARM INS, CA
STACEY A. STONE, AUTO ETCH, INC, MD
STACEY ALLES, COLORADO DIV CRIMINAL JUSTICE, CO
STACEY ALLES, COLORADO DIV OF CRIMIANL JUSTICE, CO
STACEY G. SEBA, TX
STACEY PEARSON, LOUISIANA STATE POLICE, LA
STAN E. JABLONSKI, CT
STAN ROPER, TX
STAN ZAKRZEWSKI, PA
STANLEY A. KANTERMAN, INVESTIGATIVE RESOURCE CTR, NJ
STANLEY G. YOUNG, NY
STANLEY R. DOSS, NICB, FL
STANLEY R. WILLIAMS, LA
STEFAN JENSEN, NEW YORK CITY SANITATION P D, NY
STEFAN Z. SWIERKOSZ, NY
STEPHANIE FASONE, STATE FARM INS, IL
STEPHEN A. GARRETT, VIRGINIA DMV, VA
STEPHEN B. THOMPSON, MO
STEPHEN C. ALU, NY
STEPHEN C. MYERS, STATE FARM INS, IA
STEPHEN D. TROLLOPE, MISSOULA (MT) P D, MT
STEPHEN DIFEDE, STATE FARM INS, NY
STEPHEN E. HORNE, STATE FARM INS, NY
STEPHEN J. HOSKING, MI
STEPHEN J. KERSHAW, PA
STEPHEN M. CHELSTOWSKI, NJ
STEPHEN M. KOWALEWSKI, CALIFORNIA HWY PATROL, CA
STEPHEN M. REINHARDT, NY
STEPHEN S. REAVES, LEE CO (FL) S O, FL
STEPHEN W. COOK, FL
STEVE ARNDT, FARMERS INS, MI
STEVE AVERETTE, STATE FARM INS, VA
STEVE BROWN, STATE FARM INS, KS
STEVE D. WATTS, REPUBLIC INS, TX
STEVE ENGEL, STATE FARM INS, CO
STEVE FULLER, WINDSOR GROUP, FL
STEVE GARDNER, CA
STEVE GILBERT, TX
STEVE J. GRILLO, NY
STEVE JAYNE, STATE FARM INS, MI
STEVE MARK EMBERTON, KANECO (IL) ATTF, IL
STEVE McADAMS, TX
STEVE NEMEC, NICB, WA
STEVE RENALDI, NYS DCJS, NY
STEVE THARALDSEN, FORT MYERS (FL) P D, FL
STEVE W. JONES, NORTH TEXAS AUTO THEFT TF, TX
STEVEN A. DUVALL, INDIANA STATE POLICE, IN
STEVEN APPLIN, TOLEDO (OH) P D ATU, OH
STEVEN ARP, DuPAGE CO(IL) STATES ATT'YS OFF, IL
STEVEN BITTICKS, SIERRA VISTA (AZ) PD, AZ
STEVEN COBB, FL
STEVEN E. JOHNSON, MD
STEVEN F. SCHWENN, STATE FARM INS, WA
STEVEN G. BARGER, IA
STEVEN H. LERMAN, FT LAUDERDALE (FL) P D, FL

STEVEN J. REDWINE, STATE FARM INS, AZ
STEVEN K. JOHNSON, IL
STEVEN KELBICK, NEW YORK CITY POLICE DEPT, NY
STEVEN KING, BALTIMORE CO (MD) P D, MD
STEVEN L. McQUEEN, MARYLAND STATE POLICE, MD
STEVEN L. MILLER, V I N, INC, IN
STEVEN L. POE, ILLINOIS STATE POLICE, IL
STEVEN LAMPE, HOWARD CO (MD) P D, MD
STEVEN M. KELLEY, NEW YORK STATE POLICE - AUTO THEFT UNIT, NY
STEVEN M. MYERS, PENNSYLVANIA STATE POLICE, PA
STEVEN M. NASSIVERA, NY
STEVEN M. TEMPLE, CA
STEVEN MYERS, PENNSYLVANIA STATE POLICE, PA
STEVEN NOVACEK, HARRISBURG (PA) BUREAU OF POLICE, PA
STEVEN P. FULLER, ARBELLA MUTUAL INS, MA
STEVEN P. McNABB, NC
STEVEN R. CARMAN, IN
STEVEN R. DAY, LEECH LAKE BAND OJIBWE-DPS, MN
STEVEN R. FRIEDMAN, SAFECO INS, CA
STEVEN R. REID, WISCONSIN STATE POLICE, WI
STEVEN R. THAU, NY
STEVEN STELTER, DUPAGE COUNTY (IL) AUTO THEFT, IL
STEVEN STROBLE, CA
STEVEN V. KOLB, ID
STEWART C. FINK, NY
SUE CUCUZZA, CA
SN BENNETT, NICB, IL
SN CIANI, SCHENECTADY CO (NY) DA, NY
SN CLINGMAN, VA
SN FLUD, TX
SN J. MacKAY-HIGGINS, MA
SN JEDLOVEC, STATE FARM INS, MO
SN JOHNSON, MANHEIM REMARKETING SOLUTIONS, TN
SN L. LUDER, MARICOPA CO (AZ) ATTORNEYS OFFICE, AZ
SN SAMPSON, TX
SWAV HERMANOWSKI, PROGRESSIVE INS, NY
SYLVESTER D'ANGELO, NY
SYLVIA J. CARNETT, ILLINOIS STATE POLICE, IL
T. C. McCARTHY, GEICO DIRECT, LA
T. G. JERRY MESTAS, NATIONWIDE INS, NC
T. PATRICK BOSTICK, TX
T. REX GREEN, IDAHO DOT - DLR OPS, ID
TAMARA ROSSITER, NEW YORK STATE POLICE, NY
TANI MARUYAMA, 3M SECURITY MARKET CENTER, MN
TANYA S. SCHWARTZ, BURNSVILLE (MN) P D, MN
TED C. HOMIAK, VIRGINIA STATE POLICE, VA
TED LIPKA, NV
TED W. KRAUS, ROBERT PLAN CORP, CT
TERENCE D. JACKSON, TN
TERRANCE DOBROSKY, CA
TERRELL L. RHONE, TX
TERRELL R. ADKINS, NC
TERRENCE L. CRAMER, ORANGE CO (CA) S O, CA
TERRI KEANE, PENNSYLVANIA ANTI CR THEFT COMMITTEE, PA
TERRY A. SEIBERT, IL
TERRY C. DAVIS, FLORIDA HWY PATROL, FL
TERRY CORRINNE, MD
TERRY D. LANE, ALABAMA DEPT REVENUE - MVD, AL
TERRY E. SUTTON, STATE FARM INS, NY
TERRY FIELD, TX
TERRY J. PERSING, SIOUX FALLS (SD) P D, SD
TERRY K. PARKS, SC
TERRY M. KELLY, PA
TERRY M. LEMMING, IL
TERRY STARNER, ARIZONA DPS, AZ
TERRY W. DICKEY, TN
THADDEUS A. DUTKOWSKI, ALLEGHENY CO (PA) D A, PA
THEDWARD R. O'NEAL JR., NC
THEODORE ARMAS, NY
THEODORE J. BOWMAN, RAYTOWN (MO) PD, MO
THEODORE J. PECK, IL
THEODORE J. RYAN, PA
THEODORE MARZANI, PA
THOMAS A. BISHOP, PENNSYLVANIA STATE POLICE, PA
THOMAS A. COX, VA
THOMAS A. DE ROSSETT, JR, AMERICAN GLASS ETCHING SYS, GA
THOMAS A. DeROSSETT JR., AMERICAN GLASSETCHING SYSTEMS, INC, GA
THOMAS B. BOCK, IN
THOMAS B. KEATING, CA
THOMAS B. LANDRUM, PRUDENTIAL P & C, TX
THOMAS BARRY, DEPT OF ENVIRONMENTAL MANAGEMENT, RI
THOMAS C. KRUMPTER, NY
THOMAS CALANDRILLO, STATE FARM INS, NY

THOMAS CLEARY, NY
THOMAS CORNELISSEN, NJ
THOMAS D. COBB, JR, STATE FARM INS, TN
THOMAS D. MURRAY, MN
THOMAS D. POLLACK, NY
THOMAS EVANS, PHILADELPHIA (PA) P D, PA
THOMAS G. MILLER, FBI, FL
THOMAS G. NEARY, SAN MATEO CO (CA) VEH THEFT TF, CA
THOMAS H. HARDEMAN, SAN ANTONIO (TX) P D, TX
THOMAS H. O'CONNOR, C N A INS, NJ
THOMAS J ADAMS, JR, AUCTION INS AGENCY, AL
THOMAS J HORRIGAN, MD
THOMAS J. DITRANO, NY
THOMAS J. GUTHAT, MI
THOMAS J. HOLMES, NJ
THOMAS J. McCARTHY, BUFFALO (NY) P D, NY
THOMAS J. MONKO, NY
THOMAS J. PAVIS JR., TRIFACTOR CONSULTANTS, MD
THOMAS J. PEPE, TRAVELERS INS, NY
THOMAS J. PFEIFFER, SR, ROYAL & SUN INS, SC
THOMAS J. SMOOT, DETROIT (MI) P D, MI
THOMAS J. SULLIVAN, GEICO, NY
THOMAS J. TOLSTOY, PA
THOMAS J. WHELAN, PROGRESSIVE INS, DE
THOMAS K. MAROUARDT, WI
THOMAS KIERNAN, STATE FARM INS, NY
THOMAS L KUJAWA, TN
THOMAS M HAGAN, PALM BEACH CO (FL) S O, FL
THOMAS M. HOLLAND, FAIRFAX COUNTY (VA) POLICE, VA
THOMAS M. LOJEWSKI, PA
THOMAS M. MILLER, NY
THOMAS MORSE, AVIS, NY
THOMAS NEWSOME, NV
THOMAS P. CLANCY, CA
THOMAS P. CURRAN, ST LOUIS CO (MO) P D, MO
THOMAS R. JAKUBOWSKI, NY
THOMAS R. KINGRY, VIRGINIA BEACH (VA) P D, VA
THOMAS R. MANFRE, NY
THOMAS R. MORTON, GREAT AMERICAN INS, MO
THOMAS R. PEAL, BECKLEY FIRE DEPT, WV
THOMAS R. PETERS, TX
THOMAS R. RICHESON, Jr, STATE FARM INS, AL
THOMAS R. TURNER, MD
THOMAS SCALLY, MD
THOMAS SINCICH, STATE FARM INS, CA
THOMAS W. DASH, NORFOLK (VA) P D, VA
THOMAS W. GATES, MANHEIM AUTO AUCTION, PA
THOMAS W. HORTON, SC FARM BUREAU CAS INS, SC
TIM BROSAM, BLOOMINGTON (MN) PD, MN
TIM FILES, AR
TIM P. FRAZER, NM OFF OF INSP GENL, NM
TIM STEWART, NORTH TEXAS ATTF, TX
TIM WIEDEMANN, ARIZONA VEHICLE THEFT TASK FORCE, AZ
TIMOTHY A. UPRIGHT, TX
TIMOTHY C. HOEGLER, AMERICAN AUTO AUCTIONS, MA
TIMOTHY D. BRAATZ, ATLAS INVESTIGATIONS, MN
TIMOTHY G. BRADY, NY
TIMOTHY GAHAN, STATE FARM INS, MI
TIMOTHY GOODWIN, TX
TIMOTHY J. ANDREWS, IN
TIMOTHY J. PALMER, CT
TIMOTHY L. ALLEN, GA
TIMOTHY L. ALLIGOOD, NC
TIMOTHY LUNDQUIST, NIAGARA CO (NY) DA'S OFF, NY
TIMOTHY MORRISON, FT LAUDERDALE (FL) P D, FL
TIMOTHY NOLAN, CONNECTICUTT STATE POLICE, CT
TIMOTHY P. HERNDON, HERNDON & ASSOC, MI
TIMOTHY R. BEACH, OH
TIMOTHY S. BROWN, ANNE ARUNDEL CO (MD) PD, MD
TIMOTHY W. HERSHBERGER, MT
TIMOTHY W. KAPPS, NC
TOBY CHESS, CA
TODD A. HESTER, TEXAS DPS, TX
TODD A. HOWARD, BREVARD CO (FL) S O, FL
TODD D. BEARD, GAIN-AUTO THEFT INV NETWORK, MI
TODD GARRISON, LEE CO (FL) S O, FL
TODD LEPPERT, HOWARD CO (MD) P D, MD
TODD M. BLAIR, VOLUSIA CO (FL) S O, FL
TOM ASHMORE, TOM ASHMORE ENTERPRISES, CT
TOM BERGREN, ST PAUL (MN) PD, MN
TOM CARVELLI SR, MN
TOM E. SHARPE, NC
TOM E. STRZYRYTZ, AIG SPECIALTY AUTO, PA
TOM FATZYRYTZ, STATE FARM INS, NJ
TOM JAMES, PROGRESSIVE INS, AR
TOM McNAMARA, HARD FACTS ENGINEERING, NJ
TOM O'BRIEN, TEMPE (AZ) P D, AZ
TOM OSREDKAR, STATE FARM INS, WA
TOM VICKERS, GLENDALE (AZ) P D, AZ

TOM WAITE, YTX
TOMMIE COOPER, FL
TOMMY HANSEN, TX
TOMMY L. SHORT, TX
TOMMY MAY, TX
TOMMY ROACH, TEXAS ATTORNEY GEN'L OFF, TX
TONY COLATRUGLIO, STATE FARM INS, MI
TONY D. COOK, STATE FARM INS, OK
TONY D. NIX, GA
TONY DeCIANNI, IL
TONY FERNANDEZ, FL
TONY J. RAMIREZ, NY
TONY PULLINGS, Jr, TX
TONY RANIERI, A INS, NJ
TONYA K. THEIL, STATE FARM INS, LA
TONYA SPRECHER, ND
TRACEY UTSEY, NORTH TEXAS ATTF, TX
TRACIE S. MORTENSON, 3M SECURITY MARKET CENTER, MN
TRACY FUTCHER, PENNSYLVANIA STATE POLICE, PA
TRACY LYNN DAVIS, NORTH CAROLINA DMV, NC
TRACY T. LASCARO, LA
TRAVIS FEYEN, ARIZONA VTTF, AZ
TRAVIS KEISER, LA
TRENT HURLEY, PENNSYLVANIA STATE POLICE, PA
TRICIA GRIMBALL, STATE FARM INS, SC
TROY JOINER, MIDESSA METRO ATTF, TX
TROY THOMAS, SALEM (VA) P D, VA
VALDIS A. VITOLS, MICHIGAN STATE POLICE, MI
VALERIE LITTLE, TX
VAN SZETO, HOLLYWOOD (FL) P D, FL
VAUGHN A. MILES, CO
VERN McBRIDE, ILLINOIS STATE POLICE, IL
VERNAL NEWSON, DETROIT (MI) P D, MI
VERNON A. TAPPANA, OK
VERNON JONES, Jr, VIRGINIA BEACH (VA) P D, VA
VIC L. JOHNSTON, CA
VICKI D. ANDERSON, US CUSTOMS, VA
VICKIE TRIBBLE, GEICO, MA
VICKIE V. TEMONIA, STATE FARM INS, LA
VICTOR BOUDREAUX, GALVESTON CO (TX) AUTO CRIMES, TX
VICTOR EPPS, BALTIMORE CO (MD) P D, MD
VICTOR GATES, PHILADELPHIA (PA) P D, PA
VICTOR H. ROSALES, EL PASO (TX) P D, TX
VICTOR L. TRUCCO, STATE FARM INS, OR
VINCENT CASTALDO, INFINITY INS, AL
VINCENT FLYNN, AUTHORIZED SECURITY, NY
VINCENT LaPENTA, NY
VINCENT LEE ROCKEY, VA
VINCENT LUCCI, KENOSHA CO (WI) S D, WI
VINCENT MENDILLO, NJ
VIRGIL OUINTIN THOMAS, TX
VIRGLE LUKE, MS
VIVAN C. McKENZIE, GMAC INS, NY
VLADIMIR IVKOVICH, IL
W. BILL P. SMITH, TX
W. E. RUTLEDGE, CA
WADE D. WICKRE, NATIONWIDE INS, VA
WADE KERN, NY
WALT WEST, TARRANT CO (TX) ATTF, TX
WALT WOLOSZCZUK, NC
WALTER D. WAGGONER, MO
WALTER E. WASHINGTON, PA
WALTER J. McINTOSH, HI
WALTER J. PALUSZAK, NY
WALTER O. HERNDON, JR, HERNDON & ASSOC, MI
WALTER S. PUHALSKI, NY
WALTER SZAMATOWSKI, PA
WANDA S. SIMONEAUX, STATE FARM INS, LA
WARD T. ROBINSON, FORT WORTH (TX) P D, TX
WARREN A. MCGEE, FAIRFAX COUNTY (VA) POLICE, VA
WARREN J. DONALDSON, NICB, NV
WARREN L. GRAN, STATE FARM INS, NE
WAYNE BEHNKEN, NY
WAYNE J. HEWETT, OK
WAYNE JOHNSON, MN
WAYNE L. DELO, FARM BUREAU INS, MI
WAYNE L. RUBINAS, FL DIV OF LAW ENFORCEMENT, FL
WAYNE SNEED, TX
WELDON R. HAMLETT, VA
WESLEY BYE, STATE FARM INS, WA
WESLEY M. BOLAND, SC
WILBURN L. WHEELER, CO
WILEY W. SNOW, NC
WILLAIM HOLLANDSWORTH, MARYLAND STATE POLICE, MD
WILLARD BURGER, TX
WILLARD J. SLOPER, ORANGE CO (FL) S O, FL
WILLIAM A. BRUCE, ALLSTATE INS, GA
WILLIAM A. COLEMAN, STATE FARM INS, FL
WILLIAM A. LALLY, BALTIMORE CO (MD) P D, MD
WILLIAM A. LOVOLD, CA
WILLIAM B. BASKIN, ARKANSAS S, AR
WILLIAM B. CARSON, AL
WILLIAM B. FRATUS, BEAUMONT (TX) P D, TX

WILLIAM B. McCABE, NY
WILLIAM BOBBITT, LA
WILLIAM BRINKMAN, NEW YORK STATE POLICE, NY
WILLIAM C McKELVIE, PA
WILLIAM C. HOLBERT Jr., FORT WORTH (TX) P D, TX
WILLIAM C. McRAE, STATE FARM INS, AR
WILLIAM COMPETTELLO, NASSAU CO (NY) P D, NY
WILLIAM D. MCCULLOUGH, IL
WILLIAM DIEHL, CUMBERLAND CO (PA) D A, PA
WILLIAM DOUGHERTY, ONE BEACON INS, NY
WILLIAM E. AUSLEY, NC
WILLIAM E. BURNICKE, NY
WILLIAM E. SPELL, SC FARM BUREAU CAS INS, SC
WILLIAM E. THOMPSON, Jr, NC
WILLIAM E. WAGNER, MD
WILLIAM F DUFFY, MA
WILLIAM F. BANAHAN, MD
WILLIAM F. LANG, OH
WILLIAM F. SCHAEFFER, JR, CT
WILLIAM G. BORMAN, NY
WILLIAM H. BIERER, CALIFORNIA HWY PATROL, CA
WILLIAM H. MOORE, MO
WILLIAM H. WAGNER, VIRGINIA STATE POLICE, VA
WILLIAM HARDWICKE, NY
WILLIAM HIXSON, PENNSYLVANIA STATE POLICE, PA
WILLIAM I. BILL ROBERTSON, CA
WILLIAM IRWIN GRAY, NC
WILLIAM J. BONANNI, NY
WILLIAM J. DARNELL, MICHIGAN STATE POLICE, MI
WILLIAM J. KIRBY, IL
WILLIAM J. MACIOCH, NY
WILLIAM J. NEE, GOVERNOR'S A/T STRIKE FORCE, MA
WILLIAM J. NORMOYLE, NY
WILLIAM J. O'MALLEY, OH
WILLIAM J. ROBB, NJ
WILLIAM J. TULKO, NJ
WILLIAM J. WEBB, NM
WILLIAM K. VALENTINE, CA
WILLIAM KUKLA, IL
WILLIAM L. JOHNSON, CA
WILLIAM M. DEMPSEY, NY
WILLIAM M. JOBE, IRVING (TX) P D, TX
WILLIAM M. MYRKA, NY
WILLIAM M. SHALEESH, NY
WILLIAM MITZELIOTIS, NY
WILLIAM MORT, IL
WILLIAM MULLER, ST LOUIS CO (MO) P D, MO
WILLIAM N. TERRY, MICHIGAN STATE POLICE, MI
WILLIAM N. WOITOWICH, IL
WILLIAM P. COSTELLO, NY
WILLIAM P. DEVLIN, NY
WILLIAM P. HOLLAND, STATE FARM INS, MD
WILLIAM P. JACOBSEN, FT.LAUDERDALE (FL) P D, FL
WILLIAM P. POLK, OK
WILLIAM P. REID, JR, AL
WILLIAM P. SCANLAND, CA
WILLIAM S. BRANDNER, STATE FARM INS, LA
WILLIAM S. CRAIG, GA
WILLIAM S. HUMPHREY, VIRGINIA BEACH (VA) P D, VA
WILLIAM S. SURLES, NC
WILLIAM SKINNER, TX
WILLIAM SUTCH, PA
WILLIAM T. ARMSTRONG, NY
WILLIAM T. BELCH, NC
WILLIAM T. KELHOWER, JR, PA
WILLIAM T. PARRISH, VIRGINIA DMV, VA
WILLIAM T. SWANK, OH
WILLIAM V. HUTCHINSON, MANASSAS (VA) P D, VA
WILLIAM W. LATIMER, NICB, FL
WILLIAM WELLER, NEW YORK CITY POLICE DEPT, NY
WM DAVID MILLER, CARLISLE BOROUGH (PA) P D, PA
YOLANDA VELAZQUEZ, FL
YVETTE GOMEZ, STATE FARM INS, CA
YVETTE MUNIZ, TEXAS DOT, TX
ZACHARY S. McCORKLE, KANECO (IL) ATTF, IL
ZIGGY ZABLOCKI, FL

WALES
LINDSEY ANDREW WILLIAMS
RONALD CHESNEY, NTH WALES

YUGOSLAVIA
ALEKSANDAR MILOSAVLJEVIC
ZORAN BOZIC
ANTOINE ROEGIS

INDEX

The Membership Roster is not included in the index. It can be found on pages 196-206.

Langer 148
Lapasnick 141
Larned 26, 28
Larocque 13, 132, 138, 140, 142, 145, 147, 154, 160, 187, 188
Laroque 152, 160
Larson 34, 35, 36
Laws 26
Leach 147
Leestma 34, 35, 36, 38, 40, 42
Lehman 181
Lemming 118, 192
LeRoy 146, 147
Lester 24
Letterman 64, 74, 79, 80, 81, 175, 176, 177
Lewis 148
Lipe 49, 179, 180
Lloyd 168
Loe 26, 27, 35
Long 35
Longman 145, 153, 160
Longmar 147
Look 170
Lopez 46, 49
Lorton 26
Lovold 66
Lucking 12, 110, 119
Luder 147
Luke 68, 79, 175, 177
Lunsford 181
Luther 35, 179

— M —

Maasen 66
MacGillis 105, 108, 111, 175, 176, 177
MacKenzie 19, 84, 85, 88, 89, 90, 91, 92, 96, 98, 99, 101, 102, 103, 105, 107, 108, 111, 112, 113, 132, 147, 149, 151, 164, 180, 181, 184, 190
Mackie 55
MacLaughlin 149, 151, 190
Malek 132, 142, 147, 179, 180, 181
Malinak 179
Mandeville 148
Mardilla 67
Marquardt 117, 169
Martin 147
Martinez 147
Mash 110
Masur 35
Matlock 35, 38, 40
Maurice 182
Mawyer 121, 122, 124, 125, 128, 129, 132, 135, 137, 138, 140, 145, 147, 149, 152, 160, 179, 180, 183
Maxey 26
Maxwell 124, 164, 165
May 35, 179, 180
Mayhugh 46, 49
Mazyck 148
McClain 180
McCleary 38, 42, 43

McCormick 118, 126, 195
McDonald 35, 148
McDonold 151
McDowell 49
McFadden 147
McFarling 35, 46
McGillis 103
McGrail 181
McHugh 140, 141, 145, 160, 171, 172
McIntire 26, 27
McKenzie 98, 179
McKinlay 185
McLaughlin 18, 24, 26, 27, 35, 42, 43, 45, 92, 106, 149
McLeon 181
McNally 35
McNurty 186
McQuown 70, 73, 74, 75, 78, 79, 80, 81, 82, 84, 86, 89, 92, 98, 100, 103
McVay 146, 147
Mechow 116, 136
Megan 141
Melton 46
Mendenhall 147
Mendillo 171
Mendoza 147, 157
Merriman 49
Metz 12, 13, 113, 119, 120, 121, 123, 128, 129, 130, 131, 132, 135, 136, 139, 140, 143, 145, 152, 153, 159, 160
Meyer 12, 26, 49, 89, 90, 92, 96, 99, 102, 103, 105, 107, 108, 111, 112, 114, 115, 116, 126, 146, 149, 168
Micciche 147
Midgette 176, 177
Miller 35, 49, 147, 181
Mireles 182
Mitchell 88, 89, 102, 105, 107, 110, 175
Mize 181
Moats 58, 63, 64, 65, 66, 67, 68, 70, 78
Moe 179
Moizeno 147
Moncrief 18, 24, 25, 26, 34, 35, 36, 38, 40, 42, 43
Moneyhun 146, 181
Montanaro 153
Mooers 109
Moore 165, 171
Morales 147
Moree 175
Moreno 146, 159
Morgan 46, 182
Mortenson 5, 13, 120, 128, 129, 132, 135, 136, 139, 140, 143, 145, 146, 150, 151, 152, 153, 158, 160, 170, 180, 190
Mortimer 49
Morton 148, 176

Mueller 63
Mumford 26
Munoz 181, 182
Murphy 62, 63, 64
Murray 49
Myers 26

— N —

Nails 181
Navoa 153
Naylor 28
Nelson 34, 35, 36, 38, 39, 40, 117, 148, 176
Newman 179
Newsome 24
Nichol 146
Nicholes 147
Nichols 49
Nicol 166
Norman 70, 73, 74
Norris 147, 169
Novoa 147
Nutt 35
Nutter 130, 195

— O —

O' Reilly 134
Oasman 35
Oberlichnu 35
O'Byrne 142, 146, 153, 158, 160, 164, 165
O'Connor 49
Odendal 184
Oglesby 147
Oldham 35
Oliver 35, 38, 40, 42, 51, 53, 55, 61, 62, 73, 84, 87, 147, 168
Olsen 46
Olson 21, 66, 74, 75, 76, 77
O'Reilly 131
Ortiz 183
Overton 103, 171, 172
Owens 147

— P —

Paden 49
Padget 146
Page 35, 147
Painter 102, 105, 107
Palmer 46
Parker 148
Paszek 46
Patterson 35
Pavlenic 146
Payne 24
Pearson 181
Pedigo 49
Pemberton 49
Penny 186
Penton 148
Perrin 183
Perry 147
Peters 183
Peterson 24, 49
Petroski 139, 148
Petrowski 153, 154, 155
Petterd 107, 112, 117, 118, 120, 121, 122, 124, 125, 129, 135, 140, 145, 146, 152, 158, 159, 160, 164, 165
Pfoteneuor 170
Philips 101
Phillips 26, 35, 91, 94, 98, 109, 127, 136, 190
Pierce 181, 194

Pierron 115, 118, 121, 125
Pike 49, 54, 61, 69, 89, 98
Pina 25
Pinkston 46, 49, 179
Pitts 12, 13, 83, 88, 97, 100, 101, 108, 110, 111, 130, 138, 147, 155, 187, 188, 190
Platt 64
Plowden 52, 175
Pope 74, 79, 80, 81, 82, 84, 85, 88, 89, 98
Porter 118, 121, 125
Posey 49
Potts 24, 25, 35, 46, 68
Pounder 49
Powell 12, 170
Powers 35
Presley 116, 117
Price 35
Prieto 182
Prince 46
Pruett 175, 177

— Q —

Queveva 101
Quinn 14

— R —

Raban 146
Radosevich 146
Ragsdale 49
Ragusa 36
Rainone 141
Rambo 169, 170
Ramirez 180, 181
Ramos 147
Ramsey 82
Ratcliff 181
Rawlinson 131, 193
Rawls 46
Rear 35
Reardon 35
Renaldi 148
Rentschler 49
Rerie 67, 69
Rice 70
Richter 49
Rick 180
Rickards 35
Riddell 26
Riley 35, 126, 194
Rinaldi 159
Rincon 35
Rivers 61, 143
Roach 147
Roberson 46
Roberts 35, 147, 183
Robertson 12, 82, 84, 85, 92, 96, 99, 103
Robinson 46, 146, 159, 160, 169, 170
Roccaforte 111, 193
Rodrihuez 181
Roloson 80
Ronayne 172
Roper 183
Rosenbaum 168
Roske 12, 13, 110, 111, 115, 118, 119, 120, 121, 123, 125, 128, 129, 131, 135, 136, 138, 146,

149, 152, 178
Ross 17, 24, 77, 146
Rousseau 147, 180, 181
Rowayne 148, 159
Rowell 164
Rowland 183
Roy 116
Ruddell 65
Rudisey 147
Ruks 119
Rule 150, 194
Rummel 116, 188, 192
Russell 143, 148, 166
Rutherford 20
Rutledge 8, 17, 21, 60, 65, 66, 68, 69, 70, 73, 74, 75, 76, 77, 78, 79, 81, 82, 83, 86, 89, 91, 92, 93, 94, 98, 100, 101, 103, 104, 118, 127, 136, 147, 149, 166, 184, 190
Ruzicka 96, 171, 173
Ryan 30, 63, 79, 82, 84, 85, 88, 89, 90, 92, 96, 99, 100, 102, 104, 105, 107, 118, 134, 149, 190

— S —

Saavedra 147, 153
Sache 46
Sachs 49, 51
Sadler 53, 181
Salata 147
Salathe 49
Salazar 181
Sampson 147
Sanchez 126, 147
Sandberg 73
Sanders 179
Sandoval 146
Sauceda 182
Saville 171, 173
Sayles 171
Scanland 46
Scarisbrick 49, 63, 64, 65, 66, 67, 68, 70, 73, 74, 79, 80, 81, 82, 83, 84, 85, 86, 88, 171, 172, 174
Schad 175
Schaub 184
Schauman 171, 174
Schemenauer 134, 169
Schimnoski 169
Schlomas 170
Schmidt 35
Schrage 168
Schull 179, 180, 182
Schutte 184
Schwartzfopf 192
Schwartzkopf 116
Scott 185
Scroggin 35
Seahoh 183
Seaman 35, 46, 62, 65, 68, 179
Secrest 35, 42, 43, 46
Seiler 87, 168, 169
Sellers 35
Serafini 168
Seymour 35

Shaver 35
Shelby 35
Shelley 181
Shemenauer 130
Shepherd 146
Sheppard 181, 185, 186
Shepperd 35
Shruptine 26
Sides 146, 147, 152, 159, 193
Sids 144
Simet 124, 126, 134, 169, 193, 194
Simms 142, 143, 146, 160, 185, 186
Sirnus 170
Skinner 147, 151, 157, 180, 181
Slater 35, 147
Slosson 35, 43
Smart 26
Smith 46, 104, 105, 143, 147, 175, 184, 190
Soelberg 147
Southard 148, 159, 172
Spanel 8, 105, 108, 111, 115, 118, 120, 121, 124, 125, 129, 135, 138, 139, 140, 145, 146, 157
Sparkman 8, 125, 129, 134, 135, 146, 160
Spence 183
Spradley 26, 28
Springer 49
Springvloed 105, 112, 166, 167, 184
Sprinkle 49
Spry 61, 62, 63, 64, 65, 67, 68, 73, 86, 104, 171
St. Amand 171
Stasio 148
Staudt 171
Stech 147, 182
Stelter 146
Stephens 108
Sterzing 24, 26, 35, 46
Stevenson 118
Stewart 117, 176
Stoner 46
Stowell 148, 159
Streitch 35
Stringer 35
Stuart 35
Sturgeon 34, 35, 36, 38, 40, 42, 43, 51
Suelter 107
Suess 12, 13, 114, 119, 120, 123, 131, 132, 140, 145, 148, 158, 160, 194
Sullivan 18, 24, 25, 35, 40, 49
Suthard 142
Sutherland 141, 171
Swackhamer 46, 49, 51
Swick 182
Swinford 147

— T —

Talbot 170

Tatum 46
Taylor 46, 99, 103, 108, 111, 112, 143, 183, 185, 186
Temple 158
Tenagero 159
Thames 49
Thigpen 183
Tholen 146, 150, 152, 158
Thomas 46, 165
Thompson 12, 13, 121, 125, 129, 132, 135, 140
Thorne 35
Thorp 26
Thurber 35
Tinagero 146, 147
Tisdale 35
Toppel 183
Towe 136, 192
Townsend 168, 169
Townsley 26
Tranum 35
Trekell 43
Triplett 147, 182
Tristan 147
Troiano 171, 174
Troyd 136
Trujillo 146
Tuepkema 146
Turano 143
Turner 35, 179
Tyler 35

— U —

Utsey 147

— V —

Valentine 49
Van Bree 166
Van den Hoeck 119, 134, 135, 140, 142, 145, 146, 158, 160, 166, 167, 193
Van der Lee 146, 158, 160, 166, 167
Van Drew 9, 12, 110, 115, 118, 119, 121, 123, 125, 127, 128, 129, 130, 135, 136, 138, 140, 141, 142, 143, 146, 149, 150, 152, 165, 169, 180, 188
Van Natter 138, 145, 147, 160, 188
Van Raalte 61, 63, 64, 65, 67, 68, 70, 73, 81, 88, 89, 91, 92, 98, 101, 103, 104, 109, 110, 112, 126, 134, 137, 149, 155, 170, 190
Van Vlasselaer 166
VanDoleweerd 74, 79
Vanek 181
Vanorski 147
Vargas 182
Vasquez 172
Vega 153
Vickers 147
Vigel 183
Vincent 35
Vitols 146
Voelker 168

VonHoute 130

— W —

Wahl 183
Waldt 49
Walker 35, 46
Wallace 181
Ward 35, 146, 164, 165
Watson 46
Weakley 107, 176
Webb 35, 144, 146, 147, 152, 159
Weber 171, 173
Welch 126
Wells 35
Wera 107
Werra 96, 99, 102, 103, 105, 168, 169
West 147
Westbrock 168
Westbrook 35
Wheeler 8, 109, 118, 121, 124, 125, 127, 129, 130, 133, 135, 136, 138, 140, 141, 142, 145, 146, 150, 160
White 13, 46, 49
Whittle 35
Wickland 147
Wilkerson 147
Williams 26, 28, 35, 43, 46, 47, 74, 136, 191
Williamson 49
Wilson 35, 100
Wise 147
Wiseman 147
Wisner 146, 155
Woener 26
Wollenberg 49, 54
Wood 21, 76, 78, 82, 86, 99, 102, 104, 105, 107, 108, 146, 150, 166, 167, 185, 190
Woods 64, 147, 181, 183, 184
Woychesin 181
Wright 46, 147
Wyatt 180, 182

— Y —

Yeager 36
Young 109, 121
Yzaguirre 182

— Z —

Zablocki 12, 65, 66, 68, 70, 73, 74, 75, 78, 79, 80, 81, 82, 84, 88, 89, 91, 92, 98, 100, 103, 104, 109, 110, 112, 126, 134, 137, 149, 155, 170, 190
Zangar 147, 187
Zermenu 181
Zimmer 147
Zimmerhanzel 183
Zimmmerman 24
Zofkie 170
Zureck 76
Zurek 75

Printed in the USA
CPSIA information can be obtained
at www.ICGtesting.com
JSHW060052150824
68134JS00032B/2715

9 781681 625621